"If 9/11 is to be taken as a watershed in the relations between the US and the rest of the Muslim world, then there is an urgent need to understand the nature of this challenge. *The Empire and the Crescent*, presents a clear and lucid understanding of the dangers posed by a superpower unrivalled in its military strength and its implication not only for the Muslims world, but for the world community as a whole."

— **IBRAHIM ÖZDEMIR**
Professor of Islamic Studies, Ankara University, Turkey

"Powerful, concise and realistic."

— **MEDIA MONITORS NETWORK**

"... a very useful look at key issues facing all of us today."

— **BARRY LANDO**
Former producer CBS 60 Minutes

"Hegel said that the Owl of Minerva first takes flight with twilight closing in—that wisdom comes almost too late. This collection of essays is the first, not to depict the rise of an American Empire, but to portray America's rush into a night of perpetual conflict with enemies of its own making. *The Empire and the Crescent* will be an inexhaustible source of support for those who try to reverse this homicidal and suicidal rush to global war."

— **MICHAEL NEUMANN**
Professor of Philosophy, Trent University in Ontario, Canada

"... exposes the 'neo-con' agenda for US imperialism ..."

— **RAUF A. AZHAR**
Professor of Economics, University of Central Punjab, Lahore

"A book all Americans should read: a collection of dramatic perceptions on the emerging American Empire and a poignant counterpoint to the corporate controlled mainstream media from which 79% of Americans get their news. These articles clearly express what the Bush administration, the Cabal running it, and the CEOs of the transnationals do not want to hear."

— **WILLIAM A. COOK**
Professor of English, University of La Verne (Southern California)

"*The Empire and the Crescent* is a welcome respite from the constant disinformation and historical revisionism emanating from the realm of the neo-conservative media, policy launderers, and think tanks. During these troubled times, scholarship and truth telling, not propaganda, are absolute necessities. The scholars and journalists who have contributed to this important work have successfully breached the perception management wall of obfuscation and duplicity erected by the neo-conservative movement."

— WAYNE MADSEN
Author, columnist and investigative journalist, Washington, DC

"This timely book offers a rich critique of the ideology and practice of the expansive American Empire. All those who are looking for alternative interpretations and analysis, away from the suffocating conformity of the mainstream press and academia, should read this book."

— AS'AD ABUKHALIL
Associate Professor, of Political Science, California State University

"... critically engages difficult questions about a dangerous world. The chapters will expand readers' understanding of the United States, Islam and the Middle East. The honest assessment of US foreign policy in several of the chapters is crucial to understanding the magnitude of the political choices we face."

— ROBERT JENSEN
Associate Professor School of Journalism, University of Texas at Austin

"As public-minded people around the globe strive to make sense of the times we are in—especially the nature and aims of American power in relation to the Middle East—this collection is an indispensable resource."

— WENDY BROWN
Professor of Political Science, University of California, Berkeley

"As war against Iraq turns into occupation and resistance, this valuable book aids understanding of what is at stake and sheds light on the forces and ideologies that are engaged in the conflict."

— KAMIL MAHDI
Lecturer in the Economics of the ME, University of Exeter

"Indispensable for anyone seeking to understand—and overcome—the 'Us vs. Them' dynamic."

— BRIAN J. FOLEY
Visiting Associate Professor of Law, Touro College
Jacob D. Fuchsberg Law Center

THE EMPIRE AND THE CRESCENT

Speak the truth, even if it is bitter
SAYING OF THE PROPHET MUHAMMAD

If liberty means anything at all, it means the right to tell people what they do not want to hear
GEORGE ORWELL

THE EMPIRE AND THE CRESCENT

Global Implications for a New American Century

Foreword by
IBRAHIM M. ABU-RABI'

Edited by
AFTAB AHMAD MALIK

AMAL PRESS
BRISTOL • ENGLAND

First published by Amal Press (Ltd) 2003
Amal Press, PO Box 688, Bristol BS99 3ZF England

http://www.amalpress.com
info@amalpress.com

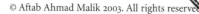
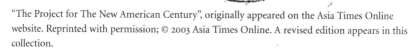

"The Project for The New American Century", originally appeared on the Asia Times Online website. Reprinted with permission; © 2003 Asia Times Online. A revised edition appears in this collection.

"The 30-Year Itch" originally appeared in the March/April 2003 issue of *Mother Jones* magazine. Reprinted with permission; © 2003, Foundation for National Progress.

"Piety, Persuasion and Politics: Deoband's Model of Islamic Activism" originally appeared on the Social Science Research Council's Website "After September 11". A revised version appeared in the volume *Understanding September 11*, edited by Craig Calhoun, Paul Price and Ashley Timmer (New York, NY: The New Press, 2002).

The right of the individual contributors to be identified as the author of the work has been asserted by them in accordance with the Copyright, Designs and Patents Act 1988.

Views expressed by different authors do not necessarily represent the views of one another, nor of Amal Press

A CIP catalogue record for this book is available from the British Library

ISBN 0-9540544-4-x paperback
ISBN 0-9540544-5-8 hardback

Cover design and typesetting by SOHAIL NAKHOODA
Cover image © REUTERS
Printed in the UK by PARTNERS IN PRINT

CONTENTS

Notes on Contributors   ix

Foreword   xv
IBRAHIM M. ABU-RABI'

Introduction   xxv
AFTAB AHMAD MALIK

PART I: THE EMPIRE

1   A Day that changed America: Did it?   3
M. SHAHID ALAM

2   The American Empire   9
WILLIAM BLUM

3   The Project for The New American Century   25
PEPE ESCOBAR

4   Global Rogue State   45
EDWARD S. HERMAN

5   The Thirty Year Itch   54
ROBERT DREYFUSS

6   Post Saddam Iraq: Linchpin of a New Oil Order   65
MICHAEL RENNER

7   Iraq and the Course of Empire   75
ANTHONY ARNOVE

8   The War Profiteers   86
FRIDA BERRIGAN

9   Lest we forget   97
LOUISE CHRISTIAN

PART II: THE CRESCENT

10 Seeing With Muslim Eyes   107
    HAMZA YUSUF

11 Islam and the West after September 11   112
    JOHN L. ESPOSITO

12 Jihad as Perpetual War   129
    ZAID SHAKIR

13 Tradition or Extradition?
    The Threat to Muslim Americans   142
    ABDAL HAKIM MURAD

14 Piety, Persuasion and Politics:
    Deoband's Model of Islamic Activism   156
    BARBARA METCALF

15 Fanaticism and its Manifestations in Muslim Societies   175
    M. HASHIM KAMALI

Appendix 1
    Security Strategy Foretold   208
    TOM BARRY AND JIM LOBE

ABDAL HAKIM MURAD is a British broadcaster, writer and preacher. His publications include several translations of classical Arabic texts. He is currently Secretary of the Muslim Academic Trust, London.

AFTAB AHMAD MALIK is a Muslim educator and writer. His book, *The Broken Chain: Reflections upon the Neglect of a Tradition* (Amal Press: 2003) examines the breadth and depth of traditional Islamic scholarship, which has now given way to certain narrow and revisionist interpretations.

ANTHONY ARNOVE is the editor of *Iraq Under Siege: The Deadly Impact of Sanctions and War* (South End Press and Pluto Press), recently updated in a new edition, and *Terrorism and War*, a collection of interviews with Howard Zinn published by Seven Stories Press. He also contributed to the introduction of *Struggle for Palestine* (Haymarket Books). An activist based in Brooklyn, he is a member of the International Socialist Organization and the National Writers Union (UAW Local 1981, New York local). His writing has appeared in *International Socialist Review, Socialist Worker, Z, Financial Times, In These Times, The Nation, Mother Jones, Left Business Observer, Monthly Review,* and other publications. He is also the co-editor of a forthcoming book with Howard Zinn, *Voices of People's History.*

BARBARA METCALF is professor of history at UC Davis and ranks among the leading experts on the Taliban and the Deoband movement. Her publications include: *Islamic Revival in British India: Deoband, 1860-1900* (Princeton U.P., 1982); *Perfecting Women: Maulana Ashraf 'Ali Thanawi's Bihishti Zewar*. Translation, annotation, and introduction (Berkeley: University of California Press) and *Tablighi Jama'at and Women* in *Travelers in Faith: Studies of the Tablighi Jama'at as a Transnational Islamic Movement for Faith Renewal* ed. M. Khalid Masud (Leiden: Brill).

EDWARD S. HERMAN is a Professor Emeritus of Finance at the Wharton School, University of Pennsylvania. He has a Ph.D. in Economics from the University of California, Berkeley, and has written extensively on economics, political economy, foreign policy, and media analysis. Among his 22 published books are: *The Political Economy of Human Rights* (2 vols, with Noam Chomsky, South End Press, 1979); *Corporate Control, Corporate Power* (Cambridge University Press, 1981); *Manufacturing Consent* (with Noam Chomsky, Pantheon, 1988); *The "Terrorism" Industry* (with Gerry O'Sullivan, Pantheon, 1990); *The Myth of the Liberal Media: An Edward Herman Reader* (Peter Lang, 1999); and with co-editor Philip Hammond, *Degraded Capability: The Media and the Kosovo Crisis* (Pluto, 2000).

FRIDA BERRIGAN is a Senior Research Associate with the Arms Trade Resource Center, (New York) a project of the New School University's World Policy Institute. The Arms Trade Resource Center was established in 1993 to engage in public education and policy advocacy aimed at promoting restraint in the international arms trade.

HAMZA YUSUF is the co-founder of Zaytuna Institute, which is dedicated to the revival of traditional study methods and the sciences of Islam. As one of the foremost contemporary spokespersons for Islam, he has taught and lectured extensively at various academic institutions worldwide. In addition, he has served as the principal lecturer at religious intensive seminars in the USA, England, Spain, and Morocco. He has translated several classical texts from Arabic and presently teaches at Zaytuna Institute in Hayward, California.

IBRAHIM M. ABU-RABI' is Professor of Islamic Studies and Christian-Muslim Relations at Hartford Seminary, Hartford, CT, USA; co-editor, *The Muslim World,* and author of *Intellectual Origins of Islamic Resurgence in the Modern Arab World* (SUNY, 1996) and *Islamism, Arabism, Socialism, and Globalization: Studies in Post 1967 Arab Intellectual History* (London: Pluto, forthcoming November 2003).

JOHN L. ESPOSITO is Professor of Religion and International Affairs and of Islamic Studies at Georgetown University. Founding Director of the

Center for Muslim-Christian Understanding: History and International Affairs in the Walsh School of Foreign Service, he has served as President of the Middle East Studies Association of North America and of the American Council for the Study of Islamic Societies as well as a consultant to governments, multinational corporations, and the media. His more than 25 books include: *Unholy War: Terror in the Name of Islam; What Everyone Needs to Know About Islam; The Islamic Threat: Myth or Reality?; Islam: The Straight Path; Islam and Democracy and Makers of Contemporary Islam* (with John Voll); *Political Islam: Radicalism, Revolution or Reform?; Iran at the Crossroads* (with R.K. Ramazani); *Islam, Gender and Social Change* (with Yvonne Haddad); and *Women in Muslim Family Law.*

LOUISE E. CHRISTIAN is a solicitor and co-founder of Christian Fisher solicitors (now known as Christian Khan), a leading human rights firm in central London. Louise is currently acting for the families of three young men detained in Guantanamo Bay (reported case R v Foreign Secretary ex parte Juma and Abassi, Court of Appeal, Nov 2002). She is also the co-author of *Inquests – A Practitioners Guide* published in 2002 by the Legal Action Group.

MICHAEL RENNER is a Senior Researcher at the Worldwatch Institute, a non-profit research organization in Washington, D.C. He serves as Project Director for *Vital Signs: The Trends that are Shaping Our Future,* a compilation of key global trends published annually. Before joining Worldwatch in 1987, he was a Corliss Lamont Fellow in Economic Conversion at Columbia University (1986–87) and a Research Associate at the World Policy Institute in New York City (1984–86). His research and writing has focused on peace, security, and disarmament issues, in particular the linkages between environment, natural resources, and violent conflict.

MOHAMMAD HASHIM KAMALI is Professor of Law at the International Islamic University of Malaysia, where he has been teaching Islamic law and jurisprudence since 1985. He is the author of numerous works, including: *Principles of Islamic Jurisprudence; Freedom of Expression in Islam; Dignity of Man in Islam; Freedom, Equality and Justice in Islam and Islamic Commercial Law* (all of which have been published by The Islamic

Texts Society: Cambridge), as well as a number of articles in reputable international journals.

M. SHAHID ALAM is Professor of Economics at Northeastern University. He has worked in the areas of trade theory, trade policy, global economy, economic growth and corruption. His book, *Poverty from the Wealth of Nations* was published by Palgrave in 2000. More recently, his interests have grown to include civilizational issues, Islam, Eurocentrism, and translating *Ghalib*.

PETRONIO ESCOBAR is a Journalist, born in Brazil in 1954 from Spanish-Dutch ancestry. Pepe has lived and worked as a foreign corres-pondent in London, Paris, Milan, Los Angeles and Asia. He currently is the senior correspondent for *Asia Times*, a news analysis website based in Bangkok and Hong Kong.

ROBERT DREYFUSS has been rated by *The Columbia Journalism Review*, as one of the "best unsung investigative journalists working in print".

WILLIAM BLUM left the State Department in 1967, abandoning his aspiration of becoming a Foreign Service Officer, because of his opposi-tion to what the United States was doing in Vietnam. He then became one of the founders and editors of the *Washington Free Press*, the first "alternative" newspaper in the capital. In 1999, he was one of the reci-pients of Project Censored's awards for "exemplary journalism" for wri-ting one of the top ten censored stories of 1998, an article on how, in the 1980s, the United States gave Iraq the material to develop chemical and biological warfare capability. His books include: *Killing Hope: U.S. Mili-tary and CIA Interventions Since World War II; Rogue State: A Guide to the World's Only Superpower; and West-Bloc Dissident: A Cold War Memoir.*

ZAID SHAKIR accepted Islam in 1977, while serving in the United States Air Force. Upon completion of his military service, in 1981, he enrolled in The American University in Washington, DC, where he earned a BA Degree in International Relations, with honors. He subsequently obtained an MA in Political Science from Rutgers University in 1986. After spending seven years in Syria studying Arabic and Islamic Sciences, he returned to the United States in November 2001, resuming the leadership of Masjid al-Islam. He also returned to Southern Connecticut State University, where he currently teaches both Arabic and Political Science. Zaid Shakir has lectured extensively on issues related to both Islam and African American life. He has also written numerous articles, which have been published in leading Islamic and academic periodicals. He has translated three books from Arabic into English, and is considered a leading authority on Islam in the American context.

FOREWORD
IBRAHIM M. ABU-RABI'

The United States bestrides the globe like a colossus. It domi-
nates business, commerce and communications; its economy
is the world's most successful, its military might second to
none.[1]

One of the central themes of American historiography is that
there is no American Empire. Most historians will admit, if
pressed, that the United States once had an empire. They then
promptly insist that it was given away. But they also speak
persistently of America as a World Power.

> —*William Appleman William*
> *"The Frontier Thesis and American Foreign Policy."*[2]

To my knowledge there is no institute or major academic
department in the Arab world whose main purpose is the study
of America, although the United States is by far the largest
outside force in the Arab world.

> —*Edward W. Said*
> *"Ignorant Armies Clash by Night."*[3]

S INCE THE END of World War Two, the United States has emerged
as the world's main superpower. The eclipse of the Soviet Union at
the beginning of the 1990s left the United States in the driver's seat
with respect to international affairs with no real challenger. The Muslim
world is not one block or unified political and economic entity. Still, it is
important to examine the relationship between the United States and the
larger Muslim world since World War Two. The various essays contained
in this volume offer a critical understanding of the United States' position and its expansionist hegemony in the world, especially in the wake

---

[1] Editorial, "America's World." *The Economist*, October 23, 1999, p.15.
[2] *Pacific Historical Review* 24 (November 1955), p.379.
[3] *The Politics of Dispossession* (New York: Vintage Books, 1995), p.229.

of the fall of the Ba'ath regime in Iraq in April 2003. The following factors were considered when choosing the essays to be included in this volume: (1) Since World War Two, the United States has inherited Europe's colonial status; (2) the United States made tremendous advances in capitalist modernity in both the nineteenth and twentieth centuries; (3) America has, since the nineteenth century, directly or indirectly involved itself militarily in the Muslim world or regions where Muslims have a substantial presence; (4) the twentieth century saw the increasing migration of Muslims to the United States and the emergence of the African-American Muslim movement in the 1950s and 60s; and (5) the world has become increasingly polarized since the tragic attacks on the USA on September 11, 2001, especially in relation to the discussion of 'our values' as opposed to 'theirs.' The fact is, some American quarters have placed the burden of these attacks solely on the shoulders of Muslims and Islam.

Many mainstream American political scientists and media commentators disagree with the thesis that America has inherited the European colonial project in the wake of the defeat of Nazi Germany in World War Two and the decline of traditional colonial European powers; neither do they subscribe to the idea that the United States currently is emerging as a mighty Empire, one which is able to circumvent the authority of the United Nations and most European nations. Harvard political scientist Joseph Nye, Jr., for example, does not see America emerging as a mighty and coercive Empire. Instead, he extols the virtues of American power since, more or less, the end of the Second War. He argues in a recent book that, "Today the foundations of power have been moving away from the emphasis on military force and conquest. Paradoxically, nuclear weapons were one of the causes. As we know from the history of the Cold War, nuclear weapons proved so awesome and destructive that they became muscle bound—too costly to use except, theoretically, in the most extreme circumstance."[4] The American occupation of Iraq clearly contradicts Nye's first thesis, however. As most articles in this volume ably show, the United States possesses tremendous political and military power that could potentially be unleashed against its enemies at the whim of the American political elite.

---

[4] Joseph S. Nye, Jr., *The Paradox of American Power: Why the World's Only Superpower Can't Go It Alone* (New York: Oxford University Press, 2002), p.5.

According to many American commentators, America has "soft power" in addition to having enormous military power. Nye defines "soft power" as "the ability to set the political agenda in a way that shapes the preferences of others ... Soft power arises in large part from our values. These values are expressed in our culture, in the policies we follow inside our country, and in the way we handle ourselves internationally."[5] The American political elite have clearly squandered American "soft power" since their threat to invade Iraq, which, as we all know, was actually carried out. Deep resentment and in some cases real hatred of American values is at its highest not just in the Muslim world, Africa and Latin America, but in Europe as well.[6]

The above analysis brings to the fore the whole issue of modernity and globalization and the impact they have had on the Muslim world in the past century. It is important to emphasize that modernity and its recent manifestation, referred to as globalization, came to the Muslim world with an onerous colonialist and neo-colonialist package. Capitalist modernity has been the dominant discourse worldwide for at least the past two hundred years. However, contrary to the perception in the West, the world is far from being dominated by one culture. That is to say, it is important that the US support existing cultural diversity while pursuing the expansion of its Empire. The world is teeming with cultures that possess their own unique internal dynamism which ensures survival and profusion. This must be protected. The good news is that the multiplicity of cultures is not likely to disappear in the future. Ultimately, cultural diversity is much more interesting than monolithic and standardized global capitalism, and provides a healthy environment for cultural dynamism and interaction among people from differing backgrounds. One may define globalization as a world system with two sets of components: financial and technological, on the one hand, and cultural, political, and ideological, on the other. In addition to being an extension of capitalist modernity, as it developed in Europe in the eighteenth century, contemporary globalization has been dominated by both the cultural and

---

5 Ibid., p.9.
6 See Lewis H. Lapham, "Notebook: Shock and Awe." *Harper's Magazine*, May 2003, pp.7–9. Also, Muhammad 'Abid al-Jabiri, "al-'Arab wa'l 'awlamah: al-'awlamah wa'l hawiyyah al-thaqafiyyah." In *al-'Arab wa'l 'awlamah* (Beirut: Markaz Dirasat al-Wihdah al-'Arabiyyah, 1998), p.298.

xviii   *Ibrahim M. Abu-Rabi'*

ideological models of the United States. Many will agree that the export of American culture has had a myriad of deleterious effects on the integrity of the social and ethical systems of the Third World, and that American culture is dominated by corrosive individualism and rampant materialism. Globalization is then a universal ideology that reflects America's desire for universal hegemony.

Contemporary Moroccan philosopher Muhammad Abid al-Jabiri draws an interesting distinction between globalization (*'awlamah*) and universalism (*'alamiyyah*). To al-Jabiri, the former implies American containment of other world cultures, whereas the latter implies openness to and reciprocity among cultures. Globalization has entailed a sophisticated process of American penetration of other cultures for the purpose of domination. In this quest to dominate the world, American ideology is supported by the media, which preaches individualism and consumerism as basic "American values."[7] Many Arab and Muslim thinkers have expressed the opinion that the internationally dominant American mass media promotes Western ideas of consumerist capitalism in its blatant and sometimes insidious quest to dominate the material and intellectual preferences of people in the Third World.[8] Frederic Jameson echoes al-Jabiri's concerns in his critique of American globalization, "This is consumerism as such, the very linchpin of our economic system, and also the mode of life in which all our mass culture and entertainment industries train us ceaselessly day after day, in an image and media barrage quite unparalleled in history."[9]

Globalization of the 1990s directly resulted from the tremendous economic changes and breakthroughs achieved by the capitalist system since

[7] According to Lebanese thinker Paul Salem, the United States has exported 'low culture' to the world since 'high culture' has a limited market overseas. See Paul Salem, "al-Wilayat al-mutahidah wa'l 'awlamah: ma'alim al-haymanah fi matla' al-qarn al-hadi wa'l 'ishrin." In Markaz Dirasat al-Wihdah al-'Arabiyyah, *al-'Arab wa'l 'awlamah*, p.221.

[8] See 'Abd al-Basit 'Abd al-Mu'ti, *al-I'lam wa tazyif al-wa'y* (Cairo: Dar al-Thaqafah al-Jadidah, 1979) and Mahmud Amin al-'Alim, *al-Wa'y wa'l wa'y al-zai'f fi'l fikr al-'arabi al-mu'asir* (Cairo: Dar al-Thaqafah al-Jadidah, 1986), pp.117–138.

[9] Frederic Jameson, "Notes on Globalization as Philosophical Issue." In Frederick Jameson and Masao Miyoshi, eds., *The Cultures of Globalization* (Durham: Duke University Press, 1999), p.64. Jameson also notes that, "We do not here sufficiently notice … the significance, in the Gatt and Nafta negotiations and agreements, of the cultural clauses, and of the struggle between immense US cultural interests, who want to open up foreign borders to American films, television, music, and the

the end of World War Two. Contemporary capitalism, similar to that Marx described so eloquently in the nineteenth century, is still subject to "constant revolutionizing of production, and uninterrupted disturbance of all social relations." As Aijaz Ahmad rightly notes, world capitalism, especially American capitalism, was able to make the transition from extensive industrialization to intensive technological revolution after World War Two.[10] This fact has enabled the United States to become the leading hegemonic power with a level of accumulation outpacing what both France and Britain "had enjoyed even at the height of the colonial period."[11] In the words of Noam Chomsky, the United States with its immense economic resources was able to "execute a global vision" after World War Two.[12] This global vision was based on an expanded military and economic power.[13] The unfolding of the technological revolution of post-World War Two capitalism coincided with another significant process taking place in the world at large: the deep crisis and later failure of the socialist project, which so far has had a tremendous impact on the Third World. The decade of the 1990s saw both a recession in the socialist project and a concerted effort to absorb China, the only remaining socialist country of any significant power, into the world capitalist market.[14]

The Third World, and especially the Muslim world, which began a vibrant decolonization process in the name of nationalism in the 1950s

like, and foreign nation-states who still place a premium on the preservation and development of their national languages and cultures and attempt to limit the damages—both material and social caused by the leveling power of American mass culture: material on account of the enormous financial interests involved; social because of the very change in values likely to be wrought by what used to be called—when it was a far more limited phenomenon—Americanization." Ibid., p.59.

[10] Aijaz Ahmad, *In Theory: Classes, Nations, Literatures* (New Delhi: Oxford U. Press, 1994), p.25.

[11] Ibid., p.21.

[12] Noam Chomsky, *World Orders Old and New* (New York: Columbia U. Press, 1994), p.83.

[13] See David Henrickson, *The Future of American Strategy* (New York: Holmes and Meier, 1988), and Annelise Anderson, and Dennis Bark, eds., *Thinking about America: The United States in the 1990s* (Washington, DC: Hoover Institution Press, 1988). In his economic vision of the 1940s, President Truman promised a new economic age with the 'old imperialism': "We must embark on a bold new program for making the benefits of our scientific advances and industrial progress available for the improvement and growth of underdeveloped areas. The old imperialism—exploitation for foreign profit—has no place in our plans. What we envisage is a program of development based on the concepts of democratic fair dealing. Greater production is the key to prosperity and peace." Quoted by Arturo Escobar, *Encountering Development: The Making and Unmaking of the Third World* (Princeton: Princeton University Press, 1995), p.3.

[14] For an elaboration on some of these points, see John L. Mearsheimer, *The Tragedy of Great Power Politics* (New York: W. W. Norton, 2002).

and 60s, now faces a major impasse. The nationalist project in many Third World countries seemed to have lost its energy by the end of the 1970s and the Islamist project, especially in Iran, began to pose a major challenge to Western, especially American, hegemony. However, it is important to note that as the twentieth century drew to a close, the Muslim world became entangled in what Eric Hobsbawm calls "the global fog"[15] surrounding the world economic and political system in general.

As several chapters in this book show, *Pax Americana* seems to be a *de facto* system of hegemony that no one in the Third World or even Europe dares challenge.[16] Whereas a mere thirty years ago there were no American troops in the Gulf, today the American military presence seems to be firmly entrenched.[17] Whether invited or not, American troops will remain in the Gulf as long as that area is defined as one that meets the strategic interests of the United States. However, the question facing us is this:

[15] "As the citizens of the *fin de siecle* tapped their way through the global fog that surrounded them into the third millennium, all they knew for certain was that an era of history had ended. They knew very little else." Eric Hobsbawm, *The Age of Extremes: A History of the World, 1914-1991* (New York: Vintage, 1994), pp.558–59.

[16] *Pax Americana* was enhanced after the attacks on the United States on September 11, 2001. According to one author, "In the months before September 11 [2001] the Bush Administration matched its surprisingly ideological programs with what Democrats politely described as a 'go-it-alone foreign policy'. Bush officials called a halt to negotiations with North Korea and withdrew from attempts to negotiate peace in the Middle East. They refused to sign the Kyoto Protocol on global warming and blocked a series of international arms control treaties. Then, while promising to make cuts in US strategic nuclear weapons, they declined to make an agreement with Russia on mutual reductions ... In a speech on June 1 [2002] Bush announced a new doctrine of preemptive warfare ... Apparently he had decided to let Sharon deal with the Palestinians while he went ahead with an attempt to bring down Saddam Hussein." Frances Fitzgerald, "George Bush and the World." *The New York Review of Books*, vol. XLIX, September 26, 2002, p.80. On the roots of American power, see Fareed Zakaria, *From Wealth to Power: The Unusual Origins of America's World Role* (Princeton: Princeton University Press, 1998), and Warren Zimmermann, *First Great Triumph: How Five Americans Made Their Country a World Power* (New York: Farrar, Straus and Giroux, 2001). It should be noted that some leading American thinkers opposed the idea of *Pax Americana* after World War Two. See the moving biography of American expert on China, Owen Lattimore. Robert P. Newman, *Owen Lattimore and the Loss of China* (Berkeley: University of California Press, 1992). In his comment on Asia after World War Two, Lattimore says, "All of these countries [India, Pakistan and Afghanistan] can be made allies, and very reliable allies, but they cannot be made puppets. In all of them, the passion that runs through men's veins is a passion for freedom from foreign rule. All of them are repelled by any policy that looks like restoration of colonial rule." Ibid., p.299.

[17] In achieving its goals in Iraq during the 1991 Gulf war, the United States, according to British political scientist Peter Gowan, "campaigned to criminalize the Saddam Hussain regime. (Just as the US first decided to support the regimes of Israel and Indonesia and *then* ensured the decriminalization of these countries' actions in occupying and annexing.) This process involved anthromorphising the

Will American military presence solidify authoritarianism or open the way for democratic practices in the area? This question is the more valid in view of the fact that within the United States, most people are led to believe that the United States acts with good intentions in the international arena. In the words of Edward Said, "Thus the notion that American military power might be used for malevolent purposes is relatively unthinkable within the consensus, just as the idea that America is a force for good in the world is routine and normal."[18] Some sophisticated liberal political theoreticians, such as Mark Lilla of the Committee on Social Thought at the University of Chicago, do not see much connection between the rise of new tyrannies in the post-Cold War era and American foreign policy. All Lilla can do is bemoan the inadequacy of American political language in dealing with what he terms the "new geography of tyranny" forming in the Arab and Muslim worlds lately.[19] The United States is truly a hegemonic power in the Arab world. Besides its military and economic prowess, the United States, through its advanced educational institutions, has begun to write the history of the Arab world in a scientific way. Military and economic hegemony are thus supported by intellectual power.

The first nine chapters of this book more or less treat the subject of American Empire and the ramifications of the increasing US hegemony worldwide. In the first chapter, M. Shahid Alam sheds important light on the American official and media discourse, which is rarely critical of American foreign policy. The 9/11 tragedy has not promoted any significant public debate about American foreign policy, how people overseas view American power and society, and why so many are angry with the United States. Alam concludes that America's outrage was placated by "talk of evil antagonists, promises of vengeance, and wars without end." Instead of

Iraqi state and its political-administrative organization into a single person—Saddan Hussain, criminal. And the more his human features were enlarged, the more other men and women in the 'criminal' state were dehumanized. The army of conscripts became the murder weapon, the lives of millions of Iraqis the various limbs and resources of their leader. Hence they were fair game; or else they became collateral, in the sense of standing alongside the criminal—bystanders in the police shoot-out." Peter Gowan, "The Gulf War, Iraq, and Western Liberalism." *New Left Review*, Number 187, May–June 1991, p.31.

18 Edward W. Said, "The Formation of American Public Opinion on the Question of Palestine." In his *The Politics of Dispossession* (New York: Vintage Books, 1995), p.57.

19 Mark Lilla, "The New Age of Tyranny." *The New York Review of Books*, Oct. 24, 2002: pp.28–29.

leading to a critical public debate, the 9/11 tragedy has given the neo-conservative ruling elite their golden opportunity to expand American hegemony overseas and contain dissent at home. The recent events in Iraq attest to this. In spite of the mass protest, both in the world and America, against the United States' attack on Iraq, the ruling elite did not heed any call for restraint or patience. Now that the war is over and Iraq is occupied by American troops, what is the next step in expanding American hegemony? Syria is already under attack and it would not be surprising if by the end of the year, the US demands a regime change in Syria, as it did in Iraq. All of this goes on while the United States continues in its failure to find a concrete solution to the Palestine/Israel question, the most unsettling and wide-reaching problem in the region.

In the second chapter, William Blum takes up the subject of Empire, which mainstream historiography of the United States refuses to address critically, as mentioned above. America has imposed many of its doctrines on others over the past several decades, in order to ensure its military and political preeminence. Blum takes us through the steps of the evolution of the American doctrine of military preparedness from the end of the 1991 Gulf War to the present. The White House's "National Security Strategy," published in 2002, stipulates that the United States must deter and defend against any threat before it is unleashed. What comes to mind is the unprecedented amount of money spent on defense and whether military might is the most effective way to ensure the safety of the world! Arguably, the world would have been better off had these trillions of dollars been spent on improving health and educational systems. Pepe Escobar continues the theme of Empire by discussing the ideological masterminds behind the Project for The New American Century, a think tank established in Washington, D.C. in 1997. Until a few years ago, the people behind this Project were relatively unknown in American foreign policy making. Recently, they have emerged as the most powerful ideological group on earth. This assembly of hawkish men includes such people as Paul Wolfowitz, Richard Perle, Donald Kagan, and Elliott Abrams, to mention but a few. It is composed of men who are bent on the shaping the map of the world on behalf of American interests. Arab oil is major target of this group and the security of Israel is another.

In the fourth chapter, Edward Herman takes the question of Empire in a new direction: his thesis is that America is the most dangerous rogue state in the world because of the danger it poses to world security. This certainly reflects the feeling of most people in the Arab and Muslim worlds at the moment.

The chapters on American Empire encourage open and honest debate about the importance of the United States in world politics, and about finding ways to enlighten both the American and Muslim peoples about the dangers that open-ended and unchecked American power can cause to the world and ultimately to itself as well.

The next sets of articles are written by a number of Muslim and American scholars, who bring different perspectives and treat different topics. Hamza Yusuf and John Esposito are more or less interested in the subject of inter-religious and inter-cultural dialogue between Islam and the West. Leading American Muslim thinker Zaid Shakir is concerned with finding a theological solution to or interpretation of some of the challenges facing Muslim communities worldwide. He offers an enlightening discussion of the Islamic meaning of *jihad*, an overused term that has elicited heated debate in Western intellectual circles. Shakir argues that "even in its classical formulation, *jihad* does not present a scheme of perpetual warfare."

I think that one of the most enlightening essays in this section is Abdal Hakim Murad's "Tradition or Extradition? The Threat to Muslim Americans." Murad addresses the sensitive subject of Muslim migration to the West (especially to the United States) and the social, cultural, religious, and psychological implications of the Muslim presence in the United States. He points out that there has been a history of negative American reaction to 'foreigners' from the nineteenth century on, and that the treatment American Muslims currently receive is somewhat reminiscent of that of Jews in America in the nineteenth century. The Muslim community has been subject to a consistent uninformed attack on its faith and ideological bases by the evangelical Right Wing, from whom some leading members of the current American political elite receive their support. However, Murad asks the Muslim community to rise to the challenge and train the proper religious and intellectual cadre in order to explain the concerns of the community to the larger society and help Muslim people adjust to the challenges of living in American society. Murad argues that "Regrettably … our community leadership has invested much energy in Islamic education, but has spent little time studying American culture to locate the multiple elements within it which are worthy of Muslim respect." One must agree that Muslims cannot afford to cut themselves off from the larger American society. On the contrary, they must take an active role in all aspects, especially as the American Constitution protects freedom of worship and speech. One also has to agree with Murad that some of the solutions Muslims have brought from 'back-home' do not serve the community well here. Muslims must develop their own American Muslim discourse(s). Although it is still important to read and benefit from the works of previous Muslim thinkers, Muslim intellectuals must develop a solid intellectual discourse that reflects the varieties of Muslim experience in the United States.

The editor is to be commended for assembling such articles in one volume. This book comes on the heels of a previous one, also edited by Aftab Malik, and released last year under the title of *Shattered Illusions: Analyzing the War on Terrorism* (Bristol [England]: Amal Press, 2002). Although both target an international audience, it is important for Muslim leaders, activists, thinkers, and speakers to heed the messages in these two books. An increasing number of Muslims live in what we call 'minority conditions.' As a matter of fact, around 35% of the Muslim population worldwide lives as a minority in such regions as South Asia, Africa, Western Europe and North America. Muslims must heed the editor's advice to develop their own discourse, which should be consistent with both their own tradition and the demands of modern life. We live in critical times indeed and the future will bring many surprises, both pleasant and unpleasant. The global Muslim community cannot afford to bury its head in the sand; it needs to play an active role in order to 'fix a broken world.'

AFTAB AHMAD MALIK

"The West won the world not by the superiority of its ideas or values or religion but rather by its superiority in applying organized violence. Westerners often forget this fact, non-Westerners never do."

— *Samuel Huntington*

PAX AMERICANA?

WITHIN NINE DAYS of 9/11, a group of neo-conservatives[1] had written a letter to Bush informing him on how "the war on terrorism" should proceed. It stated that Saddam Hussein needed to be overthrown, and that Syria and Iran should be targeted. In short, Bush was instructed to "exploit the attacks of 9/11 to launch a series of wars on Arab regimes," none of which had attacked the US.[2] The ex-Pentagon official, Michael Ledeen, wrote, "We must bring down the terror regimes [...] Iran, Iraq and Syria. And then we have to come to grips with Saudi Arabia." He continued to explain that by "destroying" the old orders of the day, this would "advance our historic mission."[3] When the

---

[1] "Neo-conservatives constitute an intellectual current that emerged from the cold war liberalism of the Democratic Party. Unlike other elements of the conservative mainstream, neo-conservatives have historical social roots in liberal and leftist politics. Disillusioned first with socialism and communism and later with new Democrats (like George McGovern) who came to dominate the Democratic Party in the 1970s, neo-conservatives played a key role in boosting the New Right into political dominance in the 1980s. For the most part, neoconservatives—who are disproportionately Jewish and Catholic—are not politicians but rather political analysts, activist ideologues, and scholars who have played a central role in forging the agendas of numerous right-wing think tanks, front groups, and foundations. Neo-conservatives have a profound belief in America's moral superiority, which facilitates alliances with the Christian Right and other social conservatives. But unlike either core traditionalists of American conservatism or those with isolationist tendencies, neo-conservatives are committed internationalists. As they did in the 1970s, the neo-conservatives were instrumental in the late 1990s in helping to fuse diverse elements of the right into a unified force based on a new agenda of US supremacy". See: http://www.foreignpolicy infocus.org/papers/02men/index.html.

[2] Patrick J. Buchanan, "Whose War?" *The American Conservative*, March 24, 2003.

[3] Ibid.

Bush administration proceeded to release its *New Security Strategy* document, on September 20th 2002,[4] which crystallized its foreign policy objectives, it was likened by the *Moscow Times* to Hitler's *Mein Kampf*, and described by the *New York Times*, as Bush's "how I'll rule the world" blueprint. The *Washington Monthly* commented that the Bush administration's "realist" foreign policy was based upon "the belief that the world is a nasty place; that it is morally and strategically misguided to try to "police" the world; that military muscle should be used solely to further America's national security interests; and that doing so will sometimes entail exercising power in ways that are themselves nasty and brutal."[5]

Rather than seizing the opportunity to provide balanced, thoughtful and even visionary leadership, the Bush administration has plunged the world into a foreseeable cycle of violence. The initial reaction to 9/11 was the carpet bombing of the poorest nation on earth, resulting in the deaths of more innocent civilians than on September 11th. While the US continues to increase military missions necessary to preserve *Pax Americana* and increases its permanent military presence in the world, as well as forging alliances with "unsavory regimes to advance national security interests,"[6] it is clear that such actions will only pave the way for a future generation of people which has every possibility of creating the very

---

[4] Produced every few years, the National Security Strategy often acts as a blueprint for US foreign policy. Given the events of 9/11, this document attracted considerable attention. Called "a romantic justification for easy recourse to war whenever and wherever an American president chooses," the document does not hide the fact that this administration believes "military power to be America's most effective instrument of statecraft." See: Andrew J. Bacevich, "Bush's Grand Strategy": http://www. amconmag.com. The document justifies striking at adversaries before they are able to attack, and does not rule out responding to an attack with biological or chemical weapons. The strategy reads, "The United States will continue to make clear that it reserves the right to respond with overwhelming force—including through resort to all of our options—to the use of WMD against the United States, our forces abroad, and friends and allies." In fact, the Bush administration is researching a new generation of nuclear weapons that are able to destroy targets buried deep beneath the earth. The document talks about how the US must "reaffirm the essential role of American military strength" and how it should "build and maintain our defenses beyond challenge." It must maintain forces "strong enough to dissuade potential adversaries" from the dream of ever "surpassing, or equaling, the power of the United States." In short, the document explicitly asserts a *Pax Americana*: US dominance, unrivalled and unchallenged. Those who do attempt to challenge the lone superpower, will be squashed by its military might and technological superiority.

[5] Joshua Green, "God's Foreign Policy: Why the biggest threat to Bush's war strategy is not coming from Muslims, but from Christians," *The Washington Monthly*, November 2001: http://www. washingtonmonthly.com/features/2001/0111.green.html.

[6] Ibid.

"blowback" that was seen on September 11th 2001.[7] The current method of using force, pre-emptive strikes, unilateral action and "regime change" only adds fuel to the fire that has been steadily burning in the Middle East, and has every chance of spreading.

DOUBLE STANDARDS, AGAIN

There already exists a great deal of anger and resentment in the Middle East stemming from the double standards, moral hypocrisy and political expediency shown to this region by the very powers professing to promote freedom and democracy. Their interventions and talk of "peace" have always raised suspicion in Muslim and Arab minds.[8] Faisal Bodi, writing in *The Guardian*, correctly asserts that "what the Muslim world needs right

---

7 To understand the phenomenon of 'blowback' and its connection to September 11th, see: Jeff Sommers, "The Middle East and Blowback against the US," in *Shattered Illusions: Analyzing the War on Terrorism* (Ed) Aftab A. Malik, (Amal Press, 2002) Bristol, p 189

8 The Muslim world questions why suddenly, the US and UK have shown such concern for the Iraqis well being, when all along, they continued to provide Saddam with weapons that have been used against his own people, as well as supporting him financially. The sanctions that have been in place, largely at the behest of the US and UK governments, have been the direct cause of the deaths of hundreds of thousands of innocent Iraqi civilians, a conclusion of the UN's own reports. There was no outcry by the Bush and Blair governments at the rampant cancers that have affected thousands of children, as a result of the depleted uranium tipped shells used back in the first Gulf War. The Muslim world does not fail to see behind the masquerade of "human rights" and "liberation", when all they see is a selective promotion of them. There can be no discussion of the Muslim and Arab world's skepticism towards the West, without discussing Israel in the Muslim psyche. The Muslim world continues to see the US consistently defend and support Israel economically and militarily, while it continues to be in breach of over sixty UN resolutions. While the US may verbally condemn acts which cause outrage, this is seen to be hypocritical, since the US continues to provide the military hardware that is often used against the Palestinians. Describing this approach in policy toward Israel, the former Conservative leader William Hague recently wrote: "They (the US) pursue a 'one-sided' policy on Israel because without it the Jews would be driven into the sea." The implication here is that Arabs and Muslims want to commit genocide and ethnic cleansing. See: William Hague, "The resentments of old Europe," *The Spectator*, 15 March, 2003. This is quite startling, in light of outlandish comments made by the Zionist founders and supporters of Israel: "We must do everything to ensure they [the Palestinian refugees] never do return." David Ben-Gurion, in his diary, 18 July 1948, quoted in Michael Bar Zohar's *Ben-Gurion: The Armed Prophet* (Prentice-Hall, 1967), p.157; "If I was an Arab leader I would never make [peace] with Israel. That is natural: we have taken their country." David Ben Gurion, quoted in *The Jewish Paradox*, by Nahum Goldmann, Weidenfeld and Nicolson, 1978, p.99; "In our country there is room only for the Jews. We shall say to the Arabs: Get out! If they don't agree, if they resist, we shall drive them out by force." Professor Ben-Zion Dinur (1954), one of Israel's founding Ministers of Education and Culture (quoted from: http://www. amandashome.com/why.html); "We walked outside, Ben-Gurion accompanying us. Allon repeated his question, 'What is to be done with the Palestinian population?' Ben-Gurion waved his hand in a gesture which said 'Drive them out!'" Leaked censored version of Rabin memoirs, published in the

now, is a long period of calm and stability, not one based on security apparatuses and dictators, but on the free expression of the collective will of its peoples."[9] This period of calm will not come from having invaded and occupied Iraq. Despite there being no link or connection between Iraq and 9/11,[10] a recent poll revealed that "one in two American's now believe Saddam was responsible for the attack on the World Trade Centre."[11] The advisors around Bush, who have been insistent from the outset that the administration should go to war, such as Perle, Wolfowitz and even Bush

New York Times, 23 October 1979; "Everybody has to move, run and grab as many hilltops as they can to enlarge the settlements because everything we take now will stay ours … Everything we don't grab will go to them." Ariel Sharon, Israeli Foreign Minister, addressing a meeting of militants from the extreme right-wing Tsomet Party, Agence France Presse, November 15, 1998. There are many such outlandish statements, and it should be quite clear exactly *who* is attempting to drive out whom. The myth that the Israeli-Palestinian conflict is one that has continued because of "mindless Arab hatred of the Jews" has been repudiated by work mostly carried out by Israeli academicians and journalists. They conclude that the dynamics of the conflict is not rooted "in mindless Arab anti-Semitism but in Zionism's insistence that a Jewish state must be created in Palestine, despite the fact that for over 1,300 years it has been overwhelmingly inhabited by Arabs." See: Jerome Slater, "What Went Wrong? The Collapse of the Israeli-Palestinian Peace Process," *Political Science Quarterly*, Volume 116, Number 2, Summer 2001, pp.172–173.

9 Faisal Bodi, "Of course it's a war on Islam," *The Guardian*, October 17, 2001.

10 When one tries to understand why the "coalition of the willing" were so willing to wage war with Iraq, one cannot help but question the flimsy arguments put forward. Donald Rumsfeld told the world that he had "bullet-proof evidence" that Iraq was behind the September 11 attacks. In fact, not a shred of evidence has been produced since. A campaign was then launched to link Iraq to the anthrax attacks in the US in 2001, and after it became clear that Iraq was not responsible for these attacks, the media interest all but vanished. To date, the anthrax cases remain unsolved. In one of the dossiers produced by the Blair government, it noted how Saddam's son tortured the Iraqi football team at half time to make them play better in the second half. However, FIFA, the international football authority told the government that they had investigated this and found that it was an "obvious falsehood." See: George Galloway, "Galloway Speaks on Iraq: Another Century of Slavery," IslamOnline: http://www.islam-online.net/English/Views/2002/12/article10.shtml. The last dossier prepared was exposed as having parts plagiarized from a decade old PhD thesis, verbatim in parts. While presenting this dossier, UK officials gave the impression that it was the most recent intelligence that had been gathered on Saddam Hussein and his regime. The truth was far from that. Officials did not even bother to correct typographic mistakes that appeared in the original thesis, written by Ibrahim al-Marashi, a postgraduate student from California. (You can read a sample of the plagiarized dossier at: http://www.channel4.com/news/home/z/stories/20030206/#1). The editing of 8,000 pages from Iraq's 11,800-page dossier on weapons (by US officials) caused considerable anger within the international community. While the US told the world that the pages deleted were rehashed statements and repetitive comments, we were not told that the pages included a list of 150 companies, 24 of them US based, that helped Saddam develop his weapons program, some of them companies we all know well. (For the complete list of companies see: http://www.taz.de/pt/2002/12/19/a0080.nf/text). When the US produced the Niger papers, proving that Saddam had actively sought to acquire uranium to make nuclear reactors, UN inspectors quickly exposed the papers as "crude fakes."

11 John Le Carré, "The United States of America has gone mad." Times Online: http://www.times-online.co.uk/article/0,,482-543296,00.html.

himself, have not been in a war, nor served their country in one. While it was clear that they had over-rated their ability to "shock and awe" the Iraqis into a quick submission, or to have hoped for a Shi'a insurrection, one wonders what the real reason was behind Perle's resignation, which only attracted scant press coverage here in the UK.[12]

It appears that the very governments who have been talking about empowering the Iraqi people, wishing them to have freedom and liberation, have forgotten how they have treated the very same people with utter contempt. Robin Cook, in his resignation speech, spoke of the hypocrisy of how during the 1980s "[…] the US sold Saddam the anthrax agents and then the British government built his chemical munitions factories."[13] Just eleven months after Saddam had gassed between 6,000 and 8,000 Iraqi Kurds at Halabjah in 1988, the US Assistant Secretary of State, James Kelly, flew to Baghdad and told Saddam of how he was seen by his government as a source of "moderation" in the region, and how the US wanted to "broaden" their relationship with him. While Saddam continued to use his chemical weapons, both against Iran and the Iraqis, recent declassified documents show how Donald Rumsfeld, then special "peace" envoy to the Middle East, traveled regularly to Baghdad, and continued to provide financial assistance to Saddam. There also seems to be some timely amnesia about how the UK, when a colonial power, dealt with attempts by Kurds to establish their own independent state, in the wake of the demise of the Ottoman Empire. It was Winston Churchill,[14] who

---

[12]   Richard Perle, dubbed "the Prince of Darkness," by some, and a man of "integrity and honor" according to Rumsfeld, was one of the chief architects of the war on Iraq. His resignation from his post as chairman of the influential Defense Policy Board came amidst a controversy of his private lobbying efforts. As chair of the Defense Policy Board, Perle sat with former government officials (such as former national security advisors Henry Kissinger and Richard Allen, former defense secretaries, Harold Brown and James Schlesinger, former Vice President Dan Quayle, former Secretary of State George P. Shultz and former CIA Director, James Woolsey) to offer advice on planning and "major matters of defense policy." Perle is among the group of neo-conservatives that pressed Bush for pre-emptive military action and to change regimes that may threaten the US. If his dismissal was caused by a conflict of interests between his business and governmental roles, one wonders why other members of the board haven't also resigned, such as Dick Cheney, who secured Halliburton's lucrative reconstruction projects of post Saddam Iraq.

[13]   Robin Cook, "Why I Had to Leave the Cabinet," *The Guardian*, March 18, 2003. Ralph Nader joked that the US and UK were so sure that Saddam had these WMD's, since they had kept the receipts!

[14]   Winston Churchill is credited with having "invented" what we know today as modern day Iraq over dinner. Previously, no such name existed. At the post-war carve up of the Ottoman Empire, Iraq was comprised of three provinces: Mosul in the North, Baghdad in the centre and Basra in the south.

in 1919 authorized the use of chemical weapons on the Kurds. He stated coldly that "I am strongly in favor of using poisoned gas against uncivilized tribes." He further explained that chemical weapons were merely "the application of western science to modern warfare."[15] Science has certainly improved since, and so have its war tools. Monstrous inventions such as cluster bombs, bunker busters, daisy cutters and the new, "Mother of All Bombs" (MOAB),[16] are used to ensure that the civilized nations can bring freedom and justice to those most deserving. Simple, cruder and out dated weapons of mass destruction, such as poisonous gas, are sold off to third world tyrants and thugs, knowing that they will be used to suppress their own people.[17] The Iraqi people certainly have much to be thankful for, being liberated by Britain and America, who have such honorable intentions.

As soon as oil was discovered in large quantities in Kurdish areas, Churchill joined Kurdistan to Iraq, bringing it under British Control. As soon as the Kurds objected and pressed for independence, RAF bomber squadrons were enlisted to crush the Kurdish "rebellion". As now, war provided an opportunity for the British to experiment with their latest weapons. Air to ground missiles, phosphorous bombs, metal crows feet, man-killing shrapnel, liquid fire and delay action bombs were all unleashed upon the Kurds. The impression that the British wanted to convey to new Iraq of wanting to liberate them from the shackles of the Ottoman Empire, and to bring them democracy (sounds very familiar) was clearly a false one. The then Secretary of State, Sir Laming Worthington-Evans, noted that "if the Arab population realize the peaceful control of Mesopotamia depends upon our intention of bombing women and children, I am very doubtful if we shall gain the acquiescence of the fathers and husbands of Mesopotamia to which the Secretary of State for the Colonies [Churchill] looks forward." Cf. Noam Chomsky, *Deterring Democracy* (Vintage, 1992) pp.181–2 and 254.

[15] Ibid., pp.62, and 258.

[16] The acronym "MOAB" ("mother of all bombs") is also, interestingly, a name for an old Biblical city in the Sinai desert that was the scene for many important events in Bible history. We are told that "Many prophets condemned Moab for scoffing and boasting against Israel" and it was the scene of many battles. (see: http://www.aboutbibleprophecy.com/s21.htm). Moab is also related to the Biblical prophet "Job" who was known in the Muslim world as in the Christian world, for his patience. The medieval Hanbali Muslim scholar, Ibn al-Qayyim al-Jawziya, in his "Patience and Gratitude" writes of the numerous benefits and importance of being patient. There is a Prophetic saying of Muhammad, may God bless him and grant him peace, who said: "There is no gift better than patience." MOAB, the destructive device, is known as a "smart" bomb, whereas the Daisy Cutter is called a "Dumb bomb." The MOAB bomb is the most powerful conventional bomb in the US arsenal to date. It is 40% more powerful than the 15,000 pound Daisy Cutter. Officials have said that the bomb was partly designed to be a "psychological weapon designed to instill fear."

[17] "The US has supplied arms, security equipment and training to governments and armed groups that have committed torture, political killings and other human rights abuses in countries around the world." *Amnesty International* report in "United States of America – Rights for All" October 1998. Britain continues to supply weapons to countries that have been marred by internal conflict. When questioned about supplying weapons to Israel, in light of continued condemnation by the UN for their treatment of Palestinians, Blair remarked that if they (Britain) didn't sell them to Israel, some-

THE WRONG MESSAGES

Despite both Bush and Blair stating that this war on terrorism is not about a war with Islam, many Muslims have seen what has been taking shape globally and have not reached the same conclusion. In a report entitled, *Opportunism in the face of Tragedy: Repression in the name of Anti-Terrorism*, Human Rights Watch stated that "many countries around the globe cynically attempted to take advantage of this struggle (of fighting terrorism) to intensify their own crackdowns." It listed a number of countries that had used 9/11 as an excuse to conveniently connect all Muslims of their choice to al-Qaʿida, and hence to term them all terrorists.[18] Other alarming developments included anti-Islamic rhetoric from White House officials and the confrontational postures taken by advisors that surrounded Bush. Christian fundamentalists were insisting that Islam was at war with Christianity and the general tone of the American media made Muslims feel that they were constantly under scrutiny.

Kenneth Adelman, who serves on the Pentagon's Defense Policy board, remarked that calling Islam a peaceful religion was an "increasingly hard argument to make." He explained that "The more you examine the religion, the more militaristic it seems. After all, its founder Muhammad was a warrior, not a peace advocate like Jesus." Paul Weyrich, an activist who

one else would. Britain continued to supply machine guns used by General Suharto's regime in East Timor, after it had been identified as the source of the worst human rights abuses, including massacre and torture. On the day of 9/11, the Blair government was hosting an arms fair in the Docklands area of East London, which was visited by a number of human rights abusers. In stark contradiction to his own policy, while conducting an interview with David Frost in the UK, Tony Blair mentioned that the way to defeat terrorists would be by stopping "the people who gave them the weapons". John Pilger made the point that both the American and British arms industry boomed after 9/11. He pointed out that Lockheed Martin secured a $200 billion contract, the biggest military order in history. In Britain, the Labor government gave its backing to a BAE sale worth £40 million to one of the world's poorest countries, Tanzania, which was opposed by the World Bank. See John Pilger, *The New Rulers of the World*, (Verso, 2002) pp.128–32.

18   The countries cited where this occurred included Uzbekistan, China, Kashmir, Chechnya, Israel and Malaysia. It was no surprise that Ariel Sharon, citing the 9/11 tragedy as an attack on "our common values", unleashed an all out attack upon the Palestinians, and reoccupied six Palestinian towns beginning with Jenin. Vladmir Putin quickly capitalized on the moment by declaring that, "Bin Laden's people are connected with the events currently taking place in Chechnya [...] so we have a common foe." With that, the Chechen freedom-fighters became terrorists and no distinction was made between them and al-Qaʿida. China soon moved to crush the Uigher struggle for autonomy in the Xinjiang Uighur Autonomous Region, where the fighters are now known as "violent terrorists." See: Fatema Gulamhussein, "Ever shifting identity of Bush's campaign against terror," *The Muslim News*, 25th October 2002.

has a considerably degree of influence in the White House, wrote "Islam is at war against us." He went on to express his concern at the "administration's constant promotion of Islam as a religion of peace and tolerance just like Judaism or Christianity. It is neither." Jerry Falwell, a religious conservative, was bold enough to declare that Muhammad was a "terrorist." He later apologized, which few others have done. The evangelist Franklin Graham called Islam "evil" and a faith that encouraged violence. The religious broadcaster, Pat Robertson, complained in his interview with the *Washington Times*, that Bush "is not elected as chief theologian" and like those before him, objected to Bush's portrayal of Islam as peaceful. Even when Bush's own Attorney General, John Ashcroft, the one responsible for implementing the anti-terrorism laws against Muslims, made the remarkably ignorant assertion that, "the difference between Christianity and Islam is that in Christianity God sent His son to die for humankind, but in Islam God demands that humans send their sons to die for Him"[19]—there was no apology. Daniel Pipes, a political analyst and author of *Militant Islam Reaches America*, seen as America's leading "Islamophobe", saw "analogies between militant Islam and communism and fascism." He continued to proclaim, "This is a virulent, hostile ideology that is in our midst." Pipes, who claimed that between 10 to 15 percent of Muslims are "potential killers," has recently been nominated by Bush to join the board of the United States Institute of Peace, a federal institution created by Congress that was formed to promote the peaceful resolution of international conflicts. This appointment will surely stoke the fires of controversy and cause serious concern, since it is common knowledge that Pipes has a history of fierce anti-Islamic rhetoric.[20] As the PBS documentary "Muhammad: Legacy of a Prophet" was aired in the US, he called it an "outrage" and urged people to sue the channel for misuse of public funds, and for attempting to convert people to Islam. Writing in the *Jerusalem Post* in January of this year, Pipes actually argued for increased surveillance of American Muslim citizens. He wrote "There is no escaping the unfortunate fact that Muslim government employees in law enforcement, the military, and the diplomatic corps need to be watched for

---

[19] Khaled Abou El Fadl, "Introduction", *Shattered Illusions*, op. cit., p.22.
[20] For Daniel Pipes' articles on the dangers and threats of Islam, see www.amisraelhai.org.

connections to terrorism, as do Muslim chaplains in prisons and the armed forces [...] Muslim schools require increased oversight to ascertain what is being taught to children [...]" [21] The President's choice of Pipes is far from perfect, and will continue to send out the wrong messages to the Muslim hearts and minds that he so desperately wants to win.

Many Muslims now see their "post 9/11" function in the West simply reduced to defending Islam from clichés and stereotypes that have become entrenched in the minds of the public, accentuated by various elements of the media. For example, there was outrage amongst Muslims as a spate of cartoons emerged depicting Islam as either a backward or a violent religion. In one editorial cartoon headlined "What Would Mohammed Drive?" it depicted the Prophet Muhammad driving a nuclear bomb-laden truck.[22] Despite continued efforts to extract an apology, none materialized. As one professor noted in the US, 9/11 seemed to have opened the floodgates of anti-Islamic literature that was not simply restricted to articles in newspapers and magazines. There appeared to be a "virtual avalanche of publications that express unrestrained animosity towards Islam as a religion, and Muslims as a people," which seemed to reflect the way that the public discourse has been set in the US.[23]

It is hard *not* to believe that these neo-conservatives and fundamentalist Christians that surround Bush are determined to set up a civilizational conflict with Islam. Rather than expressing outrage or condemning this unrelenting flow of religious bigotry, Bush has merely noted his disagreement, but has not taken steps to distance himself from those who continue to preach intolerance against Islam. In a poll conducted in

---

[21] To read more on Daniel Pipes see: http://www.cair-net.org/misc/people/daniel_pipes.html.

[22] See http://www.cair-net.org/images/mohammeddrive.gif.

[23] Professor Khaled Abou El Fadl, writing in the introduction to *Shattered Illusions*, compiled a list of some books that were either published or reissued after 9/11 that demonized Islam and the Muslims. He included two books which he deemed to be "particularly sinister works that attempt to demonize all politically active Muslim individuals or organizations" which are: Steven Emerson, *American Jihad: The Terrorists Among Us* (New York: Simon & Schuster, 2002), & Daniel Pipes, *Militant Islam Reaches America* (New York: W.W. Norton Co., 2002). Books that clearly conveyed their Islamophobia include: Dan Benjamin, *The Age of Sacred Terror: Radical Islam's War Against America* (New York: Random House Publishers, 2002); Anthony J. Dennis, *The Rise of the Islamic Empire and the Threat to the West* (New York: Wyndham Hall Press, 2001); Mark A. Gabriel, *Islam and Terrorism: What the Qu'ran Really Teaches About Christianity, Violence, and the Goals of the Islamic Jihad* (New York: Charisma House, 2002); George Grant, *The Blood of the Moon: Understanding the*

December 2002 by the BBC, it was revealed that more than two-thirds of British Muslims considered the war on terrorism to be a war against Islam. Ironically, when Bush and Co. met in the Azores, they did so on an island that was "originally settled by a Portuguese Crusader whose goal was to encircle the Muslim world with Christian armies."[24] Whatever the situation or statements made, it seems as though the efforts of Bush and Blair to convince the Muslim world that this is not a war against Islam have failed dramatically.

WMD: WORDS OF MASS DECEPTION

In his State of the Union address earlier this year, Bush asserted that Saddam's regime was "assembling the world's most dangerous weapons" which included the ability to produce "as much as 500 tons of sarin, mustard and VX nerve agent" capable of killing "untold thousands." Bush stated that US intelligence indicated that "Saddam Hussein had upwards of 30,000 munitions capable of delivering chemical agents" and biological materials such as anthrax and botulinum toxin.[25] Britain was told that Saddam's WMD could be ready within 45 minutes, and the Prime Minister told Parliament that his "weapons of mass destruction program is active, detailed and growing [...] it is up and running now." Jack Straw, the Foreign Secretary, summed up the case for war when he affirmed that "Saddam's removal is necessary to eradicate the threat from his weapons of mass destruction."[26] In short, the case for war was built upon the

Historic Struggle Between Islam and Western Civilization (New York: Thomas Nelson Press, rev. ed. 2001); David Earle Johnson, *Conspiracy in Mecca: What You Need to Know About the Islamic Threat* (New York: David Johnson Books, 2002); Sumrall Lester, *Jihad—The Holy War: Time Bomb in the Middle East* (New York: Sumrall Publishing, 2002); John F. MacArthur, *Terrorism, Jihad, and the Bible* (New York: W Publishing Co., 2001); John F. Murphy Jr., *The Sword of Islam: Muslim Extremism from the Arab Conquests to the Attack on America* (New York: Prometheus Books, 2002); Adam Parfrey (ed.), *Extreme Islam: Anti-American Propaganda of Muslim Fundamentalism* (New York: Feral House, 2002); Robert Spencer, *Islam Unveiled: Disturbing Questions About the World's Fastest Growing Faith* (New York: Encounter Books, 2002); Larry Spargimino, *Religion of Peace or Refuge for Terror?* (New York: Hearthstone: 2002); Marvin Yakos, *Jesus vs. Jihad* (New York: Creation House, 2001). For a scholarly study on the subject of holy war in Islam, see John Esposito, *Unholy War: Terror in the Name of Islam* (Oxford: Oxford University Press, 2002).

24 Robert Sheer, " A Naked Bid To Redraw World Map", *Los Angeles Times*, March 18th, 2003.

25 For a transcript of the 2003 State of the Union Address made by Bush and a detailed response to it, see the Institute for Public Accuracy: http://www.accuracy.org/2003/.

26 All quotes, unless stated, are taken from "Weapons of Mass Destruction: Who Said What When" compiled by CounterPunch. See: http://www.counterpunch.org

premise that Saddam Hussein posed an immediate threat to the world with his arsenal of WMD.

It is remarkable then, after occupying Iraq, no WMD have yet been found. Donald Rumsfeld, addressing the Council on Foreign Relations in New York in May, stated that the Pentagon did not "know what happened" to Iraq's alleged arsenal of WMD. It was only in March that Rumsfeld positively confirmed that "we know where they are." Rumsfeld's only suggestion was that Saddam might have destroyed the WMD stockpiles just before the war. However, only two months prior to this, Blair responded to suggestions that Saddam's WMD had been destroyed as "palpably absurd." In his interview with the Spanish daily, *El Pais,* Hans Blix, the Chief UN Weapons Inspector, doubted that the US themselves believed that Saddam actually possessed any WMD.[27] David Blunkett, the British Home Secretary, made the confession in a BBC radio interview that no chemical, biological or nuclear WMD may after all be found. Regardless of whether they were found or not, Blunkett went on to say that the world could rejoice at the "fall" of Saddam Hussein and his regime. Recall that the former Chief UN Inspector, Scott Ritter, stated repeatedly that Iraq's chemical, biological and nuclear programs had been "destroyed or rendered harmless." By depriving the last UN inspection team of the time they needed to uncover these WMD, one can't help but think that perhaps the hawks feared that the inspectors were doing their work too well. Perhaps with even a little more time, they would have robbed them of their excuse for going to war.

In the weeks that followed the invasion of Iraq, it became progressively apparent that Bush and Blair misled people in order to build support for the invasion. It seems that their campaign for war involved exaggerating and distorting documents and reports. While we were informed of an overriding and immediate threat from the WMD Saddam possessed, a leaked top secret pre-war report by America's Defense Intelligence Agency concluded there was "no reliable information" that Iraq had chemical weapons.[28] It dates from September 2002 when Donald

---

[27] Cf. "Iraq War was planned long in advance, says Hans Blix" in *The News International,* (London Edition) April 11, 2003, p.11.

[28] "Why America is waking up to the truth about WMD": http://www.sundayherald.com/34463.

Rumsfeld was publicly claiming Saddam had huge WMD stockpiles. In February 2003, *The New York Times* reported, "Some analysts at the Central Intelligence Agency have complained that senior administration officials have exaggerated the significance of some intelligence reports about Iraq, particularly about its possible links to terrorism, in order to strengthen their political argument for war."[29]

A recent article investigated how British Intelligence was based upon skewed information which contributed towards the dossiers that were published to convince the parliament and people of the necessity of war. Established by the Defense Intelligence Staff within the Ministry of Defense in 1991, "Operation Rockingham" provided intelligence on Iraq's WMD program but ensured that information "which indicated that Saddam's stockpiles had been destroyed or wound down" was ignored. Such "intelligence" was supplied to the Joint Inteligence Committee (JIC) which was behind the intelligence dossiers that the government published. Some connection has been made between the activities of the JIC and the Office of Special Plans (OSP) established by Donald Rumsfeld which gathered US intelligence that laid down the case for war. According to former CIA officer, Larry Johnson, the OSP was "dangerous for US national security and a threat to world peace." He added that it "lied and manipulated intelligence to further its agenda of removing Saddam."[30]

The simple fact that Saddam did not use any WMD to defend Iraq, let alone Baghdad, raises the question as to exactly how he posed a threat to the world, when he was unable to defend his own capital with any credible defense. While the US has now become the authority that will continue the search for these weapons, "who will stop the US from bringing chemical weapons from outside Iraq and moving them into the country to prove their longstanding claims?" asks Dr. Imad Jadd, international relations specialist at the Egyptian based al-Ahram Centre, echoing the growing suspicion of many in the Arab world. It would not be surprising if some rusting barrels of "weaponizable" chemicals were to be found and

---

[29] How Bush, Bliar, Howard Lied About "Iraqi WMD": http://www.greenleft.org.au/back/2003/541/541p14.htm.

[30] "Revealed: The secret cabal which spun for Blair": http://www.sundayherald.com/34491.

both Bush and Blair could claim their victory at saving civilization. It would be one thing if the UN found WMD in a country controlled by Saddam, and it would be quite another story if WMD are to be found in the country controlled by the coalition forces. Summing up the allied case for war, former Chief UN Weapons Inspector, Scott Ritter said "not one single piece of information was proved. We went to war based on garbage." This is not so far from the "official" position. Recently, Paul Wolfowitz candidly remarked that it was "for bureaucratic reasons, we settled on one issue, weapons of mass destruction (as justification for invading Iraq) because it was the one reason everyone could agree on."

ERASING HISTORY IN THE LIGHT OF VICTORY

As images were beamed across the globe of Iraqis rejoicing in Baghdad, Rumsfeld remarked in a press conference that such scenes were "breathtaking." He continued to say that "Saddam Hussein is now taking his rightful place alongside Hitler, Stalin, Lenin, Ceaucescu in the pantheon of failed, brutal dictators [...]" The world should not fail to recognize that the US government continued to support this "brutal dictator" with weapons technology, economic aid and intelligence right up to two months prior to Iraq's invasion of Kuwait. Saddam's incredible oppression of his own people has been well documented and was well known to the US, which chose to support this tyrant, who casually used torture to oppress his people. Amnesty International detailed some thirty ways in which Saddam carried this out, which ranged from "beating to mutilation, from rape to electrocution, including the gouging out of the eyes, the cutting off of noses, breasts, penises and limbs. Heavy-metal poisoning as a favored means of killing off undesirables. Lead and thallium [administered] to prisoners in soft drinks [...] children are routinely tortured [...] whipped, sexually abused and given electric shocks."[31] It is the height of moral bankruptcy and hypocrisy that the US now projects itself as the liberator of the people of Iraq, when all along it has aided and abetted Saddam in his crimes against his people. If the world learns one lesson, it is that

---

31 Cf. "Saddam Hussein: still crazy after all these years," (pp.114–115) in, *World Famous Villains: The worst dictators, murderers, gangsters and crooks of all time*, (Eds) Colin Rowan and Damon Wilson (Parragon: 1995).

invasion erases history.[32] In the moment of glory, all that has happened previously is now conveniently swept under the carpet.

THE NEO-CONSERVATIVES' MOMENT OF POWER

International public opinion had been vehemently against any war with Iraq[33] from the beginning, and even Iraq's own neighbors (including Kuwait and Iran but with the notable exception of Israel) did not see Iraq as an immediate threat to them. We have been told constantly that this war is not for oil, but we only need to look back at what has taken place in post-Taliban Afghanistan to see what lies in store for a post-Saddam Iraq.[34]

---

[32] I would like to thank Professor Eric Herring, Senior Lecturer in International Politics at the University of Bristol for this phrase.

[33] For instance, a document signed by 318 organizations and parliamentarians around the world against going to war with Iraq, included the signatories from the Anglican Church Worldwide (with 73 million members); the 1985 Nobel-prize winning International Physicians for the Prevention of Nuclear War; Friends of the Earth International; the International Association of Lawyers Against Nuclear Arms; The International Peace Bureau, and 70 members of parliaments from Australia, New Zealand, Canada, the UK, Egypt, Russia, Belgium, Netherlands, Sweden, Ghana and the Europarliament. There are countless other such documents.

[34] UNOCAL had plans to build a 1,000 mile pipeline from the Caspian Sea through Afghanistan to the Arabian sea, but despite the Taliban being invited to Texas, they blocked any such possible developments. John Maresca, VP of UNOCAL, testified before Congress and said that the pipeline would be impossible to build while the Taliban remained in power. After 1999, the Taliban became thought of the most evil people in the world, as seen through the eyes of America. In 2001, Bush declared war against Afghanistan, though not a single Afghan was involved in the hijacking of the planes. As soon as the Taliban government was removed, the new leader, a certain Hamid Karzai was elected. Karzai coincidently happened to previously work for UNOCAL. Bush then appointed a special envoy, Lakhdar Ibrahimi, to represent the US in dealings with the newly recognized, US-friendly government. Incidentally, he too had links with UNOCAL; he was formerly chief consultant to UNOCAL. In January 2002, the US government quietly announced that it will support the Trans-Afghan pipeline construction. In a stunning new study by the Institute for Policy Studies, based upon recent declassified diplomatic papers, the study reveals just how much of a large role oil is playing in this 'war'. Titled "Crude Vision: How Oil Interests Obscured US Government Focus on Chemical Weapons Use by Saddam Hussein," this report focuses upon the efforts by Reagan officials in the mid 1980s to win Saddam's approval for a $2 billion oil pipeline to be built by Bechtel. Interestingly, Bechtel is now likely to receive a major contract for building most of Iraq's infrastructure along with Parsons' group, which has Halliburton as a secondary contractor. Halliburton is Vice President Cheney's former company. Many of those Reagan officials, who back in the 1980s tried to convince Saddam of this Aqaba pipeline, are now deciding the fate of Iraq. The report revealed that while Rumsfeld made regular trips to Baghdad as a White House peace envoy, rather than taking Saddam to task about the chemical bombs that he was dropping on Iran, they spoke about Bechtel's proposed pipeline. Bechtel also turned up in the 11,800 paged dossier produced by Iraq, and was listed as one of the company's that had helped Saddam with equipment and knowledge for making chemical weapons.

With concern mounting that other countries in the region have been targeted for US pre-emptive strikes, the British Prime Minister and the Foreign Secretary have begun to deny such plans, despite the neo-conservatives' repeated statements, papers and articles that the mission in Baghdad "does not end there," and how after Baghdad is taken, there will be "an earthquake throughout the region [...]"[35] In Rome, US Under Secretary of State for Arms Control and International Security, John Bolton, warned Syria to heed the lessons of the US-led war in Iraq. Rumsfeld has continued to reiterate charges that Syria was sending military aid into Iraq. He also accused Syria of helping family members and supporters of Saddam Hussein into Syria. It appears that both Tony Blair and Jack Straw are out of sync with the rest of the US team.

Bush and Blair continually changed reasons as to why the invasion of Iraq was justified, and the reason finally used, that of WMD, seems to have lost its significance since the occupation of Iraq. "The only path to peace and security is the path of action" is the Bush doctrine. In other words, the US is ready to wage perpetual war, because without it, the Bush administration perceives that there can be no peace. The Bush administration has mapped out a world that essentially consists of two camps: the good and the evil. "The good is civilized and, naturally, the evil is not ... [E]ither one had to join the good guys, the upholders of civilization and civility, or conversely, be counted among the evildoers, the dwellers in the darkness of barbarity."[36] There is no space for dissent or for critical analysis of the current Bush plan. This has been all but muted. Anyone brave enough to speak out is painted as "a) anti-Semitic b) anti-American, c) with the enemy, and d) a terrorist."[37]

Uncertainty and anxiety prevail as to what will happen to post-Saddam Iraq, and many questions remain to be answered. For example, what role will ex-CIA Director, James Woolsey, have in Iraq's reconstruction? Woolsey declared that it is US policy to go after Syria and Iran and destabilize Saudi Arabia and Egypt. Speaking at UCLA, for Americans for Victory over Terrorism, Woolsey declared that the war on Iraq was about more

---

35 Robert Dreyfuss "Just the Beginning," *The American Prospect*, vol. 14, 4 April 1, 2003.

36 Khaled Abou El Fadl, op. cit., p1.

37 John Le Carre, "The United States of America has gone mad" Times Online: http://www.times online.co.uk/article/0,,482-543296,00.html.

than the liberation of Iraq. We are fighting "World War IV," he said, "a war that will last longer than World Wars I and II." If he has a pivotal role in the new administration, are we about to see the opening of the doors of a new political order in the Middle East? How long will the US remain in Iraq? While there is no doubt that many Iraqis were, and are overjoyed that Saddam is no longer in power, this does not mean that they would tolerate an on-going presence of US troops. As Robert Jensen pointed out, "joy over the removal of Hussein does not mean joy over an American occupation." How will Iran take to having a large American presence on its doorstep, and what role will it play, if any, within Iraq, through influencing the large Shi'a population? While the US has enjoyed a military victory, fear and loathing of the US in the Islamic world is on a scale that has not been seen before. Both Osama bin Laden and al-Qa'ida emerged because of an American presence on Saudi soil; there is a possibility that a prolonged presence in Iraq could make it a fertile ground for radicalism. What about Ahmad Chalabi, a fugitive from justice in Jordan, convicted of fraud and head of the Iraqi National Congress? Will he, as the Pentagon's favorite, be nominated by the US to lead Iraq, or will the Iraqis be able to choose from their own people? In short, there exists a great deal of tension within the Muslim and Arab world as to the future of the Middle East, and the role the US will come to play in it.

While recognizing that the invasion of Iraq was part of the "war on terrorism," the United States' establishment needs to seriously reflect upon its role in the world. It must recognize that terrorism against the US is the predictable outcome of repeated and unwarranted intervention in the affairs of other nations. This should be no surprise as it was also the conclusion of the Pentagon's Defense Science Board in 1997. It has been such forceful interventions in the Muslim and Arab world that has made both Islam and the US victims of extremists on both sides.[38] We need to

---

[38] It goes without saying that the Muslim world *cannot* simply blame the US for its extremists. Since the very first century of Islam, Muslims suffered from extremist theologies that displayed severe intolerance to both non-Muslims and even Muslims who did not agree with their views. While such theologies were always pushed to the fringes in the past, the eventual dismantling of traditional places of learning by colonialists has allowed uninformed individuals to make literal and extreme interpretations of Sacred Law that are in contradiction to and radically different from the previous centuries of traditional Islamic practice and learning. The result has been examples of extreme religious practice devoid of any real knowledge and characterized by bigotry, intolerance, harshness and excessiveness—

understand that continual interventions and an unethical foreign policy will undoubtedly create more turbulence in the world today. We should recognize the *causes* of terrorism and not focus on the personalities of the perpetrators, for in doing so we only treat the superficial symptoms of terrorism, whereas diagnosis of the cause would allow us to prevent such a cancer from spreading, destroying everything and everyone in its path.

all of which are in opposition to Islam, which always advocates the "middle way". While extremist theologies complement a contemporary orientation that is anchored in profound feelings of defeat, disempowerment and frustration, these feelings are often manipulated for political ends and are cast toward those seen to be perpetuating the current circumstances of grief, humiliation and subjugation. America's national interests which lie in the Middle East are rarely in the interest of the people of the Middle East, and herein lies the problem: America will go to any lengths to protect these 'vital interests', often involving death and hardship for the people of the region. As Jimmy Carter said, some time after he left the White House:

> We sent Marines into Lebanon and you only have to go to Lebanon, to Syria or to Jordan to witness first-hand the intense hatred among many people for the United States because we bombed and shelled and unmercifully killed totally innocent villagers—women and children and farmers and housewives—in those villages around Beirut [...] As a result of that [...] we became kind of a Satan in the minds of those who are deeply resentful. That is what precipitated the taking of our hostages and that is what has precipitated some of the terrorist attacks [...]

The US is so mistrusted in the Middle East that it often becomes easy for Muslims to blame the US for all its troubles, while ignoring their own shortcomings.

We must seriously ask ourselves if the current actions of the US government reflect a nation which understands these root causes for being mistrusted and even hated. If, as seems to be the case, in this whole tragedy nothing has been learned, the actions of the "War on Terrorism" will not serve to make the US more secure—but will provoke more hostility against the US and actually nurture more terrorists.

Globally, the onus is upon Muslims to take bold steps to ensure that all forms of violent extremism are condemned, and that the inflammatory rhetoric that feeds upon emotional sensitivities is stamped out. The Muslim world faces a crisis of authority, evident when we see individuals stepping up and claiming to speak for Islam, despite having neither the religious position nor any formal religious education. Such self-indulgent, self-styled demagogues only compound the confusion in the public arena as to what Islam really stands for.

Part 1 THE EMPIRE

1 | A Day that Changed America: Did it?

M. SHAHID ALAM

IN THE AFTERMATH of September 11, 2001, the fear, foreboding and outrage of many Americans was crystallized into a single phrase: this was a "a day that changed America forever."

These words conveyed a tragic sense of loss, a sudden passage from innocence to sorrow, a descent from strength to vulnerability, an exit from exhilaration to angst. Suddenly, Americans, used to cruising at ethereal altitudes, had crash landed on the real world; they faced terror in the heart of America. It appeared that America had collided momentarily with the reality of a world mired in wars, poverty and disease; it had been struck by the shards of economies devastated, polities derailed, environments degraded by a rapacious globalization. In short, for one brief hour, Americans had been dragged through the agony endured by more than four-fifths of mankind, or what still goes by that name. It was as if, like Adam and Eve, Americans had been expelled from Eden, banished from the land of perpetual bliss.

These wounds carried revolutionary potential. Now that September 11 had rudely shattered Americans out of their unearthly bliss, ended their disconnection from the outside world, they would avidly seek to expand their knowledge about this alien world, its geography, history, politics, and, most importantly, its peoples. They would ask not only about *who* had perpetrated the horrors of September 11, but *why*? They would not rest till they had answers to two troubling questions that delve into the origins, the source, and the genesis of September 11.

The first question concerns good and evil. Why has the goodness of America been repaid by the evil of September 11? Many, if not most,

Americans believe that they are a nation of do-gooders; that their country stands at the pinnacle of human evolution; that it embodies, better than any other nation ever, the values of freedom and justice; that it is a beacon of light to all mankind, fighting foreign tyrannies, propagating democracy, and sharing its own prosperity, ideas, and technology with the world's less fortunate nations. *If* all this is indeed true, why did September 11 happen to us? Or could it be that we have been duped, that the image of American munificence was just that, an image that concealed the reality of an ugly, imperialistic power like all others before it?

The second question concerns the efficacy of America's vaunted military power. Americans know that their country is the only superpower, a distinction solidly built upon unrivalled economic strength, leadership in cutting-edge technologies, inestimably superior manpower, strengths which allow their government to gather intelligence worldwide, to deploy troops worldwide, to hit targets worldwide, and to destroy incoming missiles before they cross their borders. In short, we are convinced that we have the capacity to annihilate any country that dares to challenge us. But none of this helped us on September 11 when a handful of men, armed with nothing more lethal than box-cutters, attacked two venerable icons of American power, and within an hour killed some three thousand Americans, caused damage to property worth tens of billions of dollars, and caused still greater damage to the economy. Why was our government spending 350 billion dollars annually on military hardware, surveillance, intelligence, training and troops if it could not stop nineteen men from changing America forever?

These are the questions—and there are many more like these—that America's mass media might have asked after September 11 if they had been free from corporate control. If these questions could have been raised in the mass media, they would also have been debated on college campuses, in churches, town halls, and in the halls of the Congress. If such a discourse had occurred, it would slowly but surely effect a sea-change in our perceptions about how America projects itself overseas; about the ideals abandoned in our dealings with weaker nations; about our readiness to trample freedoms abroad, sacrifice non-American lives, devastate entire economies, in order to advance the corporate interests of a few Americans. If these changes had indeed occurred, Americans would finally wake up to the ugly reality of America abroad, and mobilize—as they had mobilized against slavery and racial discrimination before—to force their government to pursue the same ideals abroad that it honors at home. If all this had indeed come to pass, then truly we could say that America had decisively defeated the perpetrators of September 11—by changing America, and the world for the better.

But this is not how America changed after September 11. Americans could not be allowed to ask the *right* questions because these would only generate the *wrong* answers—that is, wrong for corporate America, for America's powerful oil interests, for the military establishment, for the Zionist lobby, for racists, and for religious bigots. America's outrage would not be answered with debate, discussions and dull inquiry. It would be placated by righteous indignation, by talk of evil antagonists, by promises of vengeance, and wars without end. America's grief would be hijacked by groups whose interests, security, power and profits batten on paranoia, bigotry, racism, conflicts and war. Almost instantly, these forces responded to September 11 by orchestrating the deafening beat of war drums. On September 11, Osama bin Laden had dared America. America obliged—with wars against Afghans and Palestinians, to be followed by wars against Iraqis, Iranians, Syrians, Saudis, and many more besides.

George Bush and his neo-conservative warmongers took the lead in all this. They had found in the tragedy of September 11 the trigger for the war plans they had been hatching since the end of the Cold War in the early 1990s. Within days, George Bush *et al* had laid out their plans for global war before the American public. Even before the hijackers had been identified, they were linked to al-Qa'ida, a "collection of loosely affiliated terrorist organizations." Yet their attacks were declared to be "an act of war against our country." This was no ordinary war, however. Al-Qa'ida had launched a civilizational war: "they hate us," they were "enemies of freedom," they "hate our freedoms," they want to "disrupt and end a way of life." Al-Qa'ida's goal "is remaking the world—and imposing its radical beliefs on people everywhere." In other words, al-Qa'ida wanted to impose a fundamentalist Islam on the United States and Europe.[1]

---

[1] All the quotes in this and the next paragraph are from George Bush's speech of September 21, 2001, given to a joint session of Congress. See: www.guardian.co.uk/Print/0,3858,426-1868,00.html.

Wars spawn wars. So if al-Qa'ida had started a war, the United States would have to respond in kind. The President declared that "the *only way* to defeat terrorism as a threat to our way of life is to stop it, eliminate it, and destroy it where it grows." This global war "on terror begins with al-Qa'ida, but it does not end there. It will not end until every terrorist group of global reach has been found, stopped and defeated." In time, this war will be extended to "nations that provide aid or safe haven to terrorism." In addition, this would not be a short war: it will be a "lengthy campaign, *unlike any we have ever seen.*" It will also be a total war, including "dramatic strikes, visible on TV, and covert operations, secret even in success." The Bush strategy was clear. Magnify the terrorist threat, fuel it, and prepare the nation for a war that would be global, total and unending.

Roma locuta est; causa finite est. President Bush had spoken, and the case was closed. All the organs of the mainstream media concurred with Bush. The country was in the midst of a war, and nothing would be tolerated which carried the hint of dissent. Dissent was unpatriotic; some said, it was treasonable. The Bush doctrine—if you are not with us, you are against us—applied to individuals as well as states. The United States was now a country with one party, the party of Bush-Cheney-Rumsfeld-Ashcroft. Only the survivors among the victims of September 11 stuck to their demand for an independent investigation into September 11. When they persisted, the President reluctantly agreed, more than a year after September 11, to appoint an Independent Commission. Yet, in choosing Henry Kissinger to chair this Commission, the President ensured that it would be ineffectual. As one commentator quipped, he had put Dracula in charge of the blood bank.

Even without Kissinger chairing it, the Independent Commission on September 11 is unlikely to deliver any surprises. Its mandate only demands that it identify the factors that *allowed* the attacks on the WTC and the Pentagon to occur. The Commission will not hold any hearings in Grozny or Gaza; in Baghdad or Basra; in Kashmir or Kabul; in Cairo or Karachi; in Jakarta or Jeddah; in Caracas or Kolkata; in Nairobi or Nouakchott. It will not enter into the world the hijackers came from; it will not probe into the lives of the hijackers; it will not investigate why they committed such carnage; it will not ponder over why they took their own lives to attack

Americans; it will not ask why they could not deliver their message to Americans by less violent means?

Presumably, all these questions had been answered definitively by Bush *et al.* The perpetrators of September 11 were evil, they acted from in-eradicable spite, from a nihilistic rage against modernity, against all that America represents, her freedom, democracy, progress and prosperity. After these incontestable answers, there was only one thing that remained to be done. Send the stealth bombers, cruise missiles, daisy-cutters and bunker-busting nukes to exorcise these demons.

Now, almost two years after that tragic morning on September 11 when nearly three thousand Americans were consumed in an inferno that des-cended from the skies, after all the rubble from Ground Zero and the Pentagon has been cleared, can we say that America has changed forever? Did America embrace the potential for change contained in that terrible moment, the potential to connect with the inverse of our own world, a world whose sufferings, whose tyrannies, whose pathologies are deeply connected to ours in ways unknown to us? Were we overwhelmed by the slow dawning of the realization of the burden we bear, as the van-guard of the human enterprise, as the champions of Christian charity, were we moved to do something—even a little bit—to enrich, empower, enlighten and embrace those left behind? If Americans had taken up this challenge, if we *could* take up this challenge, *that* would be a change.

Instead, the captains of capital, the marshals of mass media, the priests of bigotry, the zealots of Zion, have laid out plans for wars, total, global and unending, to stop Americans from demanding change and to stop the rest of the world from getting the change they demand. As the wounds of global capitalism deepen, as the dark satanic mills of capitalist greed grind many of mankind deeper into poverty, as entire continents are devastated, as agro-corporations seek to chain millions of farmers to their genetic fabrications, as the middle classes in the rich countries slowly sink into poverty, as the consciousness of these depredations finally threatens to become global, the concentrated power of capital has seized upon September 11 to divert Americans with gladiatorial combats on a global scale.

Let the drums of the news networks roll, let the combats begin, let blood be spilled liberally, let entire countries be depopulated, let us make mass exterminations a spectator sport. Only death brings life. Only thus will America be diverted. After devastation there comes peace.

2 | The American Empire

WILLIAM BLUM

"We assert that no nation can long endure half republic and half empire, and we warn the American people that imperialism abroad will lead quickly and inevitably to despotism at home."

Democratic Party (United States) National Platform, 1900

FOLLOWING ITS BOMBING of Iraq in 1991, the United States wound up with military facilities in Saudi Arabia, Kuwait, Bahrain, Qatar, Oman and the United Arab Emirates.

Following its bombing of Yugoslavia in 1999, the United States wound up with military facilities in Kosovo, Albania, Bulgaria, Macedonia, Hungary, Bosnia and Croatia.

Following its bombing of Afghanistan in 2001–2, the United States wound up with military facilities in Afghanistan, Pakistan, Kazakhstan, Uzbekistan, Tajikistan, Kyrgyzstan, Georgia, Yemen and Djibouti.

"America will have a continuing interest and presence in Central Asia of a kind that we could not have dreamed of before," US Secretary of State Colin Powell declared in February 2002.[1]

This is not very subtle foreign policy. Certainly not covert. The men who run the American Empire are not easily embarrassed.

And that's the way the Empire grows—a base on every street corner, ready to be mobilized to put down any threat to imperial rule, real or imagined. Fifty-seven years after World War II ended, the United States still has major bases in Germany and Japan; forty-nine years after the end of the Korean War, tens of thousands of American armed forces are stationed in South Korea; and in the year 2002, the US Defense Department announced: "The United States Military is currently deployed to more locations then it has been throughout history."[2]

---

[1] Testimony before the House International Relations Committee, 6 February 2002.

[2] US Defense Department website: Deployment Link: 12-10-02: http://deploymentlink.osd.mil/deploy/info/info_intro.shtml

Equally unsubtle are the announcements from the early 1990s, follow-ing the demise of the Soviet Union, to the present, trumpeting Washing-ton's desire, means, and intention for world domination, while assuring the world of the noble purposes of this domination. These sentiments have been regularly put forth in policy papers emanating from the White House and the Pentagon, as well as from government-appointed com-missions and think tanks closely associated with the national security establishment. Here is the voice of the Empire in 1992:

> Our first objective is to prevent the re-emergence of a new rival, either on the territory of the former Soviet Union or elsewhere, that poses a threat on the order of that posed formerly by the Soviet Union. ... we must account sufficiently for the interests of the advanced industrial nations to discourage them from challenging our leadership or seeking to overturn the established political and economic order. ... we must maintain the mechanisms for deterring potential competitors from even *aspiring* to a larger regional or global role.[3]

1996: "We will engage terrestrial targets someday—ships, airplanes, land targets—from space. ...We're going to fight *in* space. We're going to fight *from* space and we're going to fight *into* space.[4]

1997: "With regard to space dominance, we have it, we like it, and we're going to keep it."[5] 2000:

> The new [military preparedness] standard is to maintain military superior-ity over all potential rivals and to prepare now for future military rivalries, even if they can not yet be identified and their eventual arrival is only speculative. ... Military requirements have become detached from net asses-sments of actual security threats. Generic wars and generic capabilities are proffered as the basis for planning. ... Particularities of real threat scenarios have become secondary to the generalized need to show raw US power across the globe.[6]

---

3 "Defense Planning Guidance for the Fiscal Years 1994–1999", as quoted in *New York Times*, 8 March 1992, p.14 (emphasis added).

4 General Joseph Ashy, at the time Commander in Chief of the US Space Command, cited in Aviation Week and Space Technology (New York), 5 August 1996, p.51 (emphasis in original).

5 Keith R. Hall, Assistant Secretary of the Air Force for Space and Director of the National Reconnaissance Office, speaking to the National Space Club, September 15, 1997.

6 Charles Knight, Project on Defense Alternatives, panel presentation at the Council on Foreign Relations, New York, 14 June 2000, on "US. Military-Strategic Ambitions: Expanding to Fill the post-Soviet Vacuum"; http://www.comw.org/pda/0006vacuum.html.

2001: "The presence of American forces in critical regions around the world is the visible expression of the extent of America's status as a superpower and as the guarantor of liberty, peace and stability."[7]

2001: "If we just let our own vision of the world go forth, and we embrace it entirely, and we don't try to be clever and piece together clever diplomatic solutions to this thing, but just wage a total war against these tyrants, I think we will do very well, and our children will sing great songs about us years from now."[8]

2001: The Bush administration's "Nuclear Posture Review", directing the military to prepare contingency plans to use nuclear weapons against at least seven countries—China, Russia, Iraq, Iran, North Korea, Libya and Syria—and to build smaller nuclear weapons for use in certain battlefield situations. (Thus, a willingness to dismiss a long-standing taboo against the use of nuclear weapons except as a last resort or when national survival hangs in the balance, such as the fabled doomsday confrontation with the Soviet Union.)[9]

2002: In September, the White House issued its "National Security Strategy", which declared:

> Our forces will be strong enough to dissuade potential adversaries from pursuing a military build-up in hopes of surpassing, or equaling, the power of the United States. ... America will act against such emerging threats before they are fully formed. ... We must deter and defend against the threat before it is unleashed. ... We cannot let our enemies strike first. ... To forestall or prevent such hostile acts by our adversaries, the United States will, if necessary, act preemptively.

This is of course essentially the rationale imperial Japan used to justify its attack on Pearl Harbor in 1941. To one observer, the meaning of the "National Security Strategy" was clear:

---

7 "Rebuilding America's Defenses: Strategy, Forces and Resources For a New Century" A report of the Project for the New American Century (Washington, DC), September 2000, p.14

8 Michael Ledeen, former Reagan official of Iran-Contra fame, now of the American Enterprise Institute (Washington, DC), condemned the caution of those in the CIA and the State Department who believe America should fight the war on terror one battle at a time. "No stages," he said. "This is total war." *Village Voice* (New York), 27 November 2001, p.46.

9 Submitted by the Department of Defense to Congress on 31 December 2001 as a classified document, which subsequently became public; see *Los Angeles Times*, 9 and 10 March 2002.

It dashes the aspirations of those who had hoped that the world was moving toward a system of international law that would allow for the peaceful resolution of conflicts, through covenants and courts. In place of this, a single power that shuns covenants and courts has proclaimed that it intends to dominate the world militarily, intervening preemptively where necessary to exorcise threats ... Those who want a world in which no power is supreme and in which laws and covenants are used to settle conflicts will begin a new debate—about how to contend with imperial America.[10]

So intoxicated with the idea of *dominance* is the US military that when it announced, in November 2002, the formation of a public affairs group that would travel to battlefields "to interact with journalists, assist US commanders and send news and pictures back to headquarters for dissemination," it described the operation as an attempt at "information dominance."[11]

THE COLD WAR IS OVER. LONG LIVE THE COLD WAR

It is remarkable indeed that in the 21st century the government of the United States is still going around dropping huge amounts of exceedingly powerful explosives upon the heads of innocent and defenseless people. It wasn't supposed to be this way.

In the mid 1980s, Michael Gorbachev instituted the beginning of the end for the Soviet police state. In 1989, the Berlin Wall came down, and people all over Eastern Europe were joyfully celebrating "a new day". The United States then joined this celebration by invading and bombing Panama, only weeks after the Wall fell. At the same time, the US was shamelessly intervening in the election in Nicaragua to defeat a leftist government.

Soon thereafter, South Africa freed Nelson Mandela and apartheid began to crumble, and before the year 1990 was over, Haiti held its first free election ever and chose a genuine progressive as president. It seemed like anything was possible, optimism was as widespread as pessimism is today.

---

[10] James Laxer, Professor of political science, York University, Toronto, Canada, from an article by him in the *Toronto Globe and Mail*, 24 September 2002, p.A15.

[11] *Washington Post*, 28 November 2002, p.B4.

However, when Bulgaria and Albania, "newly freed from the grip of communism", as the American media would put it, dared to elect governments not acceptable to Washington, Washington just stepped in and overthrew those governments.

Soon came the US bombing of Iraq and its people, sending the country back to a pre-industrial age, 40 days and nights without mercy, for no good or honest reason.

And that was that for our optimism, for a different and better world.

But the American leaders were not through. In 1993 they were off attacking Somalia, trying to rearrange the country's political map, more bombing and killing.

They intervened to put down dissident movements in Peru, Mexico, Colombia and Ecuador, just as if it were the Cold War in the 1950s in Latin America, and the 1960s, the 1970s, the 1980s, and still doing it in the 1990s, and into the new century.

In the latter part of the 90s, Washington could be found engaged in serious meddling in the elections in territories of its erstwhile Cold War foes: Russia, Mongolia, and Bosnia.

In 1999, they bombed the people of Serbia and Kosovo for 78 seemingly endless days, the final step in Washington's master plan of breaking up the Socialist Federal Republic of Yugoslavia.[12]

And once again, in 2001, they grossly and openly intervened in an election in Nicaragua to prevent the left from winning.

At the same time, bombarding Afghanistan, and in all likelihood killing more innocent civilians than were killed in the United States on 11 September 2001, as well as taking the lives of countless "combatants", probably none of whom had any connection to the events of that tragic day. (The great majority of those who attended an al-Qa'ida training camp in Afghanistan had come to help the Taliban in their civil war, a religious mission, nothing to do with terrorism or the United States.) The count of the dead is ever increasing as people continue to die from bombing wounds, cluster-bomb landmines, and depleted-uranium toxicity.

While continuing to savage Afghanistan in 2002, Washington found

---

[12] See William Blum, *Rogue State: A Guide to the World's Only Superpower* (Common Courage Press, Maine, 2000) for brief descriptions of the foregoing US interventions.

time to lend its indispensable support to a plot to overthrow Hugo Chavez and his populist government in Venezuela.

And all these years, still bombing Iraq and keeping their choke hold on Cuba; still, after a century of imperialist occupation, refusing to vacate Guantanamo Base in Cuba; and still providing military weapons and training to countries or armed forces guilty of serious and numerous abuses of human rights.

There was none of the "peace dividend" that had been promised, not for Americans nor for the rest of the world.

What do we have here? The American people had been taught for nearly half a century that the Cold War, including the Korean War, the Vietnam War, the huge military budgets, all the US invasions and overthrows of governments—the ones they knew about—they were taught that this was all to fight the same menace: The International Communist Conspiracy, headquarters in Moscow.

But then the Soviet Union was dissolved. The Warsaw Pact was also dissolved. The East European satellites became independent. The former communists even became capitalists.

And nothing changed in American foreign policy.

Even NATO remained, NATO which had been created—so we were told—to protect Western Europe against a Soviet invasion. Ever increasing in size and military power, now virtually a sovereign nation by itself, a NATO with a global mission. A treaty on wheels which can be rolled in any direction to suit Washington's current policy. A NATO invoking its charter to justify its members joining the US in the Afghanistan invasion, a NATO acting as a US surrogate ruling over the Balkans as a protectorate. And as Russia closed down its Cold War bases in Eastern Europe, Vietnam and Cuba, the United States was opening bases in the territories of the former Soviet Union. While Russia closed down its radio intelligence station at Lourdes, Cuba, the United States was building a powerful listening station in Latvia.

The whole thing had been a con game. The Soviet Union and something called communism *per se* had not been the object of Washington's global attacks. There had never been an International Communist Conspiracy. The enemy was, and remains, any government, movement or individual, that stands in the way of the expansion of the American Empire.

IS THE UNITED STATES AGAINST TERRORISM?

Are we now to believe that the American Empire is against terrorism? What does one call a man who blows up an airplane killing 73 people for political reasons; who attempts assassinations against several diplomats; who fires cannons at ships docked in American ports; who places bombs in numerous commercial and diplomatic buildings in the US and abroad? His name is Orlando Bosch, he's Cuban and he lives in Miami, unmolested by the authorities. The city of Miami once declared a day in his honor—Orlando Bosch Day.[13] He was freed from prison in Venezuela, where he had been held for the airplane bombing, partly because of pressure from the American ambassador, Otto Reich, who in 2002 was appointed to a high position in the State Department by President Bush.

After Bosch returned to the US in 1988, the Justice Department condemned him as a violent terrorist and was all set to deport him, but that was blocked by President Bush, the first, with the help of son Jeb Bush in Florida.[14] So is President Bush, the second, and his family against terrorism? Well, yes, they're against those terrorists who are not allies of the Empire.

The plane that Bosch bombed was a Cuban plane. He's wanted in Cuba for that and a host of other serious crimes, and the Cubans have asked Washington to turn him over to them; to Cuba he's like Osama bin Laden is to the United States. But the US has refused. Imagine the reaction in Washington if bin Laden showed up in Havana and the Cubans refused to turn him over. Imagine the reaction in the United States if Havana proclaimed Osama bin Laden Day?

Washington's support of genuine terrorist organizations has been extensive. The following are some examples of recent years:

The ethnic Albanians in Kosovo, comprising the Kosovo Liberation Army (KLA), in furtherance of their political-ethnic agenda, have carried out numerous terrorist attacks for years in various parts of the Balkans, but they've been US allies because they've attacked people out of favor

---

[13] *Dangerous Dialogue: Attacks on Freedom of Expression in Miami's Cuban Exile Community*, p.26, published by Americas Watch/The Fund for Free Expression, New York and Washington, August 1992.

[14] *New York Times*, 16 August 1989; Jane Franklin, *Cuba and the United States: A Chronological History* (Ocean Press, Melbourne, 1997), see "Bosch Avila, Orlando" in index; and chapter 30.

with Washington. This despite the fact that the KLA has had ideological and personal ties to Osama bin Laden and al-Qaʻida, and despite being categorized as a terrorist organization by the US State Department.[15]

The right-wing paramilitaries in Colombia, who have undertaken hundreds, if not thousands, of vicious attacks on civilians, could not begin to carry out their atrocities without the collaboration of the Colombian military, who are the recipients of virtually unlimited American support.

For years, anti-communist Vietnamese, Cambodians, and Laotians resident in the United States have been financing and instigating their countrymen abroad in bombings and other attacks on their governments, hoping to destabilize those governments; at times traveling from the US to those countries to carry out attacks themselves; all this with the tacit approval of the American government, which turns a blind eye to the Neutrality Act, which prohibits American citizens or residents from using force to overthrow a foreign government.[16]

As Noam Chomsky has observed, to the US government, "The criterion that distinguishes friend from enemy is obedience, not crime."

George W. Bush has also spoken out vehemently against *harboring* terrorists—"those who harbor terrorists threaten the national security of the United States".[17] Does he really mean that?

We must ask: Which country harbors more terrorists than the United States? Orlando Bosch is only one of the numerous anti-Castro Cubans in Miami who have carried out many hundreds of terrorist acts, in the US, in Cuba, and elsewhere; all kinds of arson attacks, assassinations and bombings. They have been harbored in the US in safety for decades; as have numerous other friendly terrorists, torturers and human rights violators from Guatemala, El Salvador, Haiti, Indonesia and elsewhere, all allies of the Empire.[18]

The CIA was busy looking for terrorists in caves in the mountains of Afghanistan at the same time as the Agency sat in bars in Miami having drinks with terrorists.

---

[15] Michael Parenti, *To Kill a Nation: The Attack on Yugoslavia* (Verso, London/NY 2000), chapter 10 and passim; *Washington Times*, 4 May 1999, p.1.

[16] *Washington Post*, 30 July 2001, p.1

[17] The Associated Press, 18 September 2001.

[18] *Rogue State*, op. cit., chapter 9.

THE IMPERIAL MAFIA

What are we to make of all this? How are we to understand United States foreign policy? Well, if I were to write a book called "The American Empire for Dummies", page one would say: Don't ever look for the moral factor. US foreign policy has no moral factor built into its DNA. One must clear one's mind of that baggage which only gets in the way of seeing beyond the clichés and the platitudes.

It's rather difficult for most Americans and Americophiles throughout the world to take such statements at face value. It's not easy to swallow such a message. They see American leaders on television smiling and laughing, telling jokes; they see them with their families, hear them speak of God and love, of peace and law, of democracy and freedom, of human rights and justice, and even baseball. These leaders know how to condemn the world's atrocities in no uncertain terms, with just the right words we all love to hear, just the right catch in their throat. … How can such people be moral monsters, how can they be called immoral?

They have names like George and Dick and Donald, not a single Muhammad or Abdallah in the bunch. And they all speak English. While Muhammad or Abdallah may justify amputation of the hand for a crime such as theft, Americans consider themselves too civilized for that. Instead, people named George and Dick and Donald drop sophisticated cluster bombs on cities and villages, and the many unexploded ones become land mines, and before very long a child picks one up or steps on one of them and loses an arm or leg, or both arms or both legs, and sometimes their eyesight; while the cluster bombs which actually explode create their own kind of high-velocity, jagged steel horror.

And after condemning those who commit atrocities, American leaders turn around and provide the same people the arms and the training and the equipment which their forces need to carry out further atrocities.

But these men are perhaps not so much immoral as they are amoral. It's not that they take pleasure in causing so much death and suffering. It's that they just don't care … if that's a distinction worth making. As long as the death and suffering advance the agenda of the Empire, as long as the right people and the right corporations gain wealth and power and privilege and prestige, as long as the death and suffering aren't happening to them or people close to them … then they just don't care about it happening to other people, including the American soldiers whom they throw into wars and who come home—the ones who make it back alive—with Agent Orange or Gulf War Syndrome eating away at their bodies. Our leaders would not be in the positions they hold if they were bothered by such things.

It must be great fun to be one of the leaders of an Empire, glorious in fact … intoxicating … the feeling that you can do whatever you want, to whomever you want, for as long as you want, for any reason you care to give … because you have the power … for theirs is the power and the glory.

WHEN I WAS WRITING my book *Rogue State* a few years ago I used the term "American Empire" cautiously because it was not in common usage and I wasn't sure the American public was quite ready for it. But I needn't have been so cautious. It's now being used proudly by supporters of the Empire—prominent intellectuals such as Dinesh D'Souza of the Hoover Institution, who wrote an article entitled "In praise of American Empire", in which he argued that "America is the most magnanimous of all imperial powers".[19]

Robert Kagan of the Carnegie Endowment who wrote: "And the truth is that the benevolent hegemony exercised by the United States is good for a vast portion of the world's population. It is certainly a better international arrangement than all realistic alternatives."[20]

Syndicated columnist Charles Krauthammer who spoke of America's "uniquely benign imperium."[21]

And here is the cover of the *New York Times Magazine*: "The case for a committed American imperialism".[22]

In this way are people who are wedded to American foreign policy able to live with it—they conclude, and proclaim, and may even believe, that such policies produce a benevolent force, an enlightened Empire, bringing order, prosperity and civilized behavior to all parts of the globe, and if the US is *forced* to go to war it conducts it in a *humanitarian* manner.

---

[19] *Christian Science Monitor*, 26 April 2002.
[20] "The Benevolent Empire", *Foreign Policy* (Washington, DC), Summer 1998.
[21] "The Bush Doctrine", *The Weekly Standard* (Washington, DC), 4 June 2001.
[22] *New York Times Magazine*, 28 July 2002, article by Harvard professor Michael Ignatieff.

The Empire's scribes are as amoral as the officials in the White House and the Pentagon. After all, the particles of depleted uranium are not lodging inside *their* lungs to keep radiating for the rest of their lives; the World Bank and International Monetary Fund are not bankrupting *their* economy and slashing *their* basic services; it's not *their* families wandering as refugees in the desert.

The leaders of the Empire, the imperial mafia—George W. Bush, Donald Rumsfeld, Richard Cheney, Colin Powell, Condoleezza Rice, Paul Wolfowitz, Richard Perle, et al.—and their scribes as well, are as fanatic and as fundamentalist as Osama bin Laden. *Allah Akbar*! God is great! ... USA! USA! USA!

And the "regime change" the mafiosi accomplished in Afghanistan truly went to their heads. Today Kabul, tomorrow the world.

THE LIQUID GOLD, AGAIN

The bombing, invasion and occupation of Afghanistan served the purpose of setting up a new government that would be sufficiently amenable to Washington's international objectives, including the installation of military bases and communications listening stations, and, perhaps most important of all, the running of secure oil and gas pipelines through Afghanistan from the Caspian Sea region.

For years, the American oil barons had their eyes on the vast oil and gas reserves around the Caspian Sea, ideally with an Afghanistan-Pakistan route to the Indian Ocean, thus keeping Russia and Iran out of the picture. The oilmen were quite open about this, giving frank testimony before Congress on the matter.[23]

They then turned their lust to the even greater oil reserves of Iraq. The imperial mafia staged a year-long propaganda show to convince Americans and the world that the world's only superpower had no choice but to attack a sovereign and crippled country that has not attacked the United States, that has not threatened to attack the United States, that knows it would mean instant mass suicide for them if they attacked the United States. The imperial mafia's thesis is odd not simply because Iraq is

---

[23] See, e.g., testimony of John Maresca, Unocal Corporation, Subcommittee on Asia and the Pacific, of House Committee on International Relations, 12 February 1998.

not a threat, but because the imperial mafia *know* that Iraq is not a threat, at all. They've been telling the world one story after another about why Iraq is a threat, an imminent threat, a threat increasing in danger with each passing day, a nuclear threat, a chemical threat, a biological threat, that Iraq is a terrorist state, that Iraq is tied to al-Qa'ida … only to have each story amount to nothing. They declared repeatedly that Iraq must agree to having the UN weapons inspectors back in, and when Iraq agreed to this they said "No, no, that isn't good enough."

Did any of this make sense? This sudden urgency of fighting a war in the absence of a fight? It did make sense if one understood that it was not, *per se*, about Saddam Hussein's evilness, or his alleged weapons of mass destruction, or terrorism. It's about the US replacing Hussein and installing a puppet government, as it did in Afghanistan, enabling American and other oil companies to move into Iraq to enjoy a *laissez-faire* feast; as well as opening the country to all manner of transnational corporations as Iraq takes its place in the new world order of globalized economies, and the American Empire adds another country and a few more bases from which to further control and remake the Middle East in the imperial mafia's endearing amoral style, for which, presumably, the children of the region will sing great songs in years to come.

In October, North Korea admitted that it had been conducting a major clandestine nuclear-weapons development program for the past several years, a program, declared the United States, abetted by Pakistan in return for North Korean missiles. Here were states dealing in genuine weapons of mass destruction, not simply ones alleged by Washington.[24] Surely the righteous wrath and armed might of the Empire would strike down these rogue states. Yet not even a threat of attack ensued. Can the fact that neither of the countries presents the oil paradise that Iraq offers be the explanation?

Asked what would happen if American pressure had prompted a coup against Mr. Hussein before the US invasion, a senior official replied, "That would be nice," but then went on to suggest that "the American military might enter and secure the country anyway, not only to eliminate weapons of mass destruction but also to ensure against anarchy".[25]

---

[24] *New York Times*, 18 October 2002, p.1.
[25] *New York Times*, 11 October 2002, p.1; the quote about "anarchy" is the *Times'* paraphrase.

This would appear to lend further support to the idea that the campaign was not really about Saddam Hussein.

Almost entirely absent from the discussion of this question during 2002 was the fact that over the course of several years in the 1990s, the UN inspectors had found and destroyed huge amounts of chemical, biological and nuclear weapons in Iraq. Most Americans are unquestionably convinced that Saddam got away with hiding virtually all his weapons and that he'll get away with it again in any resumption of the inspections. But that's not what happened. Scott Ritter, chief UN weapons inspector in Iraq, stated in 2002 that:

> Since 1998 Iraq has been fundamentally disarmed; 90–95% of Iraq's weapons of mass destruction have been verifiably eliminated. This includes all of the factories used to produce chemical, biological and nuclear weapons, and long-range ballistic missiles; the associated equipment of these factories; and the vast majority of the products coming out of these factories.[26]

The director general of the International Atomic Energy Agency, Mohamed El Baradei, has, moreover, reported that his agency:

> dismantled extensive nuclear weapons-related facilities. We neutralized Iraq's nuclear program. We confiscated its weapon-usable material. We destroyed, removed or rendered harmless all its facilities and equipment relevant to nuclear weapons production.[27]

However, as noted above, all this is immaterial. Washington does not care about and is not threatened by Iraq's alleged weapons. American agreement to give the UN inspectors a chance before invading Iraq was no more than a bluff to cater to unexpected world opposition to the invasion. To further underscore this we have the testimony of Richard Perle—chairman of the Pentagon's Defense Policy Board, prominent architect of belligerent US policy toward the Arab/Islamic world, member in good standing of the imperial mafia, and renowned "prince of darkness"—who declared in November 2002 that even a "clean bill of health" from UN chief weapons inspector Hans Blix would not halt a US attack.[28]

---

[26] *The Guardian*, September 19, 2002.
[27] *Washington Post*, October 21, 2002.
[28] *Daily Mirror* (UK), 22 November 2002.

IS THIS ANY WAY TO END TERRORISM?

"We leveled it. There was nobody left, just dirt and dust."
> —*US Army Major Gen. Franklin Hagenbeck,*
> *peaking of the destruction of three villages*
> *in the Shahikot Valley in Afghanistan.*[29]

The American scorched-earth bombing and military occupation of Afghanistan may turn out to be a political train wreck. Can it be doubted that the awful ruination and perceived injustice recruited thousands throughout the Muslim world as the next generation of "terrorists", blinded by their frustrations, anger and desire for vengeance, to target the US and her allies?

The invasion and bombing of Iraq—a war nobody wanted except the imperial mafia—has every likelihood of increasing terrorist numbers to the point of placing any American in mortal danger in much of the world.

Has the American power elite learned anything? Here's James Woolsey, former Director of the CIA and member of the Defense Policy Board, speaking two months after the beginning of the US bombing of Afghanistan, advocating an invasion of Iraq and unconcerned about the response of the Arab world: The silence of the Arab public in the wake of America's victories in Afghanistan, he said, proves that "only fear will re-establish respect for the US."[30]

What then, can the United States do to end terrorism directed against it? Well, it could contemplate the idea of removing the causes, the anti-American motivations of the terrorists; i.e., putting an end to the American practice of raining bombs upon the heads of countless innocent men, women and children, destroying their homes, their schools, their mosques, their hospitals, their ancient archaeological sites, their lives, their futures; poisoning the air and the gene pool with depleted uranium; imposing sanctions against the people of Iraq, truly a weapon of mass destruction; the large military presence in Islam's holiest land, Saudi Arabia, and elsewhere in the Persian Gulf region; and the central

---

[29] *Washington Post,* 17 March 2002, p.25.
[30] *Washington Post,* 27 December 2001, p.c2.

running sore: the vast and unflagging support of Israel's relentlessly cruel persecution of the Palestinians.[31]

At the time of the first anniversary of the 11 September 2001 terrorist attack on the United States, the State Department held a conference on how to improve America's image abroad in order to reduce the level of hatred. Image is what they're working on, not change of policies; (earning about the same reading on the Denial Meter as the German government studying the brains of the 1970s Red Army Faction members to divine their terrorist impulse.[32])

But the policies scorecard reads as follows: From 1945 to 2002, the United States attempted to overthrow more than 40 foreign governments, and to crush more than 30 populist-nationalist movements fighting against intolerable regimes. In the process, the US bombed some 25 countries, caused the end of life for several million people, and condemned many millions more to a life of agony and despair.

The United States wages war on the same scale other nations apply to mere survival.

Perpetual war for perpetual peace.

RECOMMENDED READING

Michael Parenti, *Against Empire* (City Lights Books, San Francisco, 1995).

Noam Chomsky, *What Uncle Sam Really Wants* (Odonian Press, Berkeley, CA, 1992).

Aftab A. Malik (Ed), *Shattered Illusions: Analyzing the war on Terrorism* (Amal Press, Bristol, UK, 2002)

"*The National Security Strategy of the United States*" (White House, 2002), readily available on the Internet.

"*Rebuilding America's Defenses: Strategy, Forces and Resources For a New Century.*" A report of the Project for the New American Century (Washington, DC), September 2000.

---

[31] See *Rogue State*, op. cit., p.30.
[32] *Washington Post*, 19 November 2002, p.15.

William Blum, *Rogue State: A Guide to the World's Only Superpower* (Common Courage Press, Maine, 2000; Zed Books, London, 2002).

Znet website <http://www.zmag.org/ZNET.htm> a treasure trove of information and analysis of The American Empire.

3 | The Project for The New American Century

PEPE ESCOBAR

HEY'VE WON. They got their war against Afghanistan. They got their war against Iraq. After Iraq, they plan to get their wars against Syria, Lebanon, Iran and Saudi Arabia. As far as their "showdown Iraq" was concerned, it was not about weapons of mass destruction, nor United Nations inspections, nor non-compliance, nor a virtual connection between Saddam Hussein and al-Qa'ida, nor the liberation of the Iraqi people, nor a Middle East living in "democracy and liberty".

The American corporate media was not inclined to spell it out, and the absolute majority of American public opinion was anesthetized non-stop by a barrage of technical, bureaucratic and totally peripheral aspects of the war against Iraq. For all the president's (sales)men, the whole game is about global preeminence, if not unilateral world domination—military, economic, political and cultural. This may be an early 21st century replay of the "white man's burden". Or this may be just megalomania. Either way, enshrined in a goal of the Bush administration, it cannot but frighten practically the whole world, from Asia to Africa, from "old Europe" to the conservative establishment within the US itself.

During the Clinton years, they were an obscure bunch—almost a sect. Then they were all elevated to power—again: most had worked for Ronald Reagan and Bush senior. Now they have pushed America—and the world—to war because they want it. Period. *This is no conspiracy theory:* it's all about the implementation of a project.

The lexicon of the Bush doctrine of unilateral world domination is laid out in detail by the Project For The New American Century, a think tank founded in Washington in 1997. The ideological, political, economic and military fundamentals of American foreign policy—and uncontested world hegemony—for the 21st century are there for all to see.

PNAC's credo is officially to muster "the resolve to shape a new century favorable to American principles and interests". PNAC states that the US must be sure of "deterring any potential competitors from even aspiring to a larger regional or global role"—without ever mentioning these competitors, the European Union, Russia or China, by name. The UN is predictably dismissed as "a forum for leftists, anti-Zionists and anti-imperialists". The UN is only as good as its support for American policy.

The PNAC mixes a peculiar brand of messianic internationalism with *realpolitik* founded over a stark analysis of American oil interests. Its key document, dated June 1997, reads like a manifesto. Horrified by the "debased" Bill Clinton, PNAC exponents lavishly praise "the essential elements of the Reagan administration's success: a military that is strong and ready to meet both present and future challenges; a foreign policy that boldly and purposefully promotes American principles abroad; and national leadership that accepts the United States' global responsibilities". These exponents include Dick Cheney, Defense Secretary Donald Rumsfeld, Deputy Secretary of Defense Paul Wolfowitz, Richard Perle, until recently, the chairman of the Defense Policy Board, an advisory panel to the Pentagon made up of leading figures in national security and defense, Florida Governor Jeb Bush and Reagan-era White House adviser Elliott Abrahms.

Already in 1997, the PNAC wanted to "increase defense spending significantly" to "challenge regimes hostile to our interests and values" and "to accept responsibility for America's unique role in preserving and extending an international order friendly to our security, our prosperity, and our principles". The deceptively bland language admitted "such a Reaganite policy of military strength and moral clarity may not be fashionable today. But it is necessary if the United States is to build on the successes of this past century and to ensure our security and our greatness in the next".

The signatories of this 1997 document read like a who's who of Washington power today: among them, in addition to those mentioned above, Eliot Cohen, Steve Forbes, Francis Fukuyama, Frank Gaffney, William Bennett, Donald Kagan, Zalmay Khalilzad, Lewis Libby, Norman

Podhoretz and Dan Quayle. The PNAC has now fulfilled its dream of invading Iraq. In the PNAC's vision of Iraq, the only vector that matters is US strategic interest. Nobody really cares about Saddam Hussein's "brutal dictatorship", nor his extensive catalogue of human rights violations, nor "the suffering of the Iraqi people", nor his US-supplied weapons of mass destruction, nor his alleged connection to terrorism.

Iraq counts only as the first strike in a high-tech replay of the domino theory: the next dominoes will be Syria, Iran and Saudi Arabia. So why not carve up Syria; let Turkey invade northern Iraq; overthrow the Saudi royal family; restore the Hashemites to the Hijaz in Arabia. And dismember Iraq altogether and annex it to Jordan as a vassal kingdom to the US: after all, Jordan's King Abdullah is a cousin of former Iraqi King Faisal, deposed in 1958. This would be one solution for the nagging question of who would have any legitimacy to be in power in Baghdad after Saddam.

WE HATE THE EU

Rumsfeld loves NATO, but he abhors the European Union. All PNAC members and most Pentagon civilians—but not the State Department—do: after all, they control NATO, not the EU. These things are not usually admitted in public. But Rumsfeld, the blunt Midwesterner and former fighter pilot, who has served former presidents Gerald Ford and Ronald Reagan, prefers John Wayne to Bismarck: even Spanish Prime Minister Jose Maria Aznar, a staunch ally of Bush, complained out loud that diplomacy is an alien concept to Rumsfeld. Rumsfeld even has his own wacky axis of evil: Cuba, Libya and ... Germany. If Rumsfeld barely manages to disguise his aversion for dovish Secretary of State Colin Powell's views, one can only imagine to what circle of hell he dispatches the pacifist couple of Jacques Chirac and Gerhard Schroeder.

Strange that no journalist has stood up to ask Rumsfeld, in one of those cosy Pentagon spinning sessions, about his 90-minute session with Saddam in Baghdad on December 20, 1983. The fuzzy photo of Rumsfeld shaking hands with Saddam, observed by Iraqi vice premier Tarik Aziz, is now a collector's item. Rumsfeld was sent by Reagan to mend relations between the US and Iraq only one month after Reagan had adopted a secret directive—still partly classified—to help Saddam fight Iran's Islamic Revolution that had begun in 1979. This close cooperation led to nothing less than Washington selling loads of military equipment and also chemical precursors, insecticides, aluminum tubes, missile components and anthrax to Saddam, who in turn used the lot to gas Iranian soldiers and then civilian Kurds in Halabja, northern Iraq, in 1988. The selling of these chemical weapons was organized by Rumsfeld.

Washington was perfectly aware at the time that Saddam was using chemical weapons. After the Halabja massacre, the Pentagon engaged in a massive disinformation campaign, spinning that the massacre was caused by Iran. Cheney, as Pentagon chief from March 1989 onwards, continued to cooperate very closely with Saddam. The military aid—secretly organized by Rumsfeld—also enabled Saddam to invade Kuwait on August 2, 1990. Between 1991 and 1998, UN weapons inspectors conclusively established that the US—as well as British, German and French firms—had sold missile parts and chemical and bacteriological material to Iraq. So much for the moral high ground defended by America and Britain in the Iraqi weapons of mass destruction controversy. September 2002's National Security Strategy (NSS) document simply delighted the members of the PNAC. No wonder: it reproduced almost verbatim a September 2000 report by the PNAC[1] which in turn was based on the now famous 1992 draft Defense Policy Guidance (DPG), written under the supervision of Wolfowitz, for then Secretary of Defense Cheney. Already in 1992, the three key DPG objectives were to prevent any "hostile power" from dominating regions whose resources would allow it to become a great power; to dissuade any industrialized country from any attempt to defy US leadership; and to prevent the future emergence of any global competitor. That's the thrust of the NSS document, which calls for a unipolar world in which Washington's military power is unrivalled.

In this context, the invasion and occupation of Iraq is just the first installment in an extended practical demonstration of what will happen to "rogue" states alleged to have or not have weapons of mass destruction, alleged to have or not have links to terrorism, and alleged connections to anyone or anything that might challenge US supremacy. The European Union, China and Russia beware: the Shock and Awe demonstration unleashed on Iraq is pure theatrical militarism.

---

[1] See Appendix I.

THE NEW "VISION THING"

It's no surprise that Bush, on February 26, chose to unveil his vision of a new Middle Eastern order at the American Enterprise Institute (AEI), a right-wing Washington think tank. The PNAC's office just happens to be on the 5th floor of the AEI building on 17th St, in downtown Washington. The AEI is the key node of a collection of neo-conservative foreign policy experts and scholars, the most influential of whom are members of the PNAC.

The AEI is intimately connected to the Likud Party in Israel—which for all practical purposes has a deep impact on American foreign policy in the Middle East, thanks to the AEI's influence. In this mutually-beneficial environment, AEI stalwarts are known as Likudniks. Thus, the depth of AEI's intellectual Islamophobia comes as no surprise. Loathing and contempt for Islam as a religion and as a way of life leads to members of the AEI routinely bashing Saudi Arabia and Pakistan. They also oppose any negotiations with North Korea—another policy wholly adopted by the Bush administration. For the AEI, China is the ultimate enemy: not a peer competitor, but a monster strategic threat. The AEI is viscerally anti-State Department (read Colin Powell). Recently, it has also displayed its innate Francophobia. And to try to dispel the idea that it is just another bunch of grumpy dull men, the AEI has been deploying its own female weapon to the BBC and CNN talk shows, one Danielle Pletka. Lynn Cheney, vice president Dick Cheney's wife, a historian and essayist, is also an AEI senior fellow.

The AEI's former executive vice president is John Bolton, one of the Bush administration's key operatives as Under Secretary of State for arms control and international security. Largely thanks to Bolton, the US unilaterally withdrew from the 1972 Anti-Ballistic Missile (ABM) treaty. Bolton has also opposed the establishment of the new International Criminal Court (ICC), recently inaugurated in the Hague. The AEI only treasures raw power as established under the terms of neoliberal globalization: the International Monetary Fund, the World Bank and the World Trade Organization. Its nemesis is everything really multilateral: the ABM treaty, the ICC, the Kyoto protocol, the treaty on anti-personnel mines, the protocol on biological weapons, the treaty on the total ban of nuclear weapons, and most spectacularly, in these past few months, the UN Security Council.

The AEI's foreign policy agenda is presided over by none other than Richard Perle. As Perle is a longtime friend and advisor to Rumsfeld, he was rewarded with the post of chairman of the Pentagon's Defense Policy Board: its 30-odd very influential members include former national security advisers, secretaries of defense and heads of the Central Intelligence Agency (CIA). Perle is also a very close friend of Pentagon number two Wolfowitz, since they were students at the University of Chicago together in the late 1960s. Until he resigned as chairman of the DPB, Perle reported to Wolfowitz.

On September 20, 2001, Perle went into overdrive, fully mobilizing the Defense Policy Board to forge a link between Saddam and al-Qa'ida. The PNAC sent an open letter to Bush detailing how a war on terrorism should be conducted. The letter says that Saddam has to go "even if evidence does not link him to the attack". The letter lists other policies that were later implemented—like the gigantic increase of the defense budget and the total isolation of the Palestinian Authority (PA), as well as others that may soon follow, like striking Hezbollah in Lebanon and yet-to-be-formulated attacks against Iran and especially Syria if they do not stop support for Hezbollah.

The Bush administration strategy in the past few months of totally isolating the PA's Yasser Arafat and allowing Israeli premier Ariel Sharon to refuse as much as a handshake, was formulated by the PNAC. Another PNAC letter states that "Israel's fight is our fight ... for reasons both moral and strategic, we need to stand with Israel in its fight against terrorism". The PNAC detested the Camp David accords between Israel and the Palestinians. For the PNAC, a simmering, undeclared state of war against Palestine, Iraq, Syria, Lebanon and Iran is a matter of policy.

ULTRA HAWKS

Perle, a former Assistant Secretary of Defense for International Security Affairs under Reagan, is also a member of the board of the *Jerusalem Post*. He wrote a chapter—"Iraq: Saddam Unbound"—in *Present Dangers*, a PNAC book. He is very close to ultra-hawk Douglas Feith, who was his special counsel under Reagan and is now Assistant Secretary of Defense for Policy (one of the Pentagon's four most senior posts) and also a partner in a small Washington law firm that represents Israeli suppliers of munitions seeking deals with American weapons manufacturers. It was thanks to Perle—who personally defended his candidate to Rumsfeld—that Feith got his current job. He was one of the key people responsible for strategic planning in the war against the Taliban and was also heavily involved in planning the war against Iraq.

David Wurmser, former head of Middle Eastern projects at the AEI, is now special assistant to PNAC founder John Bolton, the Under Secretary of State for arms control and a fierce enemy of multilateralism. Wurmser wrote *Tyranny's Ally: America's failure to defeat Saddam Hussein,* a book published by the AEI. The foreword is by Perle. Meyrav Wurmser, David's wife, is a co-founder of the Middle East Media Research Institute.

In July 1996, Perle, Feith and the Wurmser couple wrote the notorious paper for an Israeli think tank charting a roadmap for Likud superhawk and then-incoming Israeli prime minister Benjamin "Bibi" Netanyahu. The paper is called "A Clean Break: A New Strategy for Securing the Realm". Perle, Feith and the Wurmsers tell Bibi that Israel must shelve the Oslo Accords, the so-called peace process, the concept of "land for peace", go for it and permanently annex the entire West Bank and the Gaza Strip. The paper also recommends that Israel must insist on the elimination of Saddam, and the restoration of the Hashemite monarchy in Baghdad. This would be the first domino to fall, and then regime change would follow in Syria, Lebanon, Iran and Saudi Arabia. This 1996 blueprint is nothing less than Ariel Sharon's current agenda in action. In November last year, Sharon took the liberty of slightly modifying the domino sequence by growling on the record that Iran should be next after Iraq.

Bush's speech on February 26 at the AEI claimed that the real reason for a war against Iraq is "to bring democracy". Cheney endlessly repeated that Iraqis—like Germany and Japan in 1945—would welcome American soldiers with roses. For Bush, Iraq is begging to be educated in the principles of democracy: "It's presumptuous and insulting to suggest that a whole region of the world, or the one-fifth of humanity that is Muslim, is somehow untouched by the most basic aspirations of life." But this very presumption is seemingly central to the intellectual Islamophobia of both the AEI and PNAC.

The AEI and the PNAC shaped the now official Bush policy of intro-
ducing democracy—by bombing Iraq—and then "successfully transforming the lives of millions of people throughout the Middle East", in
the words of AEI scholar Michael Ledeen. At his AEI speech, Bush did
nothing but parrot the idea. Many a voice couldn't resist pointing out
the splendid American record of encouraging native democracy around
the world by supporting great freedom fighters, such as the Shah of Iran,
Sese Seko Mobutu in the Congo, Augusto Pinochet in Chile, Suharto in
Indonesia, the Somozas in Nicaragua, Zia ul-Haq in Pakistan and an array
of 1960s and 1970s Latin American dictators. Among newfound American
allies, Turkmenistan is nothing less than totalitarian and Uzbekistan is
ultra-authoritarian, and among "old" allies, Egypt and Saudi Arabia have
absolutely nothing to do with democracy.

Chalmers Johnson is president of the Japan Policy Research Institute,
based in California, and author of *Blowback: The Costs and Consequences
of American Empire*. A war veteran turned scholar, he could never be
accused of anti-Americanism. His new book about American militarism,
The Sorrows of Empire: How the Americans lost their Country, will be published in late 2003. Some of its insights are informative in confirming the
role of the PNAC in setting American foreign policy.

Johnson is just one among many who suspect that "after being out of
power with Clinton and back to power with Bush—the 'neo-cons' were
waiting for a 'catastrophic and catalyzing' event—like a new Pearl
Harbor" that would mobilize the public and allow them to put their the-
ories and plans into practice. September 11 was, of course, precisely what
they needed. National Security Adviser Condoleezza Rice called together
members of the National Security Council and asked them "to think
about how do you capitalize on these opportunities to fundamentally
change American doctrine, and the shape of the world, in the wake of
September 11th". She said, "I really think this period is analogous to 1945
to 1947 when fear and paranoia led the US into its Cold War with the
USSR".

Johnson continues: "The Bush administration could not just go to war
with Iraq without tying it in some way to the September 11 attacks. So it
first launched an easy war against Afghanistan. There was at least a visible
connection between Osama bin Laden and the Taliban regime, even

though the United States contributed more to Osama's development as a terrorist than Afghanistan ever did. Meanwhile, the White House launched one of the most extraordinary propaganda campaigns of modern times to convince the American public that an attack on Saddam Hussein should be a part of America's 'war on terrorism'. This attempt to whip up war fever in turn elicited an outpouring of speculation around the world on what the true motives were that lay behind President Bush's obsession with Iraq."

The Iraq war is above all Paul Wolfowitz's war. It's his holy mission. His cue was September 11. Slightly after Rumsfeld, on September 15, 2001 at Camp David, Wolfowitz was already advocating an attack on Iraq. There are at least three versions of what happened that day. As a reporter, the *Washington Post*'s Bob Woodward (remember Watergate) used to bring down presidents; now he's a mere presidential public relations officer. In his book *Bush at War* he writes that Bush told Wolfowitz to shut up and let the number 1 (Rumsfeld) talk. The second version, defended by the *New York Times,* says that Bush listened attentively to Wolfowitz. But a third version relayed by diplomats holds that in Bush's executive order on September 17 authorizing war on Afghanistan, there was already a paragraph giving free reign to the Pentagon to draw plans for a war against Iraq.

GARY COOPER'S EYES

Former CIA director James Woolsey, a certified five-star hawk, is a great friend of Wolfowitz. Woolsey is also the author of what could be dubbed "the High Noon" theory that defines nothing less than Bush's vision of the world. According to the theory, Bush is not a six-shooter: he is the leader of a posse.

That's how Bush described himself in a conversation last year with then Czech president Vaclav Havel. As film fans well remember, Gary Cooper in High Noon plays a village marshal who tries by all means to convince his friends to assemble a posse to face the Saddam of the times, one Frank Miller (played by Ian McDonald), who is supposed to arrive on the noon train. In the end, Cooper has to face "Saddam" Miller and his henchmen all by himself.

It's fair to argue that the Bush administration today is enacting a larger-than-life replay of a high noon. The posse is the "coalition of the willing". The logic of the posse is crystal clear. The US first defines a strategic objective (for example, regime change in Iraq). They propagate their steely determination to achieve this objective (an awesome worldwide propaganda and disinformation campaign combined with a major military deployment). And finally they assemble a posse to help them: the coalition of the willing, or "coalition of the bribed and bludgeoned", as it was dubbed by democrats in Europe and the US itself. A devastating report by the Institute for Policy Studies in Washington has detailed a "coalition of the coerced". Whatever its name, those who did not join the coalition (the absolute majority of UN member-states, as well as world public opinion) remained, as Bush said, "irrelevant".

With missionary fervor, Wolfowitz has been pursuing his Iraqi dream step by step. In late 2001, James Woolsey roamed all over Europe trying to find a connection between Saddam and al-Qa'ida. He couldn't find anything. But then in January 2002, Iraq was formally inducted in the "axis of evil" along with Iran and North Korea. Rumsfeld went into overdrive: he said that Saddam supported "terrorists" (in fact suicide martyrs in Palestine, who have nothing to do with al-Qa'ida). He said that Saddam promised US$25,000 to each of their families. The neo-cons embarked on a media blitzkrieg, and Wolfowitz's mission finally hit center stage.

During the Cold War in the 1970s, Wolfowitz learned the ropes laboring on nuclear treaties, the endless talks with the Soviets on nuclear armament limitations. At the time he also started a career for one of his better students, Lewis Libby—who today is Cheney's chief of staff. For three decades Wolfowitz has been involved in strategic thinking, military organization and political and diplomatic moves. Even former Jimmy Carter national security adviser Zbigniew Brzezinski, the author of *The Grand Chessboard* —or the roadmap for US domination over Eurasia—allegedly allows Wolfowitz to figure alongside Henry Kissinger, McGeorge Bundy or Zbig himself: that select elite of academics who managed to cross over to high office and radiate intellectual authority and almost unlimited power by osmosis because of close contact with an American president.

Wolfowitz routinely talks about "freedom and democracy"—with no contextualization. His renditions always sound like a romantic ideal. But there's nothing romantic about him. During the First Gulf War,

Wolfowitz was an Under Secretary at the Pentagon formulating policy. Cheney was the Pentagon chief. It was Wolfowitz who prepared Desert Storm—and also got the money. The bill was roughly $90 billion, 80 percent of it paid by the allies: a cool deal. It was Wolfowitz who convinced Israel not to enter the war even after the country was hit by Iraqi Scuds, so the key Arab partners of the 33-nation coalition would not run away.

But Saddam always remained his nemesis. When Bush senior lost his re-election, Wolfowitz became Dean of the School of Advanced International Studies at Johns Hopkins University in Baltimore. Later, he was fully convinced that Iraq was behind the first attack against the World Trade Center, in 1993.

Wolfowitz and Perle, though close, are not the same thing. Perle is virtually indistinguishable from the hardcore policies of the Likud in Israel. Perle thinks that the only possible way out for the US—not the West, because he despises Europe as a political player—is a multi-faceted, long-term, vicious confrontation with the Arab and Muslim world. Wolfowitz is more sophisticated: he has already served as American ambassador to Indonesia. He definitely does not subscribe to the fallacious Samuel Huntington theory of a clash of civilizations. Wolfowitz even believes in an independent Palestine—something that for Perle is beyond anathema.

Wolfowitz, born in 1943 in New York, is the son of a Polish mathematician whose whole family died in Nazi concentration camps. It was Allan Bloom, the brilliant author of *The Closing of the American Mind* and professor at the University of Chicago, deceased in 1992, who steered Wolfowitz towards political science. Wolfowitz had the honor of being cloned by Saul Bellow in the novel *Ravelstein*: the Wolfowitz character shows up under a fictional name in the same role he occupied in 1991 at the Pentagon. Messianic, and a big fan of Abraham Lincoln, Wolfowitz is a walking contradiction: his fierce unilateralism is based on his faith in the universality of American values.

THE STRAUSSIANS

Wolfowitz and his protégés are hardcore "Straussians"—after Leo Strauss, a Jewish intellectual who managed to escape the Nazis, died in 1999 as a 100-year-old and was totally anti-modern: for him, modernity was responsible for Nazism and Stalinism. Strauss was a lover of the classics—

most of all Plato and Aristotle. His most notorious disciples were Chicago's Allan Bloom, and also Harvey Mansfield—who translated both Machiavelli and Tocqueville and was the father of all things politically correct in Harvard.

Strauss believed in natural right and in an immutable measure of what is just and what is unjust. Thus the Wolfowitz credo that a vague "democracy and freedom" is a one-size-fits-all panacea to be served everywhere, even by force. Plenty of neo-hawks followed Bloom's courses at the University of Chicago: Wolfowitz of course, but also Francis Fukuyama of "end of history" fame, and John Podhoretz, who reigns over the editorial pages of the ultra-reactionary Rupert Murdoch-owned tabloid the *New York Post*. As for Mansfield, his most notorious student was probably William Kristol, the editor of the (also Rupert Murdoch-financed) magazine *Weekly Standard*. In Kristol's own formulation, all these Straussians are morally conservative, religiously inclined, anti-Utopian, anti-modern, skeptical towards the left but also towards the reactionary right.

Ronald Reagan, because of his "moral clarity" and his "virtue", is their supreme icon—rather than the devious *realpolitik* pair—Richard Nixon and Kissinger. Grasping this conceptual choice is absolutely essential to understand where the neocons are coming from. Take the crucial expression "regime change": there's nothing casual about it. Strauss used to say that "classic political philosophy was guided by the question of the best regime". Here Strauss was talking specifically about Aristotle and his notion of politeia. The "regime"—or politeia—designates not only government, but also institutions, education, morals, and "the spirit of law". In the mind of these Straussians, to topple Saddam is a mere footnote. "Regime change" in Iraq means to implant a Western Utopia in the heart of the Middle East: a Western-built politeia. Many would argue this is no more than a replay of Rudyard Kipling's "white man's burden".

Perle, also a New Yorker, is much, much rougher than Wolfowitz. No Aristotle for him. A dull man with a psychopath gaze, he recently accused New Yorker reporter Seymour Hersh of being "a terrorist"—because Hersh, in a splendid piece, unveiled how Perle set up a company that will profit immensely from war in the Middle East. Perle has repeatedly declared on the record that the US is prepared to attack Syria, Lebanon and Iran—all "enemies of Israel". One of his most notorious recent stunts was when he invited an obscure French scholar to the Defense Policy Board to bash the Saudi royal family. He casually noted that if the invasion of Iraq brings down another couple of "friendly" Arab regimes, it's no big deal. At a recent seminar organized by a New York-based public relations firm and attended by Iraqi exiles and American Middle East and security officials, Perle proclaimed that France was no longer an ally of the US; and that NATO "must develop a strategy to contain our erstwhile ally or we will not be talking about a NATO alliance". This hawk, though, is no fool, and loves *la vie en rose*: Richard Perle spends his holidays in his own house in the south of France.

If you are a Pentagon senior civilian advisor, saying all those things out loud packs a tremendous punch in Washington: it's practically official. As official as Perle musing out loud whether the US should "subordinate vital national interests to a show of hands by nations who do not share our interests", by seeking the endorsement of the UN Security Council on a major issue of policy (that's exactly what happened at the UN). Perle had been saying all along that "Iraq is going to be liberated, by the United States and whoever wants to join us, whether we get the approbation of the UN or any other institution". And Bush repeated these words almost verbatim. As for the tremendous unpopularity of the US, "it's a real problem and it undoubtedly diminishes our ability to do the things that we think are important. I think that's bad for the world, because if the United States, as the leader it has always been, has its authority and standing diminished, that can't be good for the Swiss or the Italians or the Germans. But I don't know how you deal with that problem ...".

UTOPIAN PARADISE

Perle and Wolfowitz may shape policy, but that would not enhance their mundane status among the political chattering classes if they didn't have a bulldog to disseminate their clout in the media. That's where William Kristol, the chairman of the Project For The New American Century and the director of the magazine *Weekly Standard* comes in. Kristol's co-chairman at the PNAC is Robert Kagan, former deputy for policy in the State Department in the bureau for Inter-American affairs. Kagan is the author of *Of Paradise and Power: America vs Europe in the New World Order*—where, according to a fallacious formula, Europeans living in a kind of peaceful, Utopian paradise will be forced to stomach unbridled American power. Robert is the son of Donald Kagan, ultra-conservative Yale professor and eminent historian. Kagan junior is a major apostle of nation building, as in "the reconstruction of the Japanese politics and society to America's image". He cheerleads the fact that 60 years later there are still American troops in Japan. The same, according to him, should happen in Iraq. Any strategist would remind Kagan that in Japan in 1945, the emperor himself ordered the population to obey the Americans and in Ger-many the war devastation was so complete that the Germans had no other alternative.

William is the son of Irving Kristol and Gertrud Himmelfarb, classic New York Jewish intellectuals and ironically former Trotskyites who then made a sharp turn to the extreme right. Former Trotskyites have a tendency to believe that history will vindicate them in the end. Irving, at 82 a former neo-Marxist, neo-Trotskyite, neo-socialist and neo-liberal, today is officially a neo-conservative and one of the AEI's stalwarts.

Kristol junior reportedly likes philosophy, opera, thrillers and is fond of—who else—Aristotle and Machiavelli, who not by accident were eminences behind the prince. Instead of rebelling against his parents, he sulked in his bedroom rebelling against his own generation—the anti-war, peace-and-love, Bob Dylan-addicted 1960s baby boomers. Although admitting that Vietnam was a big mistake, William did not volunteer to go to war, a fact that qualifies him as the archetypal "chicken hawk"— armchair warmongers who know nothing about the horrors of war. William wants to erect conservatism to the level of an ideology of government. His great heroes include Reagan—for, what else, his "candor" and "moral clarity". A naked imperialist? No, he's not as crass as Rumsfeld: he prefers to be characterized as a partisan of "liberal imperialism".

As media hawk-in-chief, William is just following up daddy's work: Irving Kristol was the ultimate portable think tank of Reaganism. Today, Kristol junior is convinced that the Middle East is an irredeemable source of anti-Americanism, terrorism, weapons of mass destruction and an assorted basket of evils. Kristol of course is a very good friend of Wolfowitz, Kagan and former ex-CIA chief James Woolsey, who not by accident heaps lavish praise on *The War over Iraq: Saddam's tyranny and America's mission*, a book by Lawrence Kaplan and … William Kristol. Woolsey loves how the book goes against the "narrow realists" around Bush senior and the "wishful liberals" around Bill Clinton.

Under Bush senior, William Kristol was Dan Quayle's chief of staff. Under Clinton, he was in the wilderness until he finally managed to launch the *Weekly Standard*. Who financed it? None other than Rupert Murdoch, whose tabloidish Fox News is widely known as Bush TV. The *Weekly Standard* loses money in direct proportion to the expansion of its influence. It remains invaluable as the voice of "Hawk Central".

Hawks, or at least some neo-conservatives, seem to understand the importance of a lighter touch as a key public relations strategy. That's where David Brooks comes in. Brooks, former University of Chicago, former *Wall Street Journal* and now a big fish at the *Weekly Standard,* was the one who came up with the concept of "bobos"—bourgeois bohemians, or "caviar left" as they are known in Latin countries. "Bobos", accuse the neocons, do absolutely nothing to change a social order that they seem to fight, but from which they profit. Bobo-bashing is one of the neocon's ideological strategies to dismiss their critics out of hand.

A FAMILIAR SCRIPT

In his conference at the World Social Forum in Porto Alegre, Brazil, in January 2003, Noam Chomsky demystified the mechanism through which these people, "most of them recycled from the Reagan administration", are implementing their agenda: "They are replaying a familiar script: drive the country into deficit so as to be able to undermine social programs, declare a 'war on terror' (as they did in 1981) and conjure up one devil after another to frighten the population into obedience. In the 1980s it was Libyan hit men prowling the streets of Washington to assassinate our leader, then the Nicaraguan army only two days march from Texas, a threat to survival so severe that Reagan had to declare a national emergency. Or an airfield in Grenada that the Russians were going to use to bomb us (if they could find it on a map); Arab terrorists seeking to kill Americans everywhere while Gaddafi plans to 'expel America from the world', so Reagan wailed. Or Hispanic narco-traffickers seeking to destroy our youth; and on, and on."

For both the AEI and the PNAC, the Middle East is a land without people, and oil without land—and this is something anyone will confirm in the streets or power corridors in Cairo, Amman, Beirut, Ramallah, Damascus or Baghdad. The image fits the AEI and PNAC's acute and indiscriminate loathing and contempt for Arabs. The implementation of the AEI's and the PNAC's policies has led to the transformation of Ariel Sharon into a "man of peace"—Bush's own words at the White House—and the semi-fascist Likud Party becoming the undisputed number one ally of American civilization. The occupied Palestinian territories—see never-complied with, forever-spurned UN resolution 242 plus dozens of others—became "the so-called occupied territories" (in Rumsfeld's own words). Jewish moderates, inside and outside Israel, are extremely alarmed.

One of the key excuses for the Iraq war sold by Washington was the elimination of the roots of terrorism by striking terrorists and the "axis of evil" that supports them. This is a total flaw. The excuse is undermined by the US themselves. Not even Washington believes war is the way to fight terrorism, otherwise the Bush administration would not have adopted the AEI and PNAC agenda of promoting "democracy and liberty" in the Arab world. But neither the Arabs nor anyone else is convinced that the US is committed to real democracy or to the "territorial integrity of Iraq" when key members of the administration, like Perle, signed "Clean Break" in 1996 advising Benjamin Netanyahu that Iraq and any other country which tried to defy Israel should be smashed. The message by the PNAC people to Netanyahu in 1996 and to Bush since 2001 has been the same: international law is against our interests; we fix our own objectives; we go for it and the rest will follow—or not. Even Zbig Brzezinski has recognized the American corporate press—unlike the European press—has not uttered a single word about the total similarity of the agendas. But concerned Americans have already realized the superpower has no attention span, no patience, no tact—and many would say no historical credibility—to engage in nation-building in the Middle East.

There's not much democracy on the cards either. Iraqis and the whole Arab nation view as an unredeemable insult and injury the official American plan to enforce a de facto military occupation. Iraq is already carved up on paper into three sections (just like the British did in the 1920s). Two retired generals—including Arabic-speaking, Lebanese-origin John Abizaid—and a former ambassador to Yemen—will control the three interim "civil" administrations. Abizaid studied the history of the Middle East at Harvard—and this is as far as his democratic credentials go. Everything in Iraq will be under overseer supremo Jay Garner, a retired general very close to Ariel Sharon and until a few months ago the CEO of a weapons firm specializing in missile guidance systems. Iraqis, Palestinians and Arabs as a whole are stunned: not only has the US flaunted international legitimacy in its push to war, it will also install an Israeli proxy as governor of Iraq and will keep pretending to finally be committed to respecting the never-complied-with dozens of UN resolutions concerning Palestine.

UNKNOWABLES

As much as Israel is widely regarded by most 1.3 billion Muslims as the de facto 51st American state, many responsible Americans denounce the Iraq war as Sharon's war. Washington's Likudniks—the AEI and PNAC people—allied with evangelical Christians—are running US foreign policy in the Middle East. Since autumn 2002, they have managed to convince Bush to increase the tempo—with no consultation with Congress or American public opinion—betting on a point-of-no-return scenario in Iraq. Meanwhile, Sharon, in a relentless campaign, managed to convince Bush that war on Palestine was equal to war against terrorism. But he went one step beyond: he convinced Bush that the Palestinian Intifada, al-Qa'ida and Saddam are all cats in the same bag, plotting a concerted three-pronged offensive to destroy Judeo-Christian civilization. Thus the subsequent, overwhelming Bush administration campaign to try to convince public opinion that Saddam is an ally of bin Laden. Few fell into the trap. But European strategists got the drift: they are already working with the hypothesis that the geopolitical axis in the Middle East is about to switch from Cairo-Riyadh-Tehran to Tel Aviv-Ankara-Baghdad (post-Saddam).

In a recent hearing of the Senate Foreign Relations Committee, Under-Secretary of State for Political Affairs, Mark Grossman, and Under-Secretary of Defense for Policy, Douglas Feith, talked for four hours and through 86 pages, apparently detailing how the US will rebuild Iraq after liberation through massive bombing. Feith has been on record saying that this war of course "is not about oil", while stating a few sentences later that "the US will be the new OPEC". A source confirms that it was clear at the Senate hearing that neither Feith nor Grossman had any idea of what the Arab world is all about. Senators asked how much the war would cost (Yale economist William Nordhaus said the occupation may cost between $17 billion and $45 billion a year): nobody had an answer. Feith and Grossman said it was "unknowable". Rumsfeld is also a major exponent of the "not knowable" school. The cost of war for American taxpayers—some estimates go as high as $200 billion—is "not knowable". The size of the occupation force—some estimates range as high as 400,000 troops—is "not knowable". The duration of the occupation (former NATO supreme commander Wesley Clark has mentioned no less than eight years) is "not knowable".

Arabs, Asians, Europeans—and a few Americans—warn of blowback: the whole Middle East may explode in a violent, vicious anti-imperialist struggle. As this correspondent has been hearing for months from Pakistan to Egypt and from Indonesia to the Gulf, "dozens of bin Ladens" are bound to emerge. The strategy advocated by the evangelic apostles of armed democratization—overwhelming military force, unilateral preemption, overthrow of governments, seizure of oil fields, recolonization, protectorates—is being roundly condemned by the same educated Arab elites which would be the natural leaders of a push for democratization. Many question not Washington's objective, but the method: they simply cannot stomach the "imperial liberalism" version marketed by the hawks. The current absolute mess in Afghanistan is further demonstration that "democratization" via an American proconsul is doomed to failure. Moreover, 16 eminent British academic lawyers have certified the Bush doctrine of preemptive self-defense is illegal under international law.

Even a tragically surreal, zombie regime like North Korea's has retained one essential lesson from this whole crisis: if you don't want regime change, you'd better maximize your silence, speed and cunning to build your own arsenal of WMD. Muslims for their part have understood that the unlikely Franco-German-Russian axis of peace was and still is trying to prevent what both al-Qa'ida and American fundamentalists want: a war of civilizations and a war of religion. And the world public opinion's insight is that Washington may win the war without the UN—but it will lose peace by shooting the UN down. As a diplomat in Brussels put it, "The world has voted in unison: it does not want to be reordered by a posse in Washington."

The men in the AEI and the PNAC galaxy may be accused of intolerance, the arrogance of power, undisguised fascist tendencies, ignorance of history and cultural parochialism—in various degrees. This is all open to debate. They may be "chicken hawks" like Kristol junior or attack dogs like Rumsfeld. But most of all what baffles educated publics across the world—especially the overwhelming majority of public opinion in Germany, France, the UK, Italy and Spain—is the current non-separation of Church and State in the US.

George W. Bush is not ideologically a neo-conservative. But he is certainly a man with a notorious lack of intellectual curiosity. Backed by his core American constituency of 60 to 70 million Bible-believing Christians, born-again Bush set out to do God's will on a crusade to Babylon to "fight evil"—personified by Saddam. Martin Amis, Britain's top contemporary novelist, argues that Bush, being intellectually null, had no other option than to adopt God as his foreign policy mentor. Amis wrote in the *Observer* that "Bush is more religious than Saddam: of the two presidents, he is, in this respect, the more psychologically primitive. We hear about the successful 'Texanization' of the Republican party. And doesn't Texas seem to resemble a country like Saudi Arabia, with its great heat, its oil wealth, its brimming houses of worship, and its weekly executions." For former weapons inspector Scott Ritter, Bush is "a fundamentalist who does not respect international law. The United States is becoming a crusader state." For the absolute majority of 1.3 billion Muslims, a sinister crusader it is.

The endgame revealed itself to be a cheap family farce: the Bush family delivering an ultimatum to the Hussein family. What Gore Vidal describes as "the Bush-Cheney junta" has won: Cheney, Rumsfeld, Wolfowitz, Perle, the AEI and PNAC stalwarts. Paul Wolfowitz, above all, has won his own personal crusade. Colin Powell has lost it all. It does not matter that the State Department's classified report, "Iraq, the Middle East and change: no dominoes" was unveiled by the *Los Angeles Times*. Wolfowitz and Perle will play with their dominoes. By predictable mechanisms of power as old as mankind itself (and incidentally very common in the former USSR) it was Powell—the adversary of the new doctrine of preemption—who was charged to defend it in the face of the world. Sources in New York confirm he was told to get in line: his discourse, his body language, his whole demeanor changed. Seasoned American diplomats are appalled by the devastating political and diplomatic failure of the Bush administration. They know that by deciding to go to war unilaterally—and leaving the international system in shambles—the US has squandered its biggest capital: its international legitimacy. And to make matters worse there was absolutely no debate about it—in the Senate, or in the public opinion arena.

Americans still have to wake up to the fact of how startlingly isolated they are in the world. The world, for its part, will keep deploying its weapons of mass democracy. There can be no "international community" as long as the popular perception lingers in so many parts of the world of a clash between the West and Islam. Always ready to recognize and love the best America has to offer, hundreds of millions of people would rather try to save it from the fatal unilateralism distilled by the American fundamentalists of the PNAC and the AEI. Everyone in Baghdad, the former great capital of Islam at its apex, is fond of saying how it has survived the Mongols, the barbarians at the gate. The evangelic apostles of armed democratization cannot even begin to imagine the fury a new breed of "barbarians" may unleash at the gate of the new American century.

| # Global Rogue State

EDWARD S. HERMAN

ICTIONARY SPECIFICATIONS of "rogue" include three elements: viciousness, lack of principle, and propensity to engage in unilateral action. This would certainly properly characterize Saddam Hussein's Iraq: viciousness and lack of principle were displayed, for example, in his attacking and using chemical warfare against both Iran and Iraqi Kurds in the 1980s; unilateralism in his assaults on Iran and Kuwait. But consider that the United States used chemical warfare on a far greater scale against Vietnam in the 1960s, and its overall attack on Indo-China was as vicious and far more devastating than Iraq's on its local victims. As to principle, it should be noted that the US aided Saddam Hussein during the 1980s and protected him from any international sanctions, finding his possession of "weapons of mass destruction" intolerable only after he stepped out of line and ceased to be of service. The US is also at least as prone to unilateral actions as Iraq, and commonly ignores an international consensus and international law when they stand in the way of a preferred option.

RETAIL AND WHOLESALE ROGUES

The difference between the two countries in respect of roguery is that the US is a superpower with global reach, whereas Iraq is a relatively weak regional power. The US we might say, engages in wholesale roguery, whereas Iraq is a retail rogue. But nobody in the mainstream calls the wholesale rogue by such a name, any more than they would label it a terrorist state or sponsor of terror, no matter how close the fit. If a country is sufficiently powerful, it naturally assumes the role of global policeman, and as such it designates who are terrorists and rogues. This role is accepted and internalized not only by its own media, but by politicians and the media of its allied and client states. As La Fontaine pointed out in his fable "The Wolf and the Sheep," "The opinion of the Biggest is always the best."

Under the rule of the Biggest, the law and rules of morality only apply to others, not to the ruler himself. This double standard rests on sheer power. It is effected through a variety of processes involving the main-stream media, which ignore or play down outrageous behavior and law violations by the ruler, but wax indignant at comparable or lesser enemy actions. Cuba's shooting down of a Cuban refugee plane which flew over its territory was excoriated by the media, but disclosure of multiple US attempts to assassinate Castro caused neither indignation nor reflection on "who is the terrorist." When the global rogue justified terrorizing Nicaragua in the 1980s by the "national security threat" posed by that tiny power, and bombed Baghdad in 1993 following an alleged Iraqi plot to assassinate former president George Bush, on the ground of the right to "self defense," nobody important responded with laughter or indigna-tion. The absurd rationalizations were reported "objectively" and the vio-lent acts were accepted and normalized.

MISUSING THE UN AND THE WORLD COURT

Nothing illustrates the global rogue's lack of principle and propensity to unilateralism better than its treatment of the UN and the World Court. When the UN or the Court have failed to serve its purposes, the global rogue has assailed them, refused to pay its dues (in violation of the law), withdrawn from UN organizations (UNESCO, ILO), and simply ignored a UN consensus or Court ruling. The US has used the UN as a cover for its own agenda, but not allowed the UN to function where its positions were inconsistent with that agenda.

The most notable recent case of using (and misusing) the UN was the 1990–1991 assault on Iraq, and the sanctions imposed on Iraq which con-tinue to this day. Here the US was deeply upset over an illegal occupation in violation of the UN Charter. And by the aggressive use of its power to coerce and bribe support (well described in Phyllis Bennis's valuable

Calling the Shots), the global rogue was able to get the UN to give it a free hand to crush Iraq and keep it crushed thereafter—with a cumulative civilian death toll in the hundreds of thousands. The rogue actually violated the UN charter in implementing the UN resolution giving it a free hand, by resolutely refusing to consider any peaceful settlement and insisting on a military attack. Its use of weapons like uranium-enhanced shells and fuel air bombs, the slaughter of large numbers of completely helpless and fleeing soldiers (along with many refugees), burying many of them in unmarked graves, and bulldozing sand over Iraqi trenches killing hundreds more, violated the rules of war, under UN cover.

With Iraq, the global rogue was teaching a lesson to a retail rogue who had crossed it. Clients of the global rogue are treated differently. South Africa, which illegally occupied Namibia, and used it as a jumping off place to invade Angola and support Savimbi, and also attacked and terrorized all the other front line states for several decades, was perhaps the number one retail rogue and terrorist state of the last half century. Its occupation of Namibia was condemned by the Security Council, General Assembly and World Court from the late 1960s, and it was ordered to withdraw. But it refused to obey, and no attempt was made to force the termination of that occupation. The US was "constructively engaged" with South Africa, and collaborated with it in its support of Savimbi and attacks on Angola and the front line states.

Another important case has been that of Israel, which occupied the West Bank and Gaza Strip in 1967, and although Security Council resolution 242 called upon Israel to withdraw, it has refused to do so for two decades, without penalty. Israel was also condemned for its collaboration with South Africa and maltreatment of the Palestinians in a long series of UN resolutions. But as the US supports Israel, its occupation and abuses are beyond the reach of UN authority. The US has vetoed some 40 resolutions condemning Israel, and successfully prevents any action constraining it or protecting its victims. The votes are usually in the order of 150–2, but this near unanimity cannot offset the power of the global rogue.

In the case of the World Court, the US used it effectively against Iran and other states, but when the Court ruled in favor of Nicaragua in 1986, calling for US reparations for the "unlawful use of force," the US denounced and then simply ignored the ruling. In a telling revelation of the subservience of the US media to the global rogue's prerogatives, the *New York Times* editorialized in support of the US refusal to accept the Court's ruling, calling the Court a "hostile forum." As regards the UN, also, the *Times* and its media confreres have followed the official agenda, finding the UN ineffectual and wrong-headed when not serving US interests, but finally recovering its proper role, as in the Persian Gulf war, when it functions as a US instrument.

With the collapse of the Soviet Union, and virtual US control of the Security Council, the US now regularly bypasses the World Court, and, of course, the UN General Assembly, in carrying out its agenda. Thus it was not only able to use the UN as a cover for war and retribution against Iraq, it has successfully used the Security Council to impose sanctions on Libya for refusing to turn over to the US and Britain two suspects in the bombing of Pan Am 103. Libya denies that the Security Council has jurisdiction and objects to any trial by the biased protagonists, but the World Court has deferred to the Security Council, so this US-dominated body now has a free hand to designate rogues and terrorists. No client of the global rogue has been subjected to sanctions under this regime.

GLOBAL ROGUE AGGRESSIONS

Ignoring both minor bombing raids and the numerous subversive efforts not involving military forces, since the end of World War II the United States has committed acts of aggression against Guatemala (1954), Lebanon (1958), the Dominican Republic (1965), Vietnam (1954–75), Laos (1964–1975), Cambodia (1969–1975), Nicaragua (1980–1990), Grenada (1983) and Panama (1989). I would argue that the Persian Gulf war was also a case of US aggression, as the US took advantage of Iraq's aggression against Kuwait to smash a regional power that had defied it. In short, the US has been the number one international aggressor over the past 50 years.

In the case of the Vietnam War, the global rogue was able to ignore the 1954 Geneva Accords, place a puppet in power in South Vietnam, invade and bomb all of Indo-China, killing as many as four million people over two decades, without the slightest interference from the UN or World Court. In the case of Panama, the rogue invaded in 1989 to capture its leader, Noriega, allegedly for drug dealing and authoritarian rule. But Noriega had been on the US payroll for years while dealing in drugs and ruling by terror. The real reason for the invasion was Noriega's refusal to collaborate with the US in its illegal attacks on Nicaragua. Again, the US veto and overall power allowed this multi-leveled rogue operation to go forward without impediment.

TERRORISM AND SPONSORSHIP OF REGIMES OF TERROR

As noted, the US has been able to label its targets and victims "terrorists" as well as rogues. Terrorist groups supported and sponsored by the US, like Savimbi in Angola, the Nicaraguan contras, and the Cuban refugee network—which has operated out of the US itself—are "freedom fighters," not terrorists, by right of sponsorship.

The CIA and US military forces have been outstanding direct instruments of terror: William Blum in *Killing Hope* lists 35 individuals or groups known to have been targeted by US agents in assassination attempts, some (like Castro and Qaddafi) repeatedly, and with quite a few successfully killed. Larger scale US terrorism has been carried out by its military establishment, with vastly larger civilian casualties, and the establishment terrorism expert J. Bowyer Bell acknowledged that a legitimate question had been raised as to why the "use of American B-52s over Hanoi was an appropriate military exercise, while the Palestinian use of incendiary grenades in Rome was not." Bell never answered the question, but we can do that easily: the Biggest defines what is terrorism as well as who is a rogue.

US-protected clients have also been in the forefront of world terrorism: the massacre of some 600 civilians by the Salvadoran army at the Rio Sumpul river in 1980, the killing of over 600 by South Africa in the Kassinga refugee camp in Angola in 1978, and the Phalange-Israeli massacre of over 1,800 Palestinians at Sabra-Shatila in 1982, each equaled or exceeded the collective total of the Western favorites—the PLO, Baader Meinhof gang and Red Brigades. These are just single episodes by regimes that did a lot of killing. US sponsorship of the National Security State in Latin America, and of regimes like those of Marcos, Mobutu, the

Shah of Iran, Suharto, and the Greek colonels, involved the support of serious state terrorism on a global scale. "The real terror network," described in my book of that name (South End, 1982) was a creation of US policy for its own backyard, designed to get rid of obstacles to market expansion and US-amenable rule by terror. It is the genius of the Western propaganda system that, in the face of this reality, the US was and is today portrayed as the steadfast opponent of "terrorism."

ECONOMIC TERRORISM

The economic rules of the game also apply mainly to others, not to the Biggest. During the 1980s, when the Japanese auto industry was badly outcompeting that of the US, quotas were imposed by the US in a protectionist system that was also applied in the steel and other industries. This was the same period in which the US was engaged in "aggressive unilateralism," bullying other countries into opening their markets on the ground of sacred free trade principles.

Far more gross has been the US use of food warfare and trade/investment boycotts against political targets like Vietnam, Cuba, Iran, Iraq, Nicaragua and other states that cross it. These boycotts have caused serious hunger, disease and death in the victim countries, although it is often hard to separate the effects of food warfare from those of US direct and proxy military operations. In Nicaragua in the 1980s, the two together helped reduce household real incomes by some 50 percent, contributing to widespread malnutrition, a weakened health care system, and eventually the desired ouster of the Sandinista government. The US policy of "destructive engagement" with Cuba has also substantially affected the Cuban standard of living and health conditions. The American Association of World Health recently reported that food warfare against Cuba "has contributed to serious nutritional deficits, particularly among pregnant women, leading to an increase in low birth-weight babies. In addition, food shortages were linked to a devastating outbreak of neuropathy numbering in the tens of thousands." Caloric intake fell by one third between 1989 and 1993, and curtailed access to water treatment chemicals and medicines has also taken a heavy toll.

The US boycotts of Cuba and Iran and threats to retaliate against foreign companies doing business with them—a form of secondary boycott—violates the global trade rules that the US helped put together, but it exempts itself, usually on the ground of "national security," and its power allows it to get away with self-exemption. And the mainstream media, so indignant at the Arab secondary boycott of companies doing business with Israel after the 1967 war, make no comparisons and berate the US allies for disloyalty to the Biggest.

Other countries are also expected to make national economic adjustments to reestablish equilibrium that the Biggest doesn't choose to make. A large US trade deficit, for example, could be reduced by policy changes by either the US or by Japan and other major allies. Japanese and European expansionary policies would increase their incomes and prices, and thus enlarge their imports from the US and reduce their exports. On the other hand, the US deficit could be reduced by US contractionary policies that would curtail US imports and increase US exports. The US may expect others to carry out painful contractionary policies, but it naturally does not entertain the possibility that it should be subject to similar pain. From 1945 until today the US has expected the foreign countries to do the adjusting.

Possibly the most important form of economic terrorism carried out by the global rogue has been its contribution to the ongoing aggressive imposition of the neoliberal model of economic life on peoples everywhere. The US has not been alone in pushing this program, which has the support of the community of transnational corporations across the globe, as well as many states whose governments are in thrall to this powerful community. But the Biggest, home of a sizable fraction of transnationals and effectively dominating the IMF and World Bank, has been the leader. The imposition of this model has stripped countries of autonomy and weakened the ability of national majorities to organize and seek change through traditional political processes. It has been associated with a massive upward redistribution of income and wealth and immense misery to the hundreds of millions of losers in the new class war.

Such abuse of power and exploitation by imperial top dogs is not new, as the earlier reigns of Britain and Spain make clear. What is new, however, is the hypocrisy in the exalted self-image of the US as the redeemer nation, bringing "democracy" to the world, as it fights against "protectionism" and the demon retail terrorists and rogue states, constructed to provide its sense of exoneration and purity.

EPILOGUE

This article was written in February 1998—that is, before the Kosovo war, 9/11, the Afghanistan and Iraq wars, and the post-9/11 declaration of a global "war on terror." These wars demonstrate that the rogue state has reached out to new levels of violence, disregard of international law and opinion, and threat to international stability, justice, and even survivability. The Kosovo war was not a "humanitarian war", but rather the culmination of the dismantling of an independent Yugoslavia by the NATO powers, who were primarily responsible for the outbursts of ethnic cleansing in that area, and took advantage of it to settle old scores, re-establish NATO power domination of that area and assert US domination of NATO (see Diana Johnstone, *Fools' Crusade: Yugoslavia, NATO and Western Delusions* [Pluto, Monthly Review Press, 2002]). 9/11 gave the Bush administration the excuse to aggressively push outward and repress within, in the interest of a regressive domestic program and a imperialist agenda abroad. The Afghanistan war was an opening blast outward, and as in the case of the Kosovo war was done without any sanction from the UN and in violation of international law.

The invasion and occupation of Iraq represents an important further phase of rogue state aggression and thrust toward global domination. The attack on Iraq was a blatant aggression, in which the rogue state announced many months in advance that it was going to invade, and then did so in the face of a refusal of the Security Council to give its approval and obvious massive global opposition to the attack. As Iraq poses no credible threat to the United States or its single major ally Britain, the invasion is as clear a case of illegal aggression as Hitler's attack on Poland. The failure of the United Nations Organization to stop the US-British aggression marks the same kind of terminal crisis of the UN system as was marked by the failure of the League of Nations to halt Mussolini's invasion of Ethiopia in 1936.

The world is in for serious threats from the rogue in the future. The Iraq war and occupation will generate enormous hostility from the Arab and Muslim world that will surely lead to responsive conflict, which the rogue will use to justify further militarization and violence. The rogue has already started a major new arms race by his pronouncements of an intention to dominate all military spectrums and his right to carry out preventive as well as preemptive wars. He has shown himself less than just and even-handed in designating friends and villains, with the ethnic cleansing and nuclear-armed Sharon and Israel given unstinting support, but Arab states denied the right to possess such arms. The withdrawal of the rogue from Kyoto and numerous other international agreements, and his support for the IMF, World Bank, World Trade Organization, and the neoliberal model bodes ill for both the environment and any progress in economic development and justice for the billions of global excluded. There has been growing mass resistance to the rogue in the past few years, although many governments continue to serve the rogue rather than their own citizens. We must hope that this will change in the future as people become more aware of global realities and the need to counter rogue domination.

5 | The Thirty-Year Itch

ROBERT DREYFUSS

IF YOU WERE TO SPIN the globe and look for real estate critical to
building an American empire, your first stop would have to be the
Persian Gulf. The desert sands of this region hold two of every three
barrels of oil in the world—Iraq's reserves alone are equal, by some estimates, to those of Russia, the United States, China, and Mexico combined. For the past 30 years, the Gulf has been in the crosshairs of an
influential group of Washington foreign-policy strategists, who believe
that in order to ensure its global dominance, the United States must seize
control of the region and its oil. Born during the energy crisis of the 1970s
and refined since then by a generation of policymakers, this approach is
finding its boldest expression yet in the Bush administration—which,
with its plan to invade Iraq and install a regime beholden to Washington,
has moved closer than any of its predecessors to transforming the Gulf
into an American protectorate.

In the geopolitical vision driving current US policy toward Iraq, the
key to national security is global hegemony—dominance over any and all
potential rivals. To that end, the United States must not only be able to
project its military forces anywhere, at any time. It must also control key
resources, chief among them oil—and especially Gulf oil. To the hawks
who now set the tone at the White House and the Pentagon, the region is
crucial not simply for its share of the US oil supply (other sources have
become more important over the years), but because it would allow the
United States to maintain a lock on the world's energy lifeline and potentially deny access to its global competitors. The administration "believes
you have to control resources in order to have access to them," says Chas

Freeman, who served as US ambassador to Saudi Arabia under the first President Bush. "They are taken with the idea that the end of the Cold War left the United States able to impose its will globally—and that those who have the ability to shape events with power have the duty to do so. It's ideology."

Iraq, in this view, is a strategic prize of unparalleled importance. Unlike the oil beneath Alaska's frozen tundra, locked away in the steppes of central Asia, or buried under stormy seas, Iraq's crude is readily accessible and, at less than $1.50 a barrel, some of the cheapest in the world to produce. Already, over the past several months, Western companies have been meeting with Iraqi exiles to try to stake a claim to that bonanza.

But while the companies hope to cash in on an American-controlled Iraq, the push to remove Saddam Hussein hasn't been driven by oil executives, many of whom are worried about the consequences of war. Nor are Vice President Cheney and President Bush, both former oilmen, looking at the Gulf simply for the profits that can be earned there. The administration is thinking bigger, much bigger, than that.

"Controlling Iraq is about oil as power, rather than oil as fuel," says Michael Klare, professor of Peace and World Security Studies at Hampshire College and author of *Resource Wars*. "Control over the Persian Gulf translates into control over Europe, Japan, and China. It's having our hand on the spigot."

Ever since the oil shocks of the 1970s, the United States has steadily been accumulating military muscle in the Gulf by building bases, selling weaponry, and forging military partnerships. Now, it is poised to consolidate its might in a place that will be a fulcrum of the world's balance of power for decades to come. At a stroke, by taking control of Iraq, the Bush administration can solidify a long-running strategic design. "It's the Kissinger plan," says James Akins, a former US diplomat. "I thought it had been killed, but it's back."

Akins learned a hard lesson about the politics of oil when he served as a US envoy in Kuwait and Iraq, and ultimately as ambassador to Saudi Arabia during the oil crisis of 1973 and '74. At his home in Washington D.C., shelves filled with Middle Eastern pottery and other memorabilia cover the walls, souvenirs of his years in the Foreign Service. Nearly three decades later, he still gets worked up while recalling his first encounter with the idea that the United States should be prepared to occupy Arab oil-producing countries.

In 1975, while Akins was ambassador in Saudi Arabia, an article headlined "Seizing Arab Oil" appeared in *Harper's*. The author, who used the pseudonym Miles Ignotus, was identified as "a Washington-based professor and defense consultant with intimate links to high-level US policy-makers." The article outlined, as Akins puts it, "how we could solve all our economic and political problems by taking over the Arab oil fields [and] bringing in Texans and Oklahomans to operate them." Simultaneously, a rash of similar stories appeared in other magazines and newspapers. "I knew that it had to have been the result of a deep background briefing," Akins says. "You don't have eight people coming up with the same screwy idea at the same time, independently.

"Then I made a fatal mistake," Akins continues. "I said on television that anyone who would propose that is either a madman, a criminal, or an agent of the Soviet Union." Soon afterward, he says, he learned that the background briefing had been conducted by his boss, then-Secretary of State Henry Kissinger. Akins was fired later that year.

Kissinger has never acknowledged having planted the seeds for the article. But in an interview with *Business Week* that same year, he delivered a thinly veiled threat to the Saudis, musing about bringing oil prices down through "massive political warfare against countries like Saudi Arabia and Iran to make them risk their political stability and maybe their security if they did not cooperate."

In the 1970s, America's military presence in the Gulf was virtually nil, so the idea of seizing control of its oil was a pipe dream. Still, starting with the Miles Ignotus article, and a parallel one by conservative strategist and Johns Hopkins University professor Robert W. Tucker in *Commentary*, the idea began to gain favor among a feisty group of hardline, pro-Israeli thinkers, especially the hawkish circle aligned with Democratic senators Henry Jackson of Washington and Daniel Patrick Moynihan of New York.

Eventually, this amalgam of strategists came to be known as "neo-conservatives," and they played important roles in President Reagan's Defense Department and at think tanks and academic policy centers in the 1980s. Led by Richard Perle, chairman of the Pentagon's influential

Defense Policy Board, and Deputy Secretary of Defense Paul Wolfowitz, they now occupy several dozen key posts in the White House, the Pentagon, and the State Department. At the top, they are closest to Vice President Cheney and Defense Secretary Donald Rumsfeld, who have been closely aligned since both men served in the White House under President Ford in the mid-1970s. They also clustered around Cheney when he served as Secretary of Defense during the Gulf War in 1991.

Throughout those years, and especially after the Gulf War, US forces have steadily encroached on the Gulf and the surrounding region, from the Horn of Africa to Central Asia. In preparing for an invasion and occupation of Iraq, the administration has been building on the steps taken by military and policy planners over the past quarter century.

STEP ONE: THE RAPID DEPLOYMENT FORCE

In 1973 and '74, and again in 1979, political upheavals in the Middle East led to huge spikes in oil prices, which rose fifteenfold over the decade and focused new attention on the Persian Gulf. In January 1980, President Carter effectively declared the Gulf a zone of US influence, especially against encroachment from the Soviet Union. "Let our position be absolutely clear," he said, announcing what came to be known as the Carter Doctrine. "An attempt by any outside force to gain control of the Persian Gulf region will be regarded as an assault on the vital interests of the United States of America, and such an assault will be repelled by any means necessary, including military force." To back up this doctrine, Carter created the Rapid Deployment Force, an "over-the-horizon" military unit capable of rushing several thousand US troops to the Gulf in a crisis.

STEP TWO: THE CENTRAL COMMAND

In the 1980s, under President Reagan, the United States began pressing countries in the Gulf for access to bases and support facilities. The Rapid Deployment Force was transformed into the Central Command, a new US military command authority with responsibility for the Gulf and the surrounding region from eastern Africa to Afghanistan. Reagan tried to organize a "strategic consensus" of anti-Soviet allies, including Turkey, Israel, and Saudi Arabia. The United States sold billions of dollars' worth of arms to the Saudis in the early '80s, from AWACS surveillance aircraft to F-15 fighters. And in 1987, at the height of the war between Iraq and Iran, the US Navy created the Joint Task Force-Middle East to protect oil tankers plying the waters of the Gulf, thus expanding a US naval presence of just three or four warships into a flotilla of 40-plus aircraft carriers, battleships, and cruisers.

STEP THREE: THE GULF WAR

Until 1991, the United States was unable to persuade the Arab Gulf states to allow a permanent American presence on their soil. Meanwhile, Saudi Arabia, while maintaining its close relationship with the United States, began to diversify its commercial and military ties; by the time US Ambassador Chas Freeman arrived there in the late 80s, the United States had fallen to fourth place among arms suppliers to the kingdom. "The United States was being supplanted, even in commercial terms, by the British, the French, even the Chinese," Freeman notes.

All that changed with the Gulf War. Saudi Arabia and other Gulf states no longer opposed a direct US military presence, and American troops, construction squads, arms salesmen, and military assistance teams rushed in. "The Gulf War put Saudi Arabia back on the map and revived a relationship that had been severely attrited," says Freeman.

In the decade after the war, the United States sold more than $43 billion worth of weapons, equipment, and military construction projects to Saudi Arabia, and $16 billion more to Kuwait, Qatar, Bahrain, and the United Arab Emirates, according to data compiled by the Federation of American Scientists. Before Operation Desert Storm, the US military enjoyed the right to stockpile, or "pre-position," military supplies only in the comparatively remote Gulf state of Oman on the Indian Ocean. After the war, nearly every country in the region began conducting joint military exercises, hosting US naval units and Air Force squadrons, and granting the United States pre-positioning rights. "Our military presence in the Middle East has increased dramatically," then-Defense Secretary William Cohen boasted in 1995.

Another boost to the US presence was the unilateral imposition, in 1991, of no-fly zones in northern and southern Iraq, enforced mostly by US aircraft from bases in Turkey and Saudi Arabia. "There was a massive buildup, especially around Incirlik in Turkey, to police the northern no-fly zone, and around [the Saudi capital of] Riyadh, to police the southern no-fly zone," says Colin Robinson of the Center for Defense Information, a Washington think tank. A billion-dollar, high-tech command center was built by Saudi Arabia near Riyadh, and over the past two years the United States has secretly been completing another one in Qatar. The Saudi facilities "were built with capacities far beyond the ability of Saudi Arabia to use them," Robinson says. "And that's exactly what Qatar is doing now."

STEP FOUR: AFGHANISTAN

The war in Afghanistan—and the open-ended war on terrorism, which has led to US strikes in Yemen, Pakistan, and elsewhere—further boosted America's strength in the region. The administration has won large increases in the defense budget—which now stands at about $400 billion, up from just over $300 billion in 2000—and a huge chunk of that budget, perhaps as much as $60 billion, is slated to support US forces in and around the Persian Gulf. Military facilities on the perimeter of the Gulf, from Djibouti in the Horn of Africa to the island of Diego Garcia in the Indian Ocean, have been expanded, and a web of bases and training missions has extended the US presence deep into Central Asia. From Afghanistan to the landlocked former Soviet republics of Uzbekistan and Kyrgyzstan, US forces have established themselves in an area that had long been in Russia's sphere of influence. Oil-rich in its own right, and strategically vital, central Asia is now the eastern link in a nearly continuous chain of US bases, facilities, and allies stretching from the Mediterranean and the Red Sea far into the Asian hinterland.

STEP FIVE: IRAQ

Removing Saddam Hussein could be the final piece of the puzzle, cementing an American imperial presence. It is "highly possible" that the United States will maintain military bases in Iraq, Robert Kagan, a leading neoconservative strategist, recently told the *Atlanta Journal-Constitution.* "We will probably need a major concentration of forces in the Middle East over a long period of time," he said. "When we have economic problems, it's been caused by disruptions in our oil supply. If we have a force in Iraq, there will be no disruption in oil supplies."

Kagan, along with William Kristol of the *Weekly Standard*, is a founder of the think tank Project For The New American Century, an assembly of foreign-policy hawks whose supporters include the Pentagon's Perle, *New Republic* publisher Martin Peretz, and former Central Intelligence Agency director James Woolsey. Among the group's affiliates in the Bush administration are Cheney, Rumsfeld, and Wolfowitz; I. Lewis Libby, the vice president's chief of staff; Elliott Abrams, the Middle East director at the National Security Council; and Zalmay Khalilzad, the White House liaison to the Iraqi opposition groups. Kagan's group, tied to a web of similar neo-conservative, pro-Israeli organizations, represents the constellation of thinkers whose ideological affinity was forged in the Nixon and Ford administrations.

To Akins, who has just returned from Saudi Arabia, it's a team that looks all too familiar, seeking to implement the plan first outlined back in 1975. "It'll be easier once we have Iraq," he says. "Kuwait, we already have. Qatar and Bahrain, too. So it's only Saudi Arabia we're talking about, and the United Arab Emirates falls into place."

LAST SUMMER, Perle provided a brief glimpse into his circle's thinking when he invited Rand Corporation strategist Laurent Murawiec to make a presentation to his Defense Policy Board, a committee of former senior officials and generals that advises the Pentagon on big-picture policy ideas. Murawiec's closed-door briefing provoked a storm of criticism when it was leaked to the media; he described Saudi Arabia as the "kernel of evil," suggested that the Saudi royal family should be replaced or overthrown, and raised the idea of a US occupation of Saudi oil fields. He ultimately lost his job when Rand decided he was too controversial.

Murawiec is part of a Washington school of thought that views virtually all of the nations in the Gulf as unstable "failed states" and maintains that only the United States has the power to forcibly reorganize and rebuild them. In this view, the arms systems and bases that were put in place to defend the region also provide a ready-made infrastructure for taking over countries and their oil fields in the event of a crisis.

The Defense Department likely has contingency plans to occupy Saudi

Arabia, says Robert E. Ebel, director of the energy program at the Center for Strategic and International Studies (CSIS), a Washington think tank whose advisers include Kissinger; former Defense Secretary and CIA director James Schlesinger; and Zbigniew Brzezinski, Carter's national security adviser. "If something happens in Saudi Arabia," Ebel says, "if the ruling family is ousted, if they decide to shut off the oil supply, we have to go in."

Two years ago, Ebel, a former mid-level CIA official, oversaw a CSIS task force that included several members of Congress as well as representatives from industry including ExxonMobil, Arco, BP, Shell, Texaco, and the American Petroleum Institute. Its report, "The Geopolitics of Energy into the 21st Century," concluded that the world will find itself dependent for many years on unstable oil-producing nations, around which conflicts and wars are bound to swirl. "Oil is high-profile stuff," Ebel says. "Oil fuels military power, national treasuries, and international politics. It is no longer a commodity to be bought and sold within the confines of traditional energy supply and demand balances. Rather, it has been transformed into a determinant of well-being, of national security, and of international power."

As vital as the Persian Gulf is now, its strategic importance is likely to grow exponentially in the next 20 years. Nearly one out of every three barrels of oil reserves in the world lie under just two countries: Saudi Arabia (with 259 billion barrels of proven reserves) and Iraq (112 billion). Those figures may understate Iraq's largely unexplored reserves, which according to US government estimates may hold as many as 432 billion barrels.

With supplies in many other regions, especially in the United States and the North Sea, nearly exhausted, oil from Saudi Arabia and Iraq is becoming ever more critical—a fact duly noted in the administration's National Energy Policy, released in 2001 by a White House task force. By 2020, the Gulf will supply between 54 percent and 67 percent of the world's crude, the document said, making the region "vital to US interests." According to G. Daniel Butler, an oil-markets analyst at the US Energy Information Administration (EIA), Saudi Arabia's production capacity will rise from its current 9.4 million barrels a day to 22.1 million over the next 17 years. Iraq, which in 2002 produced a mere 2 million barrels a day, "could easily be a double-digit producer by 2020," says Butler.

US strategists aren't worried primarily about America's own oil supplies; for decades, the United States has worked to diversify its sources of oil, with Venezuela, Nigeria, Mexico, and other countries growing in importance. But for Western Europe and Japan, as well as the developing industrial powers of eastern Asia, the Gulf is all-important. Whoever controls it will maintain crucial global leverage for decades to come.

Today, notes the EIA's Butler, two-thirds of Gulf oil goes to Western industrial nations. By 2015, according to a study by the CIA's National Intelligence Council, three-quarters of the Gulf's oil will go to Asia, chiefly to China. China's growing dependence on the Gulf could cause it to develop closer military and political ties with countries such as Iran and Iraq, according to the report produced by Ebel's CSIS task force. "They have different political interests in the Gulf than we do," Ebel says. "Is it to our advantage to have another competitor for oil in the Persian Gulf?"

David Long, who served as a US diplomat in Saudi Arabia and as chief of the Near East division in the State Department's Bureau of Intelligence and Research during the Reagan administration, likens the Bush administration's approach to the philosophy of Admiral Mahan, the 19th-century military strategist who advocated the use of naval power to create a global American empire. "They want to be the world's enforcer," he says. "It's a worldview, a geopolitical position. They say, 'We need hegemony in the region.'"

UNTIL THE 1970s, the face of American power in the Gulf was the US oil industry, led by Exxon, Mobil, Chevron, Texaco, and Gulf, all of whom competed fiercely with Britain's BP and Anglo-Dutch Shell. But in the early '70s, Iraq, Saudi Arabia, and the other Gulf states nationalized their oil industries, setting up state-run companies to run wells, pipelines, and production facilities. Not only did that enhance the power of OPEC, enabling that organization to force a series of sharp price increases, but it alarmed US policymakers.

Today, a growing number of Washington strategists are advocating a direct US challenge to state-owned petroleum industries in oil-producing countries, especially the Persian Gulf. Think tanks such as the American

Enterprise Institute, the Heritage Foundation, and CSIS are conducting discussions about privatizing Iraq's oil industry. Some of them have put forward detailed plans outlining how Iraq, Saudi Arabia, and other nations could be forced to open up their oil and gas industries to foreign investment. The Bush administration itself has been careful not to say much about what might happen to Iraq's oil. But State Department officials have had preliminary talks about the oil industry with Iraqi exiles, and there have been reports that the US military wants to use at least part of the country's oil revenue to pay for the cost of military occupation.

"One of the major problems with the Persian Gulf is that the means of production are in the hands of the state," Rob Sobhani, an oil-industry consultant, told an American Enterprise Institute conference last fall in Washington. Already, he noted, several US oil companies are studying the possibility of privatization in the Gulf. Dismantling government-owned oil companies, Sobhani argued, could also force political changes in the region. "The beginning of liberal democracy can be achieved if you take the means of production out of the hands of the state," he said, acknowledging that Arabs would resist that idea. "It's going to take a lot of selling, a lot of marketing," he concluded.

Just which companies would get to claim Iraq's oil has been a subject of much debate. After a war, the contracts that Iraq's state-owned oil company has signed with European, Russian, and Chinese oil firms might well be abrogated, leaving the field to US oil companies. "What they have in mind is denationalization, and then parceling Iraqi oil out to American oil companies," says Akins. "The American oil companies are going to be the main beneficiaries of this war."

The would-be rulers of a post-Saddam Iraq have been thinking along the same lines. "American oil companies will have a big shot at Iraqi oil," says Ahmad Chalabi, leader of the Iraqi National Congress, a group of aristocrats and wealthy Iraqis who fled the country when its repressive monarchy was overthrown in 1958. During a visit to Washington last fall, Chalabi held meetings with at least three major US oil companies, trying to enlist their support. Similar meetings between Iraqi exiles and US companies have also been taking place in Europe.

"Iraqi exiles have approached us, saying, 'You can have our oil if we can get back in there,'" says R. Gerald Bailey, who headed Exxon's Middle East operations until 1997. "All the major American companies have met with them in Paris, London, Brussels, all over. They're all jockeying for position. You can't ignore it, but you've got to do it on the q.t. And you can't wait till it gets too far along."

But the companies are also anxious about the consequences of war, according to many experts, oil-company executives, and former State Department officials. "The oil companies are caught in the middle," says Bailey. Executives fear that war could create havoc in the region, turning Arab states against the United States and Western oil companies. On the other hand, should a US invasion of Iraq be successful, they want to be there when the oil is divvied up. Says David Long, the former US diplomat, "It's greed versus fear."

Ibrahim Oweiss, a Middle East specialist at Georgetown University who coined the term "petrodollar" and has also been a consultant to Occidental and BP, has been closely watching the cautious maneuvering by the companies. "I know that the oil companies are scared about the outcome of this," he says. "They are not at all sure this is in the best interests of the oil industry."

Anne Joyce, an editor at the Washington-based Middle East Policy Council who has spoken privately to top Exxon officials, says it's clear that most oil-industry executives "are afraid" of what a war in the Persian Gulf could mean in the long term—especially if tensions in the region spiral out of control. "They see it as much too risky, and they are risk averse," she says. "They think it has 'fiasco' written all over it."

6 | Post-Saddam Iraq: Linchpin of a New Oil Order

MICHAEL RENNER

I
N THE RUN-UP to the recent Iraq war, very little was said about oil and some other hidden motives—in sharp contrast with the Bush administration's loud talk about terrorism, weapons of mass destruction, and democracy. And once the war started, the daily details of combat drowned out other aspects of the conflict. The Bush administration has been tight-lipped about its plans for a post-Saddam Iraq and has repeatedly disavowed any interest in the country's oil resources. But press reports indicate that US officials are considering a prolonged occupation of Iraq after their war to topple Saddam Hussein, and that top officials are looking to Iraqi oil to cover the costs of war and occupation. Contrary to official rhetoric, however, oil plays a major role. It is, in fact, likely that a US-controlled Iraq will be the linchpin of a new order in the world oil industry.

OIL FOREVER

The Bush administration's ties to the oil and gas industry are beyond extensive; they are pervasive. They flow, so to speak, from the top, with a chief executive who grew up steeped in the culture of Texas oil exploration and tried his hand at it himself; and a second-in-command who came to office with a multi-million dollar retirement package in hand from his post of CEO of Halliburton Oil. (As one of the companies that are being awarded lucrative postwar reconstruction contracts, Halliburton is likely to be one of the winners of this war.) Once in office, the vice president developed an energy policy under the primary guidance of a cast of oil company executives whose identities he has gone to great lengths to withhold from public view. Since taking office, the President and Vice President have assembled a government peopled heavily with representatives from the oil culture they came from. These include Secretary of the Army Thomas White, a former vice president of Enron, and Secretary of Commerce Don Evans, former president of the oil exploration company Tom Brown, Inc., whose major stake in the company was worth $13 million by the time he took office.

The Bush administration's energy policy is predicated on ever-growing consumption of oil, preferably cheap oil. US oil consumption is projected to increase by one-third over the next two decades. The White House is pushing hard for greater domestic drilling and wants to open the Arctic National Wildlife Refuge to the oil industry. Even so, the administration's National Energy Policy Development Group, led by Vice President Cheney, acknowledged in a May 2001 report that US oil production will fall 12% over the next 20 years. As a result, US dependence on imported oil—which has risen from one-third in 1985 to more than half today—is set to climb to two-thirds by 2020.[1]

Since the 1970s, the US has put considerable effort into diversifying its sources of supply, going largely outside of OPEC and outside the Middle East. The current administration is advocating greater efforts to expand production in such far-flung places as the Caspian area, Nigeria, Chad, Angola, and deep offshore areas in the Atlantic basin and is looking to leading Western Hemispheric suppliers like Canada, Mexico, and Venezuela.[2] West Africa is expected to account for as much as a quarter of US oil imports a decade from now.[3]

But there is no escaping the fact that the Middle East—and specifically the Persian Gulf region—remains the world's prime oil province, for the US and for other importers. Indeed, the Cheney report confirms that "by any estimation, Middle East oil producers will remain central to world oil security." The Middle East currently accounts for about 30% of global oil production and more than 40% of oil exports. With about 65% of the

---

[1] National Energy Policy Development Group, *Reliable, Affordable, and Environmentally Sound Energy for America's Future* (Washington: US Government Printing Office, May 2001), pp.x and 1–13.

[2] Ibid., pp.3–8 and 7–8.

[3] James Dao, "In Quietly Courting Africa, White House Likes Dowry," *New York Times*, September 19, 2002.

planet's known reserves, it is the only region able to satisfy the substantial rise in world oil demand predicted by the Bush administration.[4] The Cheney report projects that Persian Gulf producers alone will supply 54-67% of world oil exports in 2020.[5]

Saudi Arabia is a pivotal player. With 262 billion barrels, it has a quarter of the world's total proven reserves and is the single largest producer.[6] More importantly, the Saudis have demonstrated repeatedly—after the Iranian revolution, and following Iraq's invasion of Kuwait—that they are prepared to compensate for losses from other suppliers, calming markets in times of turmoil. Today, Riyadh could raise its production of 8 million barrels per day (b/d) to 10.5 million b/d within three months, making up for any loss of Iraqi oil during a US military assault.[7]

IRAQ: FROM PARIAH TO FABULOUS PRIZE

The pariah state of Iraq, however, is a key prize, with abundant, high-quality oil that can be produced at very low cost (and thus at great profit). At 112 billion barrels, its proven reserves are currently second only to Saudi Arabia's. The Energy Information Administration (EIA) of the US Department of Energy estimates that additional "probable and possible" resources could amount to 220 billion barrels. And because political instability, war, and sanctions have prevented thorough exploration of substantial portions of Iraqi territory, there is a chance that another 100 billion barrels lie undiscovered in Iraq's western desert. All in all, Iraq's oil wealth may well rival that of Saudi Arabia.[8]

---

4 Production and reserves are from *BP Statistical Review of World Energy 2002*; exports are from *OPEC Annual Statistical Bulletin 2001* (Vienna: 2002), Table 26.

5 National Energy Policy Development Group, *Reliable, Affordable, and Environmentally Sound Energy for America's Future* (Washington: US Government Printing Office, May 2001).

6 *BP Statistical Review of World Energy 2002*. Ultimately recoverable estimate is from US Department of Energy, Energy Information Administration (EIA), *Saudi Arabia Country Analysis Brief*, October 2002, <http://www.eia.doe.gov/cabs/saudi.html>.

7 Past Saudi production increases are from *BP Statistical Review of World Energy 2002*; potential for current increase is from Jeff Gerth, "US Fails to Curb Its Saudi Oil Habit, Experts Say," *New York Times*, November 26, 2002.

8 US Department of Energy, Energy Information Administration (EIA), *Iraq Country Analysis Brief*, October 2002, <http://www.eia.doe.gov/cabs/iraq.html>. Iraqi oil officials agree, estimating reserves at 270–300 billion barrels in "Iraq's Oil Industry: An Overview," Platts, <http://www.platts.com/features/Iraq/oiloverview.shtml>.

At present, of course, this is mere potential—the Iraqi oil industry has seriously deteriorated as a result of the 1980–88 Iran-Iraq War, the 1991 Gulf War, and inadequate postwar investment and maintenance. Since 1990, the sanctions regime has effectively frozen plans for putting additional fields into production. It has also caused a severe shortage of oil field equipment and spare parts (under the sanctions regime, the US has prevented equipment imports worth some $4 billion). Meanwhile, questionable methods used to raise output from existing fields may have damaged some of the reservoirs and could actually trigger a decline in output in the short run.[9]

But once the facilities are rehabilitated (a lucrative job for the oil service industry, including Vice President Cheney's former employer, Halliburton) and new fields are brought into operation, the spigots could be opened wide. To pay for the massive task of rebuilding, a post sanctions Iraq would naturally seek to maximize its oil production. Some analysts, such as Fadhil Chalabi, a former Iraqi oil official, assert that Iraq could produce 8–10 million b/d within a decade and eventually perhaps as much as 12 million. Other experts, however, have put forward lower figures.[10]

The impact on world markets is hard to overstate. Saudi Arabia would no longer be the sole dominant producer, able to influence oil markets single-handedly. Given that US-Saudi relations cooled substantially in the wake of the September 11, 2001, terrorist attacks—rifts that may widen further—a Saudi competitor would not be unwelcome in Washington. An unnamed US diplomat confided to Scotland's *Sunday Herald* that "a rehabilitated Iraq is the only sound long-term strategic alternative to Saudi Arabia. It's not just a case of swapping horses in mid-stream, the impending US regime change in Baghdad is a strategic necessity."[11]

Washington would gain enormous leverage over the world oil market. Opening the Iraqi spigot could eventually flood world markets. Prices

[9] US Department of Energy, Energy Information Administration (EIA), *Iraq Country Analysis Brief*, October 2002, <http://www.eia.doe.gov/cabs/iraq.html>.

[10] Fadhil J. Chalabi, "Iraq and the Future of World Oil," *Middle East Policy*, vol. vii, no. 4, October 2000, <http://www.mepc.org/public_asp/journal_vol7/0010_chalabi.asp>.

[11] Trevor Royle, "The World's Petrol Station: Iraq's Past Is Steeped in Oil ... and Blood," *Sunday Herald*, October 6, 2002, <http://www.sundayherald.com/print28226>.

could be driven substantially lower—although the US oil industry would not want to see a complete price collapse: such an outcome would render domestic production uncompetitive. But lower prices would weaken OPEC, already struggling with overcapacity and a tendency among its members to produce above allotted quotas (an estimated 3 million barrels per day above the agreed total of 24.7 million b/d), as individual exporters engage in destructive price wars against each other.[12]

Lower prices could also render Russian oil—more expensive to produce—uncompetitive, which would cloud the prospects for attracting foreign investment to tap Siberian oil deposits.[13] Russia's weak economy is highly dependent on oil export revenues. Its federal budget is predicated on prices of $24–25 per barrel.[14] Aleksei Arbatov, deputy chairman of the Russian parliament's defense committee, predicts that if a new Iraqi regime sells oil without limits, "our budget will collapse."[15]

OIL COMPANY INTERESTS

To repair and expand its oil industry, Iraq will need substantial foreign investment. Thus, for eager oil companies, Iraq represents a huge bonanza —a "boom waiting to happen," according to an unnamed industry source.[16]

Prior to the OPEC revolution in the early 1970s, a small number of companies (referred to as the "majors" or "Seven Sisters") called the shots in the industry, controlling activities from exploration and production to refining and product sales. But they lost much of their reserve base, as nationalization spread through the Middle East and OPEC nations. Today, state oil companies own the vast majority of the world's oil resources. Even though private companies still do much of the exploring,

---

[12] OPEC overproduction data is from Neela Banerjee, "As Its Members Flout Oil Quotas, OPEC Considers New Approach," *New York Times*, December 12, 2002.

[13] Dan Morgan and David B. Ottoway, "In Iraqi War Scenario, Oil Is Key Issue," *Washington Post*, September 15, 2002.

[14] Stratfor, "War in Iraq: What's at Stake for Russia?" November 22, 2002 (distributed electronically).

[15] Arbatov quoted in Sabrina Tavernise, "Oil Prize, Past and Present, Ties Russia to Iraq," *New York Times*, October 17, 2002.

[16] Quote from James A. Paul, "Iraq: The Struggle for Oil," August 2002, Global Policy Forum website, <http://www.globalpolicy.org/security/oil/2002/08jim.htm>.

drilling, and pumping, in many countries they have access to the oil only under prices and conditions set by the host government. Although oil companies have managed to adjust to this situation, a directly owned concession would offer them far greater flexibility and profitability.

The dominant private companies (ExxonMobil and Chevron-Texaco of the US, Royal Dutch-Shell and BP of Britain and the Netherlands, TotalFinaElf of France), which are largely the result of recent mega-mergers, sell close to 29 million barrels per day in gasoline and other oil products. But production from fields owned by these "super-majors" came to 10.1 million barrels per day in 2001, or just 35% of their sales volume.[17]

Although these corporations have poured many billions of dollars into discovering new fields outside the Middle East, their proven reserves stood at just 44 billion barrels in 2001, 4% of the world's total and sufficient to keep producing oil for only another 12 years at current rates.[18] Thus, the oil-rich Middle East, and particularly Iraq, remains key to the future of the oil industry.

If a new regime in Baghdad rolls out the red carpet for the oil multinationals to return, it is possible that a broader wave of denationalization could sweep through the oil industry, reversing the historic changes of the early 1970s. Squeezed by a decade of sanctions, Saddam signaled that he was prepared to provide more favorable terms to foreign companies.[19] Such an invitation by Baghdad would be in tune with larger changes that are afoot, as a growing number of oil-producing countries are opening their industries to foreign direct investment.[20]

RIVALRIES & QUID PRO QUOS

Several European and Asian oil companies have in recent years signed deals with Iraq that, if consummated, would give them access to reserves of at least 50 billion barrels and a potential output of 4–5 million barrels

---

[17] Calculated from OPEC *Annual Statistical Bulletin 2001* (Vienna: 2002), Table 77.

[18] Ibid.

[19] US Department of Energy, Energy Information Administration (EIA), *Iraq Country Analysis Brief*, October 2002, <http://www.eia.doe.gov/cabs/iraq.html>.

[20] "The Iraq Oil Industry After Sanctions," Middle East Institute conference proceedings summary, February 29, 2000, as reposted on the Global Policy Forum website, <http://www.globalpolicy. org/security/oil/2000/0229mei.htm>.

per day (another estimate says that Russian companies alone have signed deals involving about 70 billion barrels). In addition, a number of contracts have been signed for exploration in the western desert.[21]

Russian, Chinese, and French companies in particular have tried to position themselves to develop new oil fields and to rehabilitate existing ones, once UN sanctions are lifted. Russia's Lukoil, for instance, signed an agreement in 1997 to refurbish and develop the West Qurna field (with 15 billion barrels of oil reserves). China's National Petroleum Corporation signed a deal for the North Rumailah reservoir. And France's TotalFinaElf has set its eyes on the giant Majnoon deposits (holding 20–30 billion barrels).[22]

Iraq has sought to use the lure of oil concessions to build political support among three permanent Security Council nations—France, Russia, and China—for a lifting of sanctions. Although the international consensus in favor of sanctions has badly eroded, this gamble has failed to pay off in the face of determined US and British opposition. (In December 2002, Iraq cancelled a contract with three Russian companies, out of frustration that the firms—in deference to sanctions—had not commenced oil exploration work.) While Saddam Hussein remained in power, US and British companies were kept out of Iraq.

"Regime change" in Baghdad has reshuffled the cards and given US (and British) companies a good shot at direct access to Iraqi oil for the first time in 30 years—a windfall worth hundreds of billions of dollars. US companies relish the prospect: Chevron's chief executive, for example, said in 1998 that he'd "love Chevron to have access to" Iraq's oil reserves.[23]

In preface to the passage of Security Council Resolution 1441 on November 8, there were thinly veiled threats that French, Russian, and Chinese firms would be excluded from any future oil concessions in Iraq

21 Deutsche Bank estimates, reported in US Department of Energy, Energy Information Administration (EIA), *Iraq Country Analysis Brief*, October 2002, <http://www.eia.doe.gov/cabs/iraq.html>. The higher estimate is from Zarubezhneft, a Russian state-owned company. See Sabrina Tavernise, "Oil Prize, Past and Present, Ties Russia to Iraq," *New York Times*, October 17, 2002.

22 US Department of Energy, Energy Information Administration (EIA), *Iraq Country Analysis Brief*, October 2002, <http://www.eia.doe.gov/cabs/iraq.html>.

23 Speech by Kenneth T. Derr, http://www.chevrontexaco.com/news/archive/chevron_speech/1998/98–11–05.asp>.

unless Paris, Moscow, and Beijing supported the Bush policy of regime change. Ahmed Chalabi, leader of the Iraqi National Congress (INC), an exile opposition group favored by the Bush administration, said that the INC would not feel bound by any contracts signed by Saddam Hussein's government and that "American companies will have a big shot at Iraqi oil" under a new regime. US and British oil company executives have been meeting with INC officials, maneuvering to secure a future stake in Iraq's oil.[24] Meanwhile, the State Department has been coaxing Iraqi opposition members to create an oil and gas working group involving Iraqis and Americans.[25]

Nikolai Tokarev, general director of Russia's Zarubezhneft, a state-owned oil company, reflected in late 2002: "Do Americans need us in Iraq? Of course not. Russian companies will lose the oil forever if the Americans come."[26] Fears of being excluded from Iraq's oil riches and losing influence in the region have fed Russian, French, and Chinese interest in constraining US belligerence. These countries nonetheless are eager to keep their options open in the event that a pro-US regime is installed in Baghdad, avoiding the "risk of ending up on the wrong side of Washington," as the *New York Times* put it.[27]

Presumably, rival oil interests were a crucial behind-the-scenes factor as the permanent members of the UN Security Council jockeyed over the wording of Resolution 1441, intended to set the conditions for any action against Iraq. It is likely that backroom understandings regarding the future of Iraqi oil were part of the political minuet that finally led to the resolution's unanimous adoption. US promises that the other powers would get a slice of the pie, hinted at in broad terms, were apparently inducement enough to win their nod.

However, the unanimous November vote soon gave way to a major

[24] Chalabi quote is from Dan Morgan and David B. Ottoway, "In Iraqi War Scenario, Oil Is Key Issue," *Washington Post*, September 15, 2002. Also, Peter Beaumont and Faisal Islam, "Carve-Up of Oil Riches Begins," *The Observer* (United Kingdom), November 3, 2002.

[25] Stratfor, "War in Iraq: What's at Stake for Russia?" November 22, 2002 (distributed electronically).

[26] Sabrina Tavernise, "Oil Prize, Past and Present, Ties Russia to Iraq," *New York Times*, October 17, 2002.

[27] Serge Schmemann, "Controlling Iraq's Oil Wouldn't Be Simple," *New York Times*, November 3, 2002.

confrontation, as the majority of Council members rejected the US attempt to short-circuit the weapons inspection process. This fallout makes it far less likely that French, Russian, and Chinese oil companies will be invited into Iraq by a US occupation regime or by a future Baghdad government under US tutelage.

FROM SURROGATES TO DIRECT CONTROL

Throughout the history of oil, sorting out who gets access to this highly prized resource and on what terms has often gone hand in hand with violence. At first it was Britain, the imperial power in much of the Middle East, that called the shots. But for half a century, the US—seeking a preponderant share of the earth's resources—has made steady progress in bringing the Persian Gulf region into its geopolitical orbit. In Washington's calculus, securing oil supplies has consistently trumped the pursuit of human rights and democracy. US policy toward the Middle East has long relied on building up proxy forces in the region and generously supplying them with arms. After the Shah of Iran, the West's regional policeman, was toppled in 1979, Iraq became a surrogate of sorts when it invaded Iran. Washington aided Iraq in a variety of ways, including commodity credits and loan guarantees, indirect arms supplies, critical military intelligence in Baghdad's long battle against Iran, a pro-Iraqi tilt in the "tanker war," and attacks on Iran's navy.

Beginning in the 1970s, but particularly in the wake of the 1991 Gulf War, the US supplied Saudi Arabia and allied Persian Gulf states with massive amounts of highly sophisticated armaments. After the Gulf War, US forces never left the region completely. By prepositioning military equipment and acquiring access to military bases in Saudi Arabia, Kuwait, Bahrain, and Qatar, Washington prepared the ground for future direct intervention as needed.

In the Persian Gulf and adjacent regions, access to oil is usually secured by a pervasive US military presence. From Pakistan to Central Asia to the Caucasus and from the eastern Mediterranean to the Horn of Africa, a dense network of US military facilities has emerged—with many bases established in the name of the "war on terror."

Although the US military presence is not solely about oil, oil is a key reason. In 1999, General Anthony C. Zinni, then the head of the US Central Command, testified to the Senate Armed Services Committee that the Persian Gulf region was of "vital interest" to the US and that the country "must have free access to the region's resources."[28]

Bush administration officials have, however, categorically denied oil is one of the reasons why they are pushing for regime change in Iraq. "Nonsense," Defense Secretary Donald Rumsfeld told *60 Minutes'* Steve Kroft in mid-December 2002. "It has nothing to do with oil, literally nothing to do with oil."

But oil industry officials interviewed by *60 Minutes* on December 15 painted a different picture. Asked if oil is part of the equation, Phillip Ellis, head of global oil and gas operations for Boston Consulting replied, "Of course it is. No doubt."

In fact, oil company executives have been quietly meeting with US-backed Iraqi opposition leaders. According to Ahmed Chalabi, head of the Iraqi National Congress, "The future democratic government in Iraq will be grateful to the United States for helping the Iraqi people liberate themselves and getting rid of Saddam." And he added that "American companies, we expect, will play an important and leading role in the future oil situation in Iraq."

---

[28] Zinni quote is from James A. Paul, "Iraq: The Struggle for Oil," August 2002, Global Policy Forum website, <http://www.globalpolicy.org/security/oil/2002/08jim.htm>. Testimony of April 13, 1999.

7 | Iraq and the Course of Empire

ANTHONY ARNOVE

> The events of September 11 2001 fundamentally changed the context for relations between the United States and other main centers of global power, and opened vast, new opportunities.
>
> *—The National Security Strategy of the*
> *United States of America, September 17, 2002.*[1]

> I really think this period is analogous to 1945–1947, in that the events started shifting the tectonic plates in international politics. ... It's important to try to seize on that and position American interests and institutions before they harden again.
> *— National Security Adviser Condoleezza Rice.*[2]

THE WAR ON IRAQ was fought not for democracy or disarmament, but for reasons of empire that will be played out in Iraq, the Middle East, and other "main centers of global power" for years to come. The Bush administration, with the Democrats safely in tow, intended the war in Iraq, like its war in Afghanistan, to achieve a demonstration of political and military might and to signal to other states that the US government:

1. has the right to engage in "pre-emptive strikes" against countries that pose no clear threat and in cases when no attack is actually being pre-empted;

2. will not allow any restrictions on its pursuit of global domination. It will use the United Nations and other international bodies only when it suits their ends, and will dismiss them as

---

[1] *The National Security Strategy of the United States of America*, Washington, DC: The White House, September 17, 2002, p. 28. Available online at http://www.whitehouse.gov.

[2] Quoted in "Night Fell on a Different World — A Year On," *The Economist* (US edition), September 7, 2002, p.23.

"irrelevant" otherwise, and will only enter temporary alliances of convenience, allowing nothing to divert it from the pursuit of the US "national interest"; and

3. will allow no challenge to the "credibility" of US imperialism. For neo-conservatives close to the Bush administration, the fact that Saddam Hussein survived the 1991 Gulf War translated into "a lack of awe for the US," in the words of William Kristol, the editor of the *Weekly Standard* magazine.[3] The whole project of US imperialism, they argued, depended on achieving "regime change" in Iraq.

The war was not a defensive war, as Washington claimed, but an aggressive one. It was not a war of last resort, but a war that its main backers had been determined to wage for many months (and which some of them had been advocating for years). None of the stated rationale for the war (Iraq's ties to al-Qa'ida and the attacks of September 11, "evidence" of weapons of mass destruction, "democracy") could stand up to a moment's scrutiny, and from day to day the government's message shifted to suit its needs. The assault on Iraq was not a war to eliminate the dangers posed by weapons of mass destruction, but a war that will certainly increase the race for such weapons. Iraq was a target because it did *not* pose any credible nuclear threat. Countries out of favor with the United States will learn a simple lesson: develop your military strength, or potentially face a fate similar to Iraq. And rather than making the world more safe or "peaceful," as George Bush and Tony Blair assured us it would, the war has increased the likelihood of terrorist attacks against the US and the UK.

Ultimately, a combination of the immense international protests and pressure from below, US arrogance alienating potential allies, and interimperial conflict among leading Security Council countries, forced the US government to abandon the United Nations as a means of "channeling" its imperial power, as Thomas Friedman had advocated in the pages of *The New York Times*. (When fighting "a war of choice," as he called it, Friedman suggested that the "the best way to legitimize" the US's "over-

---

3 Quoted in Guy Dinmore, "Ideologues Reshape World over Breakfast," *Financial Times*, March 22, 2003, p. 1.

whelming might" is "by channeling it through the UN"[4]). In his State of the (Empire) Union address on January 27, Bush pointedly stated that "the course of this nation does not depend on the decisions of others." While some in the Bush administration saw the advantages of having a UN fig leaf, others understood that the US victory would seem more "robust" if the US in effect went it alone.[5] (The Coalition of the Bought and Paid For provided some useful cover, even though several of its members asked not to have their names released for fear of the domestic consequences. But it was not Iceland's, Azerbaijan's, Estonia's, or Eritrea's power that was demonstrated in Iraq.)

In advance of Secretary of State Colin Powell's utterly deceitful presentation to the UN, one US official explained,

> We're not going to negotiate on a second [UN] resolution, because we don't need to. ... If there is a resolution, it is because they [other Security Council members] need one, and are going to give the US what it wants. ... If the rest of the Council wants to catch up to us, we might stop briefly to sign on the dotted line.[6]

The advantages of going it alone were clear. As one unnamed "hawk" quoted in *The New York Times* put it, "By setting up our military in Iraq ... we can set an example to other countries: 'If you cooperate with terrorists or menace us in any way or even look at us cross-eyed, this could happen to you.'"[7] "An American-led overthrow of Saddam Hussein—and the replacement of the radical Baathist dictatorship with a new government more closely aligned with the United States," asserted former Bush speechwriter David Frum, "would put America more wholly in charge of the region than any power since the Ottomans, or maybe even the Romans."[8]

The Bush administration also knew it could count on a compliant corporate media that would offer little but home team coverage of the war,

---

4 Thomas L. Friedman, "Light in the Tunnel," *New York Times*, November 13, 2002, p. A29.

5 Maureen Dowd, "I Vant to Be Alone," *New York Times*, March 12, 2003, p. A25.

6 Mark Turner and Roula Khalaf, "Powell 'Not Lobbying for Second Resolution,'" *Financial Times*, February 5, 2003, p. 9.

7 Quoted in Maureen Dowd, "Desert Spring, Sprung," *New York Times*, March 9, 2003, p. 4: 15.

8 Quoted in George Packer, "Dreaming of Democracy," *New York Times Magazine*, March 2, 3003, p. 7: 49.

and stick to the script of Iraqi "liberation" (with many news networks simply adopting the slogan "Operation Iraqi Freedom" as the tagline for their war coverage, and, of course, prominently waving their flag logos). The media, even more fully co-opted through the Pentagon's brilliant strategy of "embedding" journalists with US troops, systematically down-played civilian casualties and gave a thoroughly distorted picture of the war, scarcely bothering to maintain any pretense of objectivity or inde-pendence. As Chris Hedges wrote in the pages of *The Nation,*

> The coverage of war by the press has one consistent and pernicious theme—the worship of our weapons and our military might. Retired officers, breath-less reporters, somber news anchors, can barely hold back their excitement, which is perverse and—frankly, to those who do not delight in watching us obliterate other human beings—disgusting …
>
> The reasons for war are hidden from public view. We do not speak about the extension of American empire, but democracy and ridding the world of terrorists—read "evil"—along with weapons of mass destruction. We do not speak of the huge corporate interests that stand to gain even as poor young boys from Alabama, who joined the Army because this was the only way to get health insurance and a steady job, bleed to death along the Euphrates. We do not speak of the lies that have been told to us in the past by this Administration—for example, the lie that Iraq was on the way to building a nuclear bomb …
>
> The embedding of several hundred journalists in military units does not diminish the lie. These journalists do not have access to their own trans-portation. They depend on the military for everything, from food to a place to sleep. They look to the soldiers around them for protection. When they feel the fear of hostile fire, they identify and seek to protect those who protect them. They become part of the team. It is a natural reaction. I have felt it.
>
> But in that experience, these journalists become participants in the war effort. They want to do their bit. And their bit is the dissemination of myth, the myth used to justify war and boost the morale of the soldiers and civi-lians. The lie in wartime is almost always the lie of omission. The blunders by our generals—whom the mythmakers always portray as heroes—along with the rank corruption and perversion, are masked from public view. The intoxication of killing, the mutilation of enemy dead, the murder of civilians and the fact that war is not about what they claim is ignored. But in wartime

don't look to the press, or most of it, for truth. The press has another purpose.[9]

THE MEDIA ORGANIZATION

In a survey of TV news coverage of the war, Fairness and Accuracy in Reporting found that 75 percent of US sources in a survey of TV news coverage of the war were current or former government officials. And, "At a time when 61 percent of US respondents were telling pollsters that more time was needed for diplomacy and inspections ... only 6 percent of US sources on the four networks were skeptics regarding the need for war."[10]

Toward the end of the war, the dominant media dutifully played out the government's script. The images of Iraqis cheering when US Marines toppled a statue of Saddam Hussein in Baghdad retroactively "proved" that the war was just (no matter how many lives were shattered and no matter how many "suspected sites" of weapons of mass destruction turned out to have none). The defeat of a country that had no air force, that had an army that was a shadow of what it had been in 1991 (when it was crushed in a matter of weeks), that had been subjected to twelve years of sanctions, that was destroying its own missiles in the days before the war, and that had been repeatedly struck in advance of the war by US and UK planes, and that had been surveyed by repeated intelligence over flights (the last round of which it had even approved) was absurdly hailed as "a remarkable military achievement" and compared to some of the greatest battles in military history.

Iraqis certainly had every reason to celebrate the fall of the Hussein dictatorship, and many certainly felt the understandable hope that the fall of the government would mean an end to the devastating sanctions to which they had been subjected for more than a decade. But this sense of joy quickly turned into more complicated emotions. On April 10, the *Financial Times* front-page headline read, "Saddam Toppled as Iraqis Cheer Regime's Collapse." The next day, the front-page headline announced, "Jubilation Gives Way to Violent Chaos Across Iraq." The same

---

9 Chris Hedges, "The Press and the Myths of War," *The Nation*, April 21, 2003. Available online at: http://www.thenation.com/doc.mhtml?i=20030421&s=hedges.

10 Fairness and Accuracy in Reporting (FAIR), "In Iraq Crisis, Networks Are Megaphones for Official Views," March 18, 2003. Online at http://www.fair.org/reports/iraq-sources.html.

day, the *Financial Times* reported that "The 1st battalion of the US 5th Marines in the streets of Baghdad yesterday were so unnerved by attacks from Iraqi fighters in civilian clothes that they opened fire repeatedly on unarmed men, women and children." Within a week, the *New York Times* was acknowledging that "[p]rotests against the American forces here are rising by the day."[11] In Nasiriya, 20,000 Iraqis marched in protest on April 15, chanting "No No Saddam, No No United States."[12] In Mosul, a crowd stoned a member of the so-called Iraqi opposition who praised the US marines, and American soldiers fired into Iraqi crowds, killing 17 and wounding 39 in only a few days, according to the director of the local hospital.[13] As the British reporter Robert Fisk commented, "The army of 'liberation' has already turned into the army of occupation.... Everywhere are the signs of collapse. And everywhere the signs that America's promises of 'freedom' and 'democracy' are not to be honored."[14]

Few missed the fact that the invading forces had not been able to supply safe drinking water or restore electricity to large parts of Iraq, or to stop looting of Iraq's National Museum, with its immense archeological and cultural treasures, but had immediately secured many of its oil fields. Even before the first week of the war had passed, the US government was handing out large contracts for the multibillion-dollar reconstruction of Iraq, with many "friends" and members of the administration certain to benefit financially (among them Bechtel and Halliburton). And, while we were assured the war had nothing to do with Iraq's enormous oil reserves, one of the first actions of soldiers in Iraq was to establish Forward Operating Base Exxon and Forward Operating Base Shell. When asked about this, Tom Cirigliano, a spokesman from Exxon Mobil (the world's largest publicly traded corporation) explained that it must have been because they were "naming things after what reminds them of home. And I think that's pretty neat."[15]

11 Ian Fisher, "Free to Protest, Iraqis Complain About the US," *New York Times*, April 16, 2003, p.A1.

12 Marc Santora and Patrick E. Tyler, "Pledge Made to Democracy By Exiles, Sheiks and Clerics," *New York Times*, April 16, 2003, p.A1.

13 David Rohde, "Deadly Unrest Leaves a Town Bitter at US," April 20, 2003, p.A1; David Rohde, "Marines Again Kill Iraqis In Exchange of Fire in Mosul," April 17, 2003, p.B2.

14 Robert Fisk, "For the People on the Street, This Is Not Liberation But a New Colonial Oppression," *The Independent* (London), April 17, 2003, p.1.

15 Neela Bannerjee, "Army Depots In Iraqi Desert Have Names Of Oil Giants," *New York Times*, March 27, 2003, p.C14.

There was never any doubt that the United States could militarily crush Iraq, but having done so, it now inherits all of the problems of occupying a people who have every reason to resist their presence. Iraqis also remember the support Hussein received throughout the 1980s, when London and Washington provided him with intelligence and weaponry, and before, as they supported his rise through the Baath Party structure. They recall the friendly visit of US Defense Secretary Donald Rumsfeld to Baghdad in 1983. They know that politicians in the West stood by Hussein during his worst crimes, including the brutal massacre of Kurds in Halabja in 1988, and know how Kurds and the Shia's were betrayed at the end of the Gulf War when they were encouraged to rise up, and then were left to be slaughtered by Hussein's guards. For all their grievances with their own government, most Iraqis blamed the US for the enormous suffering they experienced in the years of sanctions. And many of them know that the US government has in the past promised countries "liberation," only to deliver destruction, occupation, and civil war.

Iraqis also have good reason to distrust the rhetoric of Washington politicians who claim they have no design on Iraq's oil and seek no material advantage from the war. As Naomi Klein reported in *The Guardian* (London) on April 14, Iraq

> is being treated as a blank slate on which the most ideological Washington neo-liberals can design their dream economy: fully privatized, foreign-owned and open for business ... A people, starved and sickened by sanctions, then pulverized by war, is going to emerge from this trauma to find that their country had been sold out from under them. They will also discover that their new-found "freedom"—for which so many of their loved ones perished—comes pre-shackled by irreversible economic decisions that were made in boardrooms while the bombs were still falling. They will then be told to vote for their new leaders, and welcomed to the wonderful world of democracy.[16]

The financial stakes in Iraq are significant. Billions of dollars will be made from contracts for roads, schools, oil industry reconstruction, water, and power, with the main beneficiaries being politically connected

---

16 Naomi Klein, "Bomb Before You Buy: What Is Being Planned in Iraq is Not Reconstruction but Robbery," *The Guardian* (London), April 14, 2003, p.13.

businesses in the United States. But the geopolitical stakes of the war in Iraq are immensely greater. Iraq has at least an 11 percent share of world oil reserves, but some geologists believe Iraq has far greater reserves than have been identified, perhaps more than Saudi Arabia. As the *Financial Times* notes,

> Iraqi oil officials suspect the country's 112.5bn barrels of proven crude oil reserves … would top 300bn barrels once Iraq's entire acreage was mapped.
>
> And unlike the Caspian region—the "great new frontier" of the 1990s—Iraq's crude oil is easier to access and to export. Iraq has the added advantage of being able to transport much of its output through the Mediterranean via a pipeline to Turkey—a flexibility other Middle East producers lack.[17]

Control of Iraqi oil gives the US tremendous leverage and influence. As the energy analyst Daniel Yergin observed, "The re-emergence of Iraq will be of historic significance, because of the scale of the resources and because of the realignment it may portend among the major oil exporters."[18] The United States is likely to use its leverage over Iraqi oil to undermine the power of Saudi Arabia and Venezuela within OPEC, if not seek to make the cartel irrelevant altogether. And it will allow the US government to wield oil as a weapon against competing economic and military powers, especially in Europe and Asia. US officials are very conscious of the fact that China is on a path to soon double the energy it imports and that the country relies significantly on reserves from the Middle East.

It is important to note that as soon as the "coalition" declared victory in Iraq, Rumsfeld announced that the US would cut off an important oil pipeline running from Iraq to Syria, in a signal to other powers that the United States alone will be allowed to use oil as a weapon. Syria has emerged in the weeks since the war began as a key target in Bush's ongoing "war on terrorism." While Syria was not among the countries Bush named as the "axis of evil" (Iraq, Iran, and North Korea), a Bush administration official said that Syria is part of the "junior varsity axis of evil"

---

17 Carola Hoyos, "Baghdad Re-entry to Market 'Could Have Big Impact,'" *Financial Times* (London), February 21, 2003, p.3.

18 Hoyos, ibid.

(along with Cuba and Libya). "We've changed the geo-strategic situation in the Middle East," an administration official told *The New York Times.* "Syria can either wake up to that fact, or not. It is up to Syria to decide whether to become a part of the new Middle East that we are shaping." While sending this message to Syria, Rumsfeld and other top officials have also escalated their public threats against Iran. The rhetoric is part of "a declared strategy to consolidate the allied victory in Iraq by beginning to reshape the Middle East" in US interests, *The New York Times* reported. "The swiftness of the victory [in Iraq]," one senior administration official said in an interview, "opens all sorts of new opportunities for us."[19]

The gap between the rhetoric of democratizing the Middle East and the occupation of Iraq exposes the many contradictions of the US war. The initial gathering of handpicked "leaders" who met to determine Iraq's future did so at Tallil Air Base in a meeting "organized by and under the protection of the United States military." No one had any illusions about who was actually calling the shots. The US is now implementing plans for postwar Iraq that it drafted months before the war began. The plans call for privatizing Iraqi oil, establishing longterm US military bases in Iraq, keeping US military leaders in key positions of power, and giving prominent ministries to figures from the corrupt exile Iraqi National Congress and other exile groups that have no social base or legitimacy in Iraq. The whole arrangement will be under the supervision of retired Lt. General Jay Garner (also the former president of SYColeman, a defense contractor that worked to develop Israel's Arrow missile-defense system) and, for an indefinite period, General Tommy Franks, the head of the US Central Command.

The United States has discussed its support for elections in Iraq, but may defer them for years. Brent Scowcroft, the national security adviser to Bush I, put the matter bluntly: "What's going to happen the first time we hold an election in Iraq and it turns out the radicals win? What do you do? We're surely not going to let them take over."

Washington's goals in Iraq face many obstacles. In addition to the fact that Iraqi resentment at the US presence and its hand-picked exile bankers

19 David E. Sanger and Thom Shanker, "Bush Says Regime in Iraq Is No More; Syria Is Penalized," *New York Times*, April 16, 2003, p.A1.

and oil men is likely to increase, stabilizing and governing Iraq is not a simple matter. Washington will no doubt try to convince other countries to pay the bill for cleaning up the mess it has created, as many countries did after the last Gulf War, though far fewer are likely to do so again, given the current levels of resentment at US arrogance. *The Washington Post* noted that "[t]he 1991 Gulf war cost $61 billion, but about $50 billion of that was picked up by US allies, including Saudi Arabia, Kuwait and Japan, which are unlikely to contribute this time around."[20] The United States also faces questions of Shia and Kurdish rebellions, and potential Turkish and Iranian intervention into Iraq. Already, one Shia cleric backed by the United States has been assassinated.

Anger against the United States will also be increased by the ongoing crisis in Palestine. It is unlikely that Bush or Blair can deliver on their "road map" for a solution to the Palestine-Israeli conflict, which will generate even further opposition to the US presence in the Middle East. While the road map itself (like the broader Oslo framework) is tilted absolutely against Palestinian interests, Israel is mounting solid resistance to it. Ariel Sharon told *Ha'aretz* in April that, while Israel is not willing to halt expansion of settlements, Palestinians should be required to renounce the right of return for Palestinian refugees. Settlements, he explained, are "a sensitive issue. In the final stage of negotiations it will be brought up for discussion. We don't have to deal with it just now."[21]

The US also faces problems of imperial overextension. It has barely restored order in Kabul, Afghanistan, let alone the rest of the country, and though the media has said little about it, Afghanistan is in shambles. The US has troops engaged in Coloumbia, in the Philippines, in Georgia, in Afghanistan and elsewhere in Central Asia, and faces growing economic problems at home. Nearly every state is in fiscal crisis. At the same time as the Bush administration is spending hundreds of billions for war, it is laying off teachers, cutting Medicare programs, cutting back on child welfare services, and making other cuts to vital social programs. The extension of the war into Syria, Iran, or North Korea will generate not

---

20 James Harding and Peter Spiegel, "Bush Facing 90bn Dollars Bill for Costs of Conflict," *Financial Times* (London), February 27, 2003, p.9.

21 James Bennet, "Mideast Sides Maneuver, Expecting New Peace Effort," *New York Times*, April 14, 2003, p.A3.

only protest globally, but could easily generate even greater opposition at home than we have already seen.

The story of Iraq's liberation has already begun to go awry. As Robert Fisk rightly notes, "America's war of 'liberation' is over. Iraq's war of liberation from the Americans is about to begin."[22]

The wars in Afghanistan and Iraq are the *beginning* of wars to come, not the end of the "war on terrorism." Washington clearly intends to use the war in Iraq as a launch pad for further expansion of its military and economic power, not only in the Middle East, but globally. It is essential that we build an anti-imperialist movement in the United States and internationally that can both organize against the occupation of Iraq and build opposition to the wars that will certainly follow, unless we are organized and effective enough to prevent them.

22   Fisk, op. cit., p.1.

8 | The War Profiteers

FRIDA BERRIGAN

"Afghanistan hasn't had a direct impact on sales yet".
—*Peter Simmons, Spokesman for Lockheed*
Martin's Marietta, Georgia plan

THE STATUES OF Saddam Hussein have toppled in Iraq and the neo-conservative hawks are in full "I told you so" mode across American television screens, but the war is not over. And that is good news for big defense contractors—Lockheed Martin, Boeing, Northrop Grumman, Raytheon—and their subcontracts. That is encouraging news for the companies jockeying for position over the lucrative reconstruction contracts. The news creates an interesting tension for individuals who are personally profiting from the war while using their political positions to promote the overthrow of Saddam Hussein.

In anticipation of the war in Iraq, defense stocks enjoyed a surge in value, but once the war drew near in the early months of 2003, stock prices started to retreat.[1] "As soon as there is a conflict and tons of bombs are being dropped, there is a perception that the industry is getting rich. But it doesn't really work that way," explains Paul Nisbet, an aerospace analyst.[2] Why? For two reasons: (1) While bombs and munitions stockpiles are depleted in wartime, they are relatively inexpensive. The real profits are in big-ticket items like bombers and fighter planes, but these do not need to be replaced unless they crash or are shot down. (2) Because as Robert Friedman, aerospace and defense equity analyst for Standard and Poor's notes, "the stocks were overvalued to begin with."[3]

The weapons industry might not be expecting to make money hand

---

1 "Defense Stocks not Likely to be War Winners," *Chicago Tribune*, Mar 23, 2003.
2 Jennifer Beauprez, "Military Spending: Bush Priorities Raise Hopes," *Denver Post*, March 24, 2003.
3 "Defense Stocks not Likely to be War Winners," op. cit.

over fist in this war because it augers to be relatively short, but we should not feel too sorry for them yet. The military budget—the defense industry's share of the "pie"—keeps getting larger and larger. Immediately following the terrorist attacks of September 11, 2001, Congress passed a $343.2 billion defense budget—a $32.6 billion increase above 2001 levels. In addition, they approved a series of emergency supplemental spending bills, which totaled more than $30 billion for the Pentagon. The defense budget for 2003 is $392.9 billion. The President's military budget request for 2004 is $399.1 billion. That means that more than a billion dollars a day is being spent on the military, and that does not even include the costs of the war in Iraq. President Bush submitted a separate $74.7 billion supplemental war request to Congress in March, $62.6 billion of which is for military programs.

So, the weapons industry will get a big slice of pie from the Congress. But they are also counting on a spike in foreign sales in the aftermath of the war in Iraq. After the 1991 Gulf War, foreign weapons sales doubled according to the Congressional Research Service. In 1993 US defense contractors sold an estimated $20 billion in arms abroad, a sharp increase from $10 billion in 1992 and $11 billion in 1991.[4] The Paris Air Show, scheduled for June 2003, is likely to be crammed with weapons dealers touting their deadly wares with images of the rubble of Baghdad and Basra.

There is more than one way to make money from that rubble, as the corporations lining up for the lucrative post-war reconstruction contracts demonstrate. The name of the game is "crony capitalism" and the Bush administration is playing it well. Companies like Halliburton and Bechtel, which enjoy close ties to the administration, are gaining lucrative contracts in post-war Iraq. And Jay Garner, a close friend of the Bush White House (who is also the President of a defense company gaining new profit from the war) was tapped to administer post-war Iraq.

LOCKHEED MARTIN

Lockheed Martin fighter planes opened the war in Iraq. F-117 stealth attack fighters bombed "leadership targets" in Baghdad as part of the

4 Ibid.

opening salvo of "Operation Iraqi Freedom."[5] Lockheed Martin is the world's largest weapons contractor. The company received over $17 billion in contracts from the Pentagon in fiscal year 2002. The company did very well in the lead up to the 2003 war with Iraq. Lockheed Martin's third quarter 2002 profits jumped 36% overall, with a 15% increase in military aircraft sales alone.[6] The F-16 is the company's most lucrative export item, with more than 3,000 sold overseas since the mid-1970s. The company also makes the Hellfire missile, "bunker buster" munitions and the massive C-130 transport plane.[7]

Lockheed Martin's Paveway II bomb, which is guided to its target by a sensor, is seeing its first widespread use in this war. Versions of the Paveway are built by both Raytheon and Lockheed Martin, which spent $15 million to gain certification to begin making its version of the bombs.[8] The two companies received a $280 million order in mid-March to produce hundreds more of the weapons.[9]

The company also makes a version of the Patriot missile, known as the PAC-3, designed to destroy incoming missiles by ramming into them. In early March, the Army granted Lockheed Martin a $100 million contract for 212 PAC-3 for use in Iraq.[10] In late March, the Air Force announced it was ramping up production of the $91 million per copy missile, with a plan to increase production to 20 missiles per month in 2005. On top of that, in December 2002, the company was granted another contract for $341 million to build 88 missiles and associated hardware.[11]

Other high-tech Lockheed Martin weapons have been on display in Iraq. The Joint Air-to-Surface Standoff Missile (JASSM) uses satellite guidance and an infrared-seeking device to identify targets. The weapon has a range of 200 miles and, though it is still being tested, military analysts speculated that it served in Iraq.[12]

5 "Air Force F-117s Open Coalition Air Strikes With EGBU-27s," *Defense Daily*, March 21, 2003.

6 "Lockheed Profit Increases 36%," *New York Times*, October 26, 2002.

7 *Wall Street Journal*, October 12, 2001.

8 Renae Merle, "Battlefield Is A Showcase for Defense Firms," *The Washington Post*, Apr 1, 2003.

9 Tim Lemke, "War Likely to Bolster Defense Stocks," *Knight Ridder Tribune Business News*, March 24, 2003.

10 Ross Kerber, "In Kuwait, US Cites Early Patriot Missile Success," *Boston Globe*, March 21, 2003.

11 "DoD Officials Outline PAC-3 Production Plan," *Defense Daily*, March 21, 2003.

12 "Orlando, Fla.-Area Defense Contractors Contributed Equipment Used in Campaign," *Knight Ridder Tribune Business News*, March 24, 2003.

In late 2001, the company won what has been touted as "the largest defense contract in history," a $19 billion development contract for the $200 billion Joint Strike Fighter program. Plans call for producing variants of the JSF for the US Air Force, Navy, and Marines, as well as for the Navy and Air Force of the United Kingdom. Other countries that have been discussed as potential customers for this "world aircraft" are Germany, Turkey, and Israel.

Politically, Lockheed Martin has played a "behind the scenes" role in developing support for the Bush administration's war in Iraq. In 2002 the Coalition for the Liberation of Iraq was formed with the explicit support of the Bush administration. Former Lockheed Martin vice-president Bruce Jackson chairs the group, and he is joined by numerous other VIPS like former Secretary of State George Shultz and Senator John McCain. The group's goal is to make sure that the Bush administration isn't put on the defensive on the war issue.

Bruce Jackson's influence extends even further. In February 2003, the White House was feeling anti-war pressure from France, Germany and other members of what they derided as "Old Europe." A letter signed by 10 Central and Eastern European nations positioning themselves as the "New Europe," strongly supported Washington's war in Iraq, creating a spilt in Europe, that helped the Bush administration make a stronger case for war. Bruce Jackson, who has been working with the so-called Vilnius 10 since 2000 as they seek NATO membership, initiated and helped draft that statement.[13]

Jackson, who also runs the Project on Transitional Democracies, is a long-time supporter and active proponent of North Atlantic Treaty Organization (NATO) expansion to include former Soviet states. In that capacity, he has helped open up a whole new market to Lockheed Martin's combat aircraft and weapons systems. And in January 2003, Jackson's work began to pay off, as his former company and Poland signed a $3.5 billion contract for 48 F-16 fighter planes (which Poland will purchase with $3.8 billion in loans from the US).[14]

---

13 "US Lobbyist Helped Draft Eastern European's Iraq Statement," Agence France Presse, February 20, 2003.

14 Leslie Wayne, "Polish Pride, American Profits," *New York Times,* January 12, 2003.

BOEING

Since 1997, when Boeing acquired defense giant McDonnell Douglas, Boeing has ranked as the Pentagon's No. 2 contractor, second only to Lockheed Martin. Last year, Boeing received more than $16 billion in Pentagon contracts, up from $13 billion in 2001 and $12 billion in 2000.

In the aftermath of 9/11, when the Pentagon asked defense contractors to get ready to ramp up production in support of pending military operations, Boeing Vice Chairman Harry Stonecipher was quoted in *The Wall Street Journal* boasting that "the purse is now open."[15]

Boeing has its fingers in a lot of pots, so to speak, making fighter planes and precision munitions, operating the Space Shuttle, creating new satellite-based information and communications services, and overseeing many of the Pentagon's missile defense programs.

But in this war, it is the bombs that are bringing in the bucks. The company's Joint Direct Attack Munitions (JDAMs) are the US's preeminent "smart bomb" on display in Iraq. The $22,000 a copy JDAMs are relatively inexpensive, and make "dumb bombs" smart by fitting them with guidance devices. Boeing spokesman Robert Algarotti says that from September 2001 to October 2002, the JDAM program generated more than $1 billion dollars worth of contracts.[16] The Air Force originally ordered about 87,000 JDAM kits, but recently upped their order to more than 230,000. Boeing expects to boost production 40% to 2,800 kits per month this summer, Algarotti says.[17] And there are more to come; the Pentagon is investing more than $3.5 billion in JDAM production through FY2005.[18]

USA Today reported that Boeing also has contracts to make JDAM kits for five other countries, but Algarotti wouldn't name them.[19] And the company can expect major sales after the war. As John Pike, director of Global Security.org remarks, "Everybody has JDAM on the brain right now. I think any country with a self-respecting military in fairly short order is going to have to get in line to buy the genuine American article."[20]

15 Anne Marie Squeo and Andy Pasztor, "Defense Contractors Gear Up for Jump in Weapons Spending Following Attacks," *Wall Street Journal,* October 15, 2001.

16 Matt Kelley, "US Boosting Its High-Tech War Arsenal," Associated Press, July 16, 2002.

17 Gary Stoller, "JDAM Smart Bombs Prove to be Accurate," *USA Today,* March 24, 2003.

18 Hunter Keeter, "Pentagon Estimates 70% PGM Used in Possible War With Iraq," *Defense Daily,* March 6, 2003.

19 Gary Stoller, "JDAM Smart Bombs Prove to be Accurate," *USA Today,* March 24, 2003.

20 Renae Merle, "Battlefield Is A Showcase for Defense Firms," *The Washington Post,* Apr 1, 2003.

NORTHROP GRUMMAN

Northrop Grumman recently purchased TRW, the Cleveland based automotive and defense corporation, giving the company a depth and breadth that allows it to reap the rewards of increased military spending in a time of war. In 2002, the Los Angeles based company received $8.7 billion in Pentagon contracts, up from $5.2 billion in 2001. With the acquisition of TRW, the company now rivals Lockheed Martin as the largest military contractor in the world.

Northrop Grumman is best known for the B-2 bomber and the much-touted unmanned Global Hawk, both of which were on display during the US wars in Afghanistan and Iraq. But the company is a "trendsetter" in what are called "transformational systems"—weapons and support systems that bring together all the facets of the battlefield into a unified web. The company's $260 million per copy E-8C Joint Surveillance Target Attack Radar System (Joint STARS), a flying command platform, is loaded with sophisticated electronics that allow ground units to call in airstrikes and guide weapons to targets.[21] The company also makes high-tech systems like the Airborne Warning and Control Systems (AWACS) which serves as an "airborne nerve center."

The scope of the company's work is the result of careful planning and unprecedented political influence. Northrop Grumman CEO Kent Kresa and other executives are part of "St. Andrew's Prep," an informal network of Andrew Marshall protégés. Marshall, an iconoclastic military strategist, directs the Pentagon's Office of Net Assessment and was given wide power to define future defense priorities by Defense Secretary Donald Rumsfeld. The imperative to build and deploy missile defense and the emphasis on a more flexible, high-tech military are just a few of Andrew Marshall's ideas that Northrop Grumman is in a position to profit from.

Additionally, former Northrop Grumman executives are now in influential posts in the Pentagon. Secretary of the Air Force James Roche previously served as the head of Northrop Grumman's Electronic Sensors and Systems Sector in Maryland. Barry Watts, who once ran Northrop Grumman's influential in-house think tank, now directs the Pentagon's Office of Program Analysis and Evaluation.

21 "Orlando, Fla.-Area Defense Contractors Contributed Equipment Used in Campaign," *Knight Ridder Tribune Business News*, March 24, 2003.

RAYTHEON

As the fourth largest defense contractor, and a company that not only makes missiles, but also the new high tech weapons of war, like defense electronics and information systems, Raytheon is well positioned to benefit from war in Iraq. "Raytheon makes missiles, and it makes defense electronics, and it makes information systems, and this [military] budget is heavily oriented to all three," explains Loren Thompson, a defense analyst with the Lexington Institute.[22] In January 2003, Raytheon reported that its fourth quarter operating profit doubled. Raytheon CEO Daniel Burnham boasts that the "market is higher today than we thought a year ago. We are perfectly aligned with the defense department's priorities."[23]

Raytheon's best-known product is probably the Patriot air defense missile, which received massive publicity during the 1991 Gulf conflict. But post-war analyses indicate that the Patriots were far less accurate than US officials originally claimed, and that in fact they had missed their targets more often than not.[24] Since then, the Pentagon has spent $3 billion improving the Patriot missile. But they are still causing problems—2 Patriots have missed their targets in the 2003 Iraq war and caused "friendly fire" incidents.[25] Despite these problems, the Army ordered 230 of Raytheon's latest model.[26]

Promotional materials describe Raytheon's Tomahawk land attack missile as "the US Navy's weapon of choice." And indeed it appears to be. In the first 24 hours of war in Iraq, the US Navy fired more than 500 Tomahawk missiles—each costing $600,000—at Iraq.[27] And it is estimated that 725 of the munitions have been fired at Iraq since then.[28]

Raytheon also manufactures the "bunker buster" GBU-28, a 5,000-pound bomb and missiles like the TOW, Maverick and Javelin, all of which are being used in Iraq. The company's Joint Standoff Weapon

22   R. Schlesinger, "Extra $15b For Military Would Profit N.E. Firms," *Boston Globe*, Feb 4, 2003.

23   Anthony Velocci, "US Primes Buoyed By Weapons Procurement Sales," *Aviation Week and Space Technology*, February 3, 2003.

24   Theodore A. Postol and George M. Lewis, "Review of Army's Study on Patriot Effectiveness," September 8, 1992. http://www.fas.org/spp/starwars/docops/pl920908.htm.

25   Richard White, "Patriot Missiles are against Weapons of Choice to Defense Against Iraq Scud Attack," *Knight Ridder*, February 26, 2003.

26   Ross Kerber, "In Kuwait, US Cites Early Patriot Missile Success," Boston Globe, March 21, 2003.

27   Renae Merle, "Battlefield Is A Showcase for Defense Firms," *The Washington Post*, Apr 1, 2003.

28   Front Page of *The Independent* (Ireland), April 5, 2003.

(JSOW), a $150,000 precision-guided glide bomb, is seeing its first widespread action in Iraq, although it was used periodically in Afghanistan.[29]

OTHER COMPANIES PROFITING FROM THE WAR

The US Agency for International Development is distributing $1.6 billion in contracts to five US owned companies in the first six months of work—Bechtel, Fluor Corp., Washington Group International Inc., Louis Berger Group Inc. and Parsons Corp. These companies are now well positioned to reap millions more in future contracts. According to the *Wall Street Journal*, this could be the "largest government reconstruction effort since Americans helped to rebuild Germany and Japan after World War II." And while it is too soon to say exactly how much reconstruction will cost or how much profit is at stake, an American Academy of Arts and Sciences report estimated that the reconstruction of Iraq could cost anywhere from $30 billion to $105 billion over the next decade.[30]

Halliburton, where Vice President Dick Cheney served as CEO for five years (which continues to pay him $100,000–$1 million in "deferred compensation") was at the very top of the list of companies under consideration for the contracts.[31] But, in the face of criticism, it withdrew itself from consideration. So many press reports focused on the fact that the Vice President's former company would reap millions (possibly billions in contracts) to rebuild a country the President was bombing. It was an embarrassment. A spokesman for Halliburton said that its subsidiary KBR had not submitted bids on the lucrative reconstruction contracts. However, they will probably still gain from the contracts, as one of the other companies will hire them as a subcontractor.[32]

And there are other ways the company will benefit from the war. Halliburton's KBR was granted a contract worth an estimated $7 billion to fight oil well fires throughout Iraq, even though they did not submit a bid for the job.[33]

29 Renae Merle, "Battlefield Is A Showcase for Defense Firms," *The Washington Post*, Apr 1, 2003.

30 "War with Iraq: Costs, Consequences, and Alternatives," Academy of Arts and Sciences, December 2002.

31 Edwin Chen, "Bushes Report Net Earnings," *Baltimore Sun*, April 12, 2003.

32 David R. Baker, "US Awards Rebuilding Contracts, *San Francisco Chronicle*, April 12, 2003.

33 Michael Moore, "Pentagon Admits Halliburton Could Make $7 Billion in Iraq," *The Independent* (UK), April 12, 2003.

It is not just the war in Iraq that offers opportunities for Cheney's old company. The war on terrorism, which he warned might never end— "at least not in our lifetime," promises profits to last a lifetime too.[34] In December 2001, the company was granted an open-ended contract to provide base camp and facilities maintenance, laundry, food and airfield services and supply operations wherever the US Army and Navy go in the next 10 years.[35]

The contract is unique in that there is no ceiling on cost. So, while the deal could be worth billions, it is unclear how many billions. KBR will be reimbursed for every dollar spent, plus a base fee of 1%, which guarantees profit no matter what. On top of that, if the military is pleased with KBR's performance, they add a bonus, which is calculated as a percentage of the company's costs. Contract expert Steve Schooner described the deal as an unprecedented way of saying "come up with creative ways to spend my money and the more you spend the happier I'll be."

In addition to KBR's blank check, they have also been granted other contracts related to the war on terrorism:

- \$2 million to reinforce the United States embassy in Tashkent, Uzbekistan, November 2001.
- \$100 million to convert the Subic Bay US Navy base in the Philippines into a modern commercial port facility, November 2001.
- \$16 million to build a prison for captured Taliban fighters at Guantanamo Bay, Cuba, March 2002.

Dick Cheney is just one man who is profiting from the war. There are others—Richard Perle and Jay Garner are two others worth noting in some detail.

Richard Perle is not an appointed member of the Bush administration, but he enjoys an insider's perspective on the Pentagon, the war in Iraq, and the ongoing war on terrorism. As former chair of the Defense Policy Board, a "think tank" at the Department of Defense, he still serves as a close advisor to Defense Secretary Donald Rumsfeld.

But even as he enjoys insider access, he also benefits from outsider

---

34 Toby Harnden, "CIA gets £700m License to Kill," *The Daily Telegraph* (UK), October 22, 2001.
35 Pratap Chatterjee, "The War on Terrorism's Gravy Train," CorpWatch, May 2, 2002.

profits. As a major investor in a number of defense companies, he stands to reap considerable benefits from war and homeland security contracts. Seymour Hersh, writing in the March 17, 2003 issue of *The New Yorker*, mentions Trireme, Perle's venture capital company, which invests in companies dealing in homeland security and defense products. So far, the company has raised $45 million in capital—almost half of that coming from US defense giant Boeing.[36]

There is also the matter of The Autonomy Corporation, where Perle is the Director, with 75,000 shares of stock. The firm has developed a high-tech eavesdropping software that is capable of monitoring hundreds of thousands of email and phone conversations at the same time. In October 2002, the Department of Homeland Security granted the company a huge contract. A few months later, Autonomy was granted $1 million in contracts from a number of government agencies, including the Secret Service, and National Security Agency.[37]

When asked about the *New Yorker* article in a TV interview, Perle declared that "Sy Hersh is the closest thing American journalism has to a terrorist, frankly."[38]

A report from the Washington-based Center for Public Integrity, "Advisors of Influence," documents that at least nine of the Defense Policy Board's 30 members have ties to companies that have won more than $76 billion in defense contracts in 2001 and 2002. Four members are registered lobbyists, one of whom represents two of the three largest defense contractors.[39]

While this is bad enough, Jay Garner is even worse. Nothing embodies the Bush administration's shortsightedness and moral bankruptcy more than its plan to employ former Army Lt. Gen. Jay Garner as the head of the Pentagon's rebuilding effort for Iraq.

Garner is the president of SY Coleman, a subsidiary of L-3 Communications, a high tech defense contractor that specializes in missile-defense

36 Seymour M. Hersh, "Lunch With The Chairman: Why was Richard Perle Meeting with Adnan Khashoggi?" *The New Yorker*, March 17, 2003.

37 Seymour M. Hersh, *The New Yorker*, March 17, 2003.

38 "CNN Late Edition with Wolf Blitzer," March 9, 2003.

39 "Advisors of Influence: Nine Members of the Defense Policy Board Have Ties to Defense Contractors," Center for Responsive Politics, March 28, 2003.

systems. As the new head of the Pentagon's new Office of Reconstruction and Humanitarian Assistance, Garner, who is a personal friend of Defense Secretary Donald Rumsfeld, will oversee and coordinate relief and re-building efforts in Iraq after the war. [40]

If the Bush administration were to consciously set out to pick a person most likely to raise questions about the legitimacy of the post-war re-building process, they could not have selected a better man for the job than Jay Garner. As one observer noted, "If it's not a conflict of interest, it's certainly being tone deaf." In February L-3 announced that its revenue in the most recent quarter had soared to $1.3 billion from $705 million a year ago. They attribute the windfall to a doubling of military communi-cations and electronics sales. The company expects a 20% increase in sales and earnings this year.[41]

This is good news for the company and its stockholders, but will the people of Iraq trust a man who's company garnered millions making the targeting systems for missiles that destroyed their country?

---

[40] "The US General Waiting to Replace Saddam," *Independent,* UK, April 5, 2003.

[41] David Lazarus, "General/Defense Contractor to Rebuild Iraq: Conflict of Interest?," *San Fran-cisco Chronicle,* February 26, 2003.

9 | Lest We Forget

LOUISE CHRISTIAN

> We have no right to roam the world arresting foreigners we
> think might be dangerous and keeping them in our jails when
> we cannot show them to have committed any crime.
>
> —*Professor Ronald Dworkin,*
> *New York Review of Books, April 25th 2002*

THE WAR ON TERRORISM which George Bush declared in response to the atrocities of September 11th was said to be a war which would be fought in the name of democracy and human rights. Fifty three years after the adoption of the Universal Declaration of Human Rights on 10th December 1948, Bush issued a proclamation: "The terrible tragedies of September 11th served as a grievous reminder that the enemies of freedom do not respect or value individual human rights". He called on "the people of the United States to honour the legacy of human rights passed down to us from previous generations and to resolve that such liberties will prevail in our nation and throughout the world as we move into the 21st century". In his State of the Union address on 29th January 2002 Bush said, "America will lead by defending liberty and justice, because they are right and true and unchanging for people everywhere [...] America will always stand firm for the non-negotiable demands of human dignity [...] We choose freedom and the dignity of every life".

But these fine sounding sentiments were already being undermined even as Bush expressed them. The transfer of hundreds of prisoners captured in Afghanistan to a US military base in Guantanamo Bay, Cuba raised questions first about their treatment and conditions and then more fundamentally about the legal basis for their detention without trial or recourse to any court or access to a lawyer. In the US, there were also reports of hundreds of arbitrary arrests, while in Britain government rushed through a new terrorism law, the Anti-Terrorism Crime and

Security Act, empowering itself to detain non-UK nationals indefinitely without trial. Prisoners have also continued to be detained in Afghanistan in the Bagram air base and others have been transferred to Diego Garcia, an island in the Indian Ocean leased from Britain. There have been credible reports of torture methods used on prisoners. Another credible report alleges that there was a massacre in Afghanistan in November 2001 of hundreds of prisoners who were transported in container lorries. At the time of writing, it has been reported that hundreds of Iraqi civilians taken prisoner by the US in the war against Iraq could also be sent to Guan-tanamo. The Camp Commander was quoted in the US press as saying he had budgeted for the Camp to go on operating until 2005, but that also a twenty year plan could be drawn up.

Guantanamo, in the furthest south east corner of Cuba, may be best known for its vibrant musical tradition; the song Guantanamera, familiar to tourists everywhere, actually comes from there. Now however, Guan-tanamo Bay is assured a place in the history of international relations and human rights. Since the beginning of 2001, over six hundred prisoners from thirty different countries have been held in the US naval base there, who the US government claim are suspected Taliban and al-Qa'ida fighters. Among them are seven British citizens who have at least been identified. It is not known who many of the other prisoners are or whether their families have been notified.

In 1903 the then Cuban government signed a lease "for as long as they are needed" to the US government of two territorial areas at Guan-tanamo and Bahia Honda for the purpose of "coaling and naval stations". This agreement followed the ending of the Cuban war of independence from Spain in 1898, US intervention and the notorious Platt amendment of 1901, an amendment introduced by Senator Platt to a resolution in the US senate about Cuban independence which provided, "that the government of Cuba consents that the United States may exercise the right to intervene for the preservation of Cuban independence [...]"

Subsequently the agreement was amended to extend substantially the area on lease at Guantanamo Bay in exchange for giving back Bahia Honda to the Cuban government. Today Guantanamo Bay is a vast US naval base inaccessible from the mainland with supplies to US quarters, supermarkets, cinemas, health facilities all being flown in from the US military base in Norfolk, Virginia. The base has been used before to incarcerate prisoners of the US military; in 1994 thousands of Haitians trying to leave in boats for the US were held there, followed shortly afterwards by large numbers of Cubans who also tried to reach US shores.

The conditions at Camp X Ray caused huge consternation when they first came to light. Prisoners were shown in pictures broadcast around the world arriving at the camp in orange jump suits, shackled, mittened and hooded and clearly subject to sensory deprivation. One prisoner was shown motionless on a trolley with his legs shackled. These pictures released by the US government to play to a domestic audience demanding tough action backfired and resulted in international condemnation. It was disclosed that the prisoners were being held in wire cages of eight foot by eight foot open to the elements and lit by flood lights all night. A hunger strike started in the camp and two prisoners had to be force fed after the protest at the forcible removal of a turban from a prisoner during prayer. A British prisoner wrote to his family complaining he had lost three stone in weight, but otherwise letters received from prisoners by their families were short on information. Lawyers were refused any access to the prisoners but the British government sent MI5 officials to interrogate them in the presence of the CIA as well as Foreign Office officials. On the third such visit in May 2002, Feroz Abbassi complained that letters from his family explaining they had got him a lawyer had been withheld from him and said he would not speak without a lawyer. Notwithstanding this no lawyer was allowed him. A further problem for families of the detainees is that the only communication which is allowed by letter is taking six months or more, and some families have not heard anything for a very long time.

Following international condemnation, cells were built to house the prisoners at Camp Delta to which they have all now been transferred. Yet these still breach international standards on minimum conditions for humane imprisonment. The cells are tiny, only 8 foot by 6 foot 8 inches and the prisoners are allowed out of them only twice a week for fifteen minutes each time. International standards demand an hour's exercise a day. It is also said that the cells are lit by bright lights all night as well as in daytime. British officials have admitted that the British citizens have complained at the lack of exercise. The guards at the camp have been reported as saying that the reduction in contact between the prisoners, who are less able to talk to one another than when they were in wire cages, makes their job easier than in Camp X Ray, where there were hunger strikes and protests. However the protests have been replaced by suicide attempts, of which there have been reportedly over thirty with some inmates developing serious mental illness. Grotesquely, the military doctor in charge of the detainees health was quoted in the press as saying that the suicide attempts were a sign that the detainees were "finally showing some signs of remorse".

Despite the US Secretary of State, Donald Rumsfeld, publishing an order giving him the power to set up military tribunals with the power to impose the death penalty to try suspected members of al-Qa'ida or persons suspected of terrorism, none of the prisoners at Guantanamo Bay have been brought before such a tribunal or charged with anything. They are being imprisoned indefinitely incommunicado without access to a lawyer or to any court or tribunal. This has now been the situation for over a year. International law experts, including the UN High Commissioner on Human Rights Mary Robinson, have been more or less unanimous that this is a gross violation of international law.

The Geneva Conventions govern the treatment of prisoners taken during a war. They provide that if there is any uncertainty, the status of a prisoner should be decided by a competent tribunal, but this has not happened. If the detainees are prisoners of war then they must be released once the hostilities are at an end (which presumably those in Afghanistan now are) and cannot be prosecuted simply for fighting. They can only be prosecuted for war crimes such as crimes against humanity, genocide and ethnic cleansing. The US government says that the Guantanamo detainees are not prisoners of war, because they were not part of the official Taliban army, but instead they are "unlawful combatants". It is claimed this gives them no rights, but this ignores the provisions of Article 75 of Additional Protocol 1 to the Geneva Conventions which provides for "an impartial and regularly constituted court respecting the generally recognised principles of regular judicial procedure, which include the following:

a) the procedure shall provide for an accused to be informed without delay of the particulars of the offence alleged against him and shall afford the accused before and during his trial all necessary rights and means of defence".

The US has not ratified Additional Protocol 1, but the 1997 Operational Law Handbook of the US army states that it regards it as part of customary international law which will bind it.

On 16th December 2002, the UN Working Group on arbitrary detention concluded that so long as a competent tribunal is not convened to decide whether the Guantanamo Bay detainees are prisoners of war, then they provisionally enjoy the guarantees provided by the Geneva Conventions to persons taken on the battlefield who are not prisoners of war, i.e. the right to have the detention reviewed and a fair trial and access to a lawyer. They recalled the decision of the Inter American Court of Human Rights of 12th March 2002 urgently to request the US government to have the legal status of the Guantanamo Bay detainees determined by a competent tribunal.

In July 2002 an application for *habeas corpus* by some of the detainees to the United States District Court for the District of Columbia was thrown out on the grounds that the Court found that US courts have no jurisdiction over Guantanamo Bay, and that "aliens" (non US citizens) detained outside the sovereign territory of the US do not have any recourse to a US court to complain of breach of rights. This decision was subsequently confirmed by the Washington Court of Appeals in March 2003. From there it will be further appealed to the Supreme Court.

In the meantime, the family of Feroz Abbasi, one of the British citizens detained in Guantanamo, made an application to the Court in Britain asking for an order that the British Government make diplomatic protests to the US government. The British government had refused to take any position whatsoever on the legality of the detention, despite being the closest ally of the US in the war and therefore, it might be assumed, having more influence to protect the rights of its citizens. The application eventually went to the Court of Appeal who delivered judgment in November 2002. Although the Court of Appeal refused to make the order sought, it did make some unusually trenchant comments about the legality of the detention describing it as "objectionable" and an "arbitrary detention in a legal black hole". The judgment refers to the common legal tradition in both the US and the UK of the concept of *habeas corpus*—the principle being that any imprisonment of a person is deemed unlawful unless declared otherwise by a court. This concept goes back to the seventeenth century and the acknowledged need for the constitution to protect against arbitrary imprisonment ordered by the King. The Court quoted Lord Atkin as saying it applies in war as in time of peace. The references in the judgment to the proceedings in the USA make it clear that the Court of Appeal expect their judgment to carry weight with the US courts in persuading them to overturn the previous finding that they have no jurisdiction.

However, it was not long before the US courts were delivering a judgment in another case which suggests that they may not be prepared to intervene at all. Initially the USA appeared to be discriminating against non US citizens, in that there are no US citizens in Guantanamo and John Lindh Walker, a US citizen detained in Afghanistan, was given a trial and access to a lawyer. (After making allegations of ill treatment he entered into a plea bargain and was sentenced to fourteen years). The appearance of discrimination was one of the arguments that it was felt would mean that the US courts would have to decide they had jurisdiction over the prisoners in Guantanamo Bay. However in January 2003 the Richmond Virginia Appeals court decided that the indefinite detention in the USA of Yaser Esam Hamdi without trial or access to a lawyer, as an "enemy combatant", could not be reviewed by the US courts saying that, "to delve further into Hamdi's status and capture would require us to step so far out of our role as judges that we would abandon the distinctive deference that animates this area of law".

Hamdi is one of two US citizens now deemed unlawful combatants and arbitrarily detained in the USA. He was initially taken to Guantanamo after being held in Afghanistan. When discovered to be a US citizen he was transferred to a navy brig in Norfolk Virginia, where he is now set to remain indefinitely arbitrarily detained. The other US citizen deemed an enemy combatant, Jose Padilla, was allegedly planning to construct a radioactive bomb when arrested in Chicago in 2002. A trial court judge ruled in December 2002 that he could have access to a lawyer, but his indefinite detention without charge in a South Carolina brig "is not per se unlawful".

This rolling over of the US Courts in refusing to protect fundamental constitutional rights has been mirrored in Britain. The British government has also detained people indefinitely without trial under its new Anti Terrorism Crime and Security Act. Eleven non British citizens are currently in this position. Although the Special Immigration Appeals Commission initially ruled that the derogation from Article 5 of the Human Rights Act, enabling the British government to detain "aliens" (non British citizens) indefinitely without trial, was discriminatory because it did not apply to British citizens, this has now been overruled by the Court of Appeal, which did not accept this argument. Both judgments also accepted in its entirety the government's case that there is a state of emergency in this country allowing the derogation to take place to permit arbitrary and indefinite detention. It is not possible to derogate from Articles 2 and 3 protecting the right to life and to be free from inhuman and degrading treatment and therefore people could not be sent back to countries which persecute them—instead a derogation from Article 5 (the right to access to a court) is relied on to allow arbitrary detention.

The breach of fundamental international law by the USA and its allies in the name of democracy sends a message to other countries. In the last year, the numbers of Palestinians arbitrarily detained by the Israeli forces without trial has risen to well over 1000, while the phrase "targeted killings"—used to justify the killing of alleged Palestinian militants—was given legitimacy when the US openly trumpeted in late 2002 that it had carried out a "targeted killing" of three people said to be members of al-Qa'ida in the Yemen. Arbitrary detention and ill treatment also causes a huge feeling of injustice in the populations of countries whose nationals are disproportionately subject to it. The pressure on the Pakistan and Afghan governments have been sufficient to ensure they, unlike Britain, have made diplomatic protests about the incarceration of their citizens in Guantanamo and more than twenty of them were released from there in response.

Meanwhile, it is said that the US has arranged for the interrogation of its prisoners held in Afghanistan and elsewhere, in countries including Egypt, Morocco, Jordan and the Philippines, where full-blown torture methods are used. In addition, prisoners at Guantanamo have been subjected to sleep deprivation and shining harsh lights at them labelled "torture lite" by former US navy intelligence officer Wayne Madsen. Solitary confinement and sensory deprivation are also alleged to have been used against the 900 or more mainly Muslims detained in the USA on immigration and other charges since September 11th.

Just over a year after George W. Bush made the statements quoted at the beginning of this article, it is abundantly clear that the agenda of the "war on terror" is to abrogate fundamental human rights and to perpetrate the very abuses it is claimed we are fighting against. Disturbingly, there is little understanding or outrage about what is happening and this may well be linked to the extent to which the targets are non citizens or people who are disturbingly not really seen as citizens. In the US, anti-Muslim prejudice alone has been enough to achieve this; in Britain, hysteria has been whipped up about asylum seekers. In both countries, the Courts have failed to stand up for liberties and politicians have whipped up fears about terrorist attacks to justify human rights abuses.

Part 2 THE CRESCENT

10 | Seeing with Muslim Eyes

HAMZA YUSUF

How many a dispute could have been deflated into a single paragraph if the disputants had dared to define their terms.

—Aristotle.

THE MYSTIC POET, Rumi, tells of three foreigners traveling down a road together. They come across a drachma on the road, and picking it up together, each declares what he wishes to do with it. The first says he will buy *'inab*, which is Arabic for grapes; the second, a Persian, says, "No! We must buy *angur*," Farsi for grapes. The third, a Roman, exclaims it must be *vitis*—Latin for grapes. They begin to fight, and soon a journey distinguished by camaraderie descends into a fisticuff of animosity. Rumi remarks that all they needed was a translator to explain that they all really wanted the same thing.

A tragedy of the human condition is that at the root of much of our suffering is a simple human desire: the desire for men and women to live in human dignity, treated with respect. When people are not treated with respect, they often become angry. This anger is either expressed or repressed. When repressed, it often manifests as sorrow and grief. In order to explore why so many people in the modern world are angry, let us first define some terms.

If understood properly, many of the words we use to describe states and qualities would, in their actual definitions, explain how human states come about. Anger is an old English word that originally meant "sorrow," but this doesn't tell us much if we don't define sorrow. Webster tells us it is "mental anguish [anger's root lies hidden in that word, anguish, as well] caused by injury, loss or despair." What does all this mean?

Mental anguish is a state of mind, an overwhelming experience of pain that is not of the body, although it is certainly experienced in the body, and affects profoundly the state of the body. It results from injury, a word derived from two Latin words *in juria* meaning "unjust or wrongful." Injury is a wrong that was not deserved. One can see how a person who bumps his head on a tree branch he did not see, experiences it as an injury, a wrong that was undeserved.

King Lear remarks that he was a man "more sinned against than sinning." The irony of his remark is lost on him, as it is on most people who injure others and are in turn injured by those they initially wronged; in Lear's case, they were his daughters. Loss occurs when something we believe is ours is no longer accessible. It could be by death or by destruction, as in the loss of property, or it could be by something less tangible, such as a loss of respect.

Finally, in the definition of anger appears despair. How do we define despair? It is perhaps the easiest to define and yet the hardest. It comes from two Latin words meaning simply "without hope." *Sperare* in Latin is glossed "to hope." The Spanish have a wonderful expression, "espere me," meaning "hold on"; but etymologically, it is closer to "have hope in me." We despair of people when we no longer believe them, when they tell us to give them some more time, yet we feel we have given them enough already and that this is just another ploy to keep us hopeful of help that we know is not forthcoming.

In our attempt at understanding the anger of the Muslim world, we have to try to understand the history of the Muslim world's relationship with the West, something most people have neither the time nor the inclination to do. David Fromkin wrote a compelling and cogent book: *The Peace to End All Peace.* When it first came out, I read all five hundred and some odd small print pages, trying to understand a world I had become intimately familiar with, but deeply perplexed by, the Arab world. After September of 2001, like many other books on the Middle East, it has resurfaced in a new edition. The author painstakingly documents how the configuration in the Middle East was designed to ensure that peace would never be achieved—a rather depressing account of another chapter in the "Great Game". There is a sad but enduring myth, bantered about by supercilious journalists attempting to edify the rest of us, that "the Arab/Israeli conflict is an ancient one." If less than a century is ancient, then I suppose they have a case. For journalists, less than twenty-four hours is often ancient, which is part of the problem.

To understand the anger in the Muslim world, one must understand the Crusades, the centuries of antagonistic détente, cold war and sometimes hot war, as well as the many betrayals by the colonialists, the broken treaties and promises, burnt libraries and massacres. Indeed, I could also enumerate terrors inflicted by Muslims of the past, but as a Western convert to Islam, a multi-generational American whose father, grandfathers and great-grandfathers have worn the uniforms of this country and fought its wars, who has studied the history and traditions of both sides, I can honestly say, I did not convert to Islam for nothing. If I side at all, I side with truth not tribe.

Muslims, like many Native Americans, feel that "white men speak with forked tongues." Understanding the anger in the Muslim world requires that one attempt to understand the pain, the injury, the loss and the despair that has arisen from so much treachery, so many lies and so meager an attempt at ever acknowledging these wrongs. It requires an attempt to understand the past, the roots of what is now a moribund and desperate culture that views suicide as a glorious, albeit tragic, testimony to the spark of resistance that still lies in the almost extinguished embers of hope.

To understand anger, one must understand mental anguish, something Western people should be very adept at, given the fourth quarter returns of pharmaceuticals that produce anti-depressants and anxiolytic drugs. Anxiolytic—what a strange but interesting word: literally "anxiety loosing". Anxiety is a fear of some perceived future difficulty. The Arabs have a beautiful word for it: "*hamm.*" You can hear the worry in it if you say it, much like our "hum", which can mean "to express hesitation or doubt." The Prophet Muhammad said, "Anxiety is half of aging." We grow old faster by fearing the future. Mental anguish is often precipitated by the past, by an injury or by loss or despair, but it is in reality a fear of the future. Anguish is clinging to the past, relishing the injury, living the loss over and over and despairing of a different future. We in the West know a lot about mental anguish, but we fail to sympathize with the anguish of others in the South and in the East. Their anguish, unlike ours, is often exogenous: it relates to the very real conditions that literally surround them and leave them in despair, without hope of a better future. They no longer believe the politicians who promise that things will be different this time around; they don't believe that America will allow a democratically elected government do what is good for their country if it means the United States may lose some less than vital interests.

The anger in the West, like the East's anger, is deeply repressed and rooted invariably in sorrow. Sometimes it comes out in road rage. Road rage is usually precipitated by some slight on the road, some tragic attempt at getting somewhere too fast without care for others on the road. It is bad manners, plain and simple, but the response is almost always out of proportion. Temper, like temperature, is something we need to adjust to constantly, but most of us are not very adept at it, and we are becoming less so by the minute.

September 11th was in some ways a type of road or air rage. The first recorded case of road rage is in Sophocles' play, *Oedipus Rex.* Oedipus kills his father who slighted him on the road. What neither of them knew was that they were father and son. Oedipus' rage was a result of abandonment. He was sent by his father to die, but the father's servant took pity on him and abandoned him to the elements. This abandonment is at the root of Oedipus' sorrow, which shows up as rage later in his life. We need to understand this to comprehend the result of America using Osama bin Laden to do a job for which America was not willing to kill her sons. She decided to get others to fight her war, as did T. E. Lawrence. Known as Lawrence of Arabia, he tells us that the only reason he used the Arabs to destroy the Ottoman Empire was because he did not want young English boys to die. The Ottoman Empire was seen as the evil empire of its day as far as the Europeans were concerned, and so Lawrence used the brave but treacherous Arabs against their fellow Muslims. Similarly, America, in what was called Operation Mosquito, decided to use the Afghans to bring down the Russian Empire. Zbigniew Brzezinski (who served as the National Security Advisor to President Carter from 1977 to 1981) boasts of luring the Russians into Afghanistan. Into the web of intrigue they came only to be consumed by the spider's game. Osama worked as an operative being used by Pakistani, Saudi and American intelligence. He funneled money into the "noble" war effort. The godless Russians were clearly infidels even to the Americans because they did not believe in Western markets, and that is akin to saying "there is no God" in the West. After many years of struggle and a loss of one and a half million Afghanis, to add insult to injury, we in the West walked away and washed our hands of it. The "fathers" who produced Osama abandoned their son to the elements of Afghanistan after training him, because the hunt was over and the game bagged.

Is the Muslim world angry? Yes, it is indeed. Its people feel mental anguish from injury, loss and despair, not of God, but of a godless world that has long forgotten the strings of betrayal, the webs of deceit, the chains of broken promises. The West would do well to understand why we have so much mental anguish here. I believe it is a deep seated fear of a future conflict between the oppressed and those who either oppress them with impunity or who sit by and watch the process. We all know in our heart of hearts something is deeply wrong with the world we all share and inhabit: the injuries our lifestyles in the West cause to so many others, the loss to others caused by our Western consumption levels and the despair our deaf ears cause to the multitudinous people around the world whose cries we ignore. We cannot just sit back and watch our world disintegrate before our eyes—a beautiful, abundant and divine theater of grace in which so many suffer so needlessly because of the actions of so few. To the Muslims, I can only warn them: "the one who fights monsters might take care lest he thereby become a monster."

11 | Islam and the West after September 11: Civilizational Dialogue or Conflict?

JOHN L. ESPOSITO

T HE SEPTEMBER 11 2001 attacks against New York's World Trade Center and the Pentagon in Washington reinforced the voices of those in the West who had spoken of a "fundamentalist" holy war exported to America. Fears of radical Islam and the continued threat of global terrorism have led many to warn even more confidently of a clash of civilizations. In some ways, the Cold War attitudes of the West towards communism have been replicated in the projection of a new global threat. The tendency of many governments, the media and political analysts was to conclude the existence of an inherently anti-Western global Islamic threat. Muslim rulers in countries such as Turkey, Indonesia, and the Central Asian Republics, as well as Israel, India and the Philippines, have used the danger of Islamic radicalism to attract American and European foreign aid. Scant attention, however, is paid to the indiscriminate suppression of opposition movements, mainstream as well as extremists, in those very same countries.

In America and Europe, those who believe a clash is inevitable have maintained that today we see but the latest iteration of a centuries old confrontation and conflict between Islam and Christianity, the Muslim world and the West.

THE HISTORY OF MUSLIM-CHRISTIAN RELATIONS

Despite many common theological roots and beliefs, throughout history, Muslim-Christian relations have often been overshadowed by conflict as the armies and missionaries of Islam and Christendom have been locked in a struggle for power and for souls. This confrontation has ranged from the fall of the early Byzantine (eastern Roman) empire before the armies of Islam in the seventh century to the fierce battles and polemics of the Crusades during the eleventh and twelfth centuries. It continued with the expulsion of the 'Moors' from Spain, the Inquisition, the Ottoman threat to overrun Europe and European (Christian) colonialism and imperialism, from the eighteenth to the early twentieth centuries. Then followed the political and cultural challenge of the superpowers (America and the Soviet Union) to the Muslim world in the latter half of the twentieth century. The creation of the state of Israel, and the competition of Christian and Muslim missionaries for converts in Africa today and the contemporary reassertion of Islam in politics, have all added to tensions.

Islam's relationship to Christianity and the West has often been marked less by understanding than by mutual ignorance and conflict. Ancient rivalries and modern day conflicts, such as the Palestinian-Israeli conflict, have so accentuated differences as to completely obscure the shared theological roots and religious vision of the Judeo-Christian-Islamic tradition. Many have focused on, and reinforced differences, which have polarized, rather than united, these three great interrelated monotheistic traditions.

Islam's early expansion and success constituted a challenge, in terms of theology, politics and civilization, which proved a stumbling block to understanding and a threat to the Christian West. Both Islam and Christianity possessed a sense of universal message and mission that, in retrospect, were destined to lead to a history in which confrontation would prevail over mutual cooperation. Both have a dual history of religious propagation and conversions. In early Christianity, the apostle Paul spread the Gospel through his preaching and teaching, a peaceful example followed in later years by the Eastern Church. However, Western European Christianity was spread both by force, as evidenced by Charlemagne in Europe and the conquistadors in Latin America, as well as through peaceful means prior to the 19th century. The missionary connection to European colonialism and imperialism has been especially problematic for the Muslim world in the 19th and 20th centuries. More recently, as Christianity and Islam have continued to spread through Asia and Africa, tensions and conflicts have occurred between Muslims and Christian communities from the Sudan and Nigeria to Pakistan and Indonesia.

The history of the conquests and expansion of the Arab/Islamic Empire through military force in the early years has been emphasized in Western approaches to understanding Islam. However, many fail to distinguish between the use of the sword to expand empires and the use of religion by rulers to legitimate conquest on the one hand, versus the more complex manner in which Islam as a religion was spread by soldiers, merchants and Sufi (mystic) brotherhoods on the other. Few who talk of the early spread of Islam by the sword are cognizant of the fact that since Muslim rulers profited from special taxes paid by non-Muslims, there was often little desire or need to convert people to Islam. Moreover, Sufi networks and traders and merchants from Africa to Southeast Asia spread Islam peacefully.

In addition, for some Oriental Christians living under Byzantine rule, the arrival of Islam freed them from more onerous taxes and gave them a religious freedom that permitted them to remain as independent communities and practice their faith. In these cases, Islam was seen as a liberating political force, rather than as a menace or challenge to the Christian faith. The Muslim conquest of Europe was also more complex than is often recognized, witnessing co-existence as well as conflict. Muslims and Christians sometimes joined in political alliances with each other against common enemies or where there were common interests.

AL-ANDALUS: *CONVIVENCIA* (LIVING TOGETHER) OF CIVILIZATIONS

The most famous example of inter-religious and inter-civilizational tolerance is that of Muslim rule in Spain (*al-Andalus*) from 756 CE to about 1000 CE, often idealized as a period of interfaith harmony. Part of the attraction for Christians and Jews was the opportunity Muslim rule offered to those seeking refuge from the old ruling class system of Europe. Muslim rule brought with it the elimination of the nobility and clergy and the redistribution of their lands, creating a new class of small land holders who were largely responsible for the agricultural prosperity of Muslim Spain.

Although tensions did arise between the Jewish, Christian and Muslim communities, Christians and Jews occupied prominent positions in the court of the Caliph in the 10th century, serving as translators, engineers, physicians, and architects. Bishops were even sent by the Umayyads on important diplomatic missions. The Archbishop of Seville had the Bible translated and annotated into Arabic for the Arabic-speaking Christian community. Tolerance and social intercourse between religious groups at the upper levels was the highlight of the period: upper class Christians adopted Arab names and aspects of Arab culture, including veiling of women to reflect and enhance their status, not eating pork, and incorporating Arabic music and poetry into their own culture. Interfaith marriages also occurred at the upper class level. This example is important, but it needs to be balanced with the knowledge that the records indicate that, overall, actual contacts between Christians and Muslims were relatively limited. However, Muslims showed less tolerance towards Christians in their territories after the 10th century during the rule of the caliph al-Mansur.

RELIGIOUS/POLITICAL CONFLICT AND CONFRONTATION

Historically both Christians and Muslims have their bitter memories of conquest and intolerance. Christians experienced losses during the expansion of the Islamic and Ottoman Empires; Muslims experienced the traumatic loss of Andalusia and of independence during European colonial dominance of much of the Muslim world. Today, memories of the past, continued experience of conflicts globally in Palestine/Israel, Nigeria, Sudan, Chechnya and the emergence of Islam as the second or third largest religion in Europe and America reinforce an even stronger sense of the need for greater pluralism and tolerance to avoid the intolerance and retaliation of the past. Today, Muslims and Christians share common challenges and concerns: rampant secularism and materialism, the moral breakdown of society—the collapse of the institution of marriage and the family; problems with drugs, alcohol, and promiscuous sex; these moral and social challenges affect Christians and Muslims alike. In the twenty-first century, all are challenged to remember and build on the positive legacy of *convivencia,* living together, as well as to reinterpret and broaden their theological worldviews.

Historically, there are many examples of Muslim sponsorship of interfaith discussion and debate. The Prophet's dialogue with the Christians of Najran resulted in a mutually agreeable relationship where the Najranis were permitted to pray in the Prophet's mosque. The fifth caliph, Muawiyah (661–679 AD), initiated regular invitations to the contending Jacobite and Maronite Christians to the royal court to work out their debates with each other. The Syrian Christian John of Damascus was invited to appear in the court of the caliph to debate the divinity of Jesus and the concept of free will. Debates between both Muslims and Jews occurred in Spanish Muslim courts. In the 16th century, the Emperor Akbar presided over inter-religious theological discussion between Catholic priests and Muslim religious scholars (*ulama*) in Fatehpur Sikri. Like the debates sponsored by Christians, these debates were not always conducted between "equals" (indeed, many were held in order to "prove" that the other religion was "wrong"). However, the fact that the debate was permitted and encouraged indicates some degree of open exchange between faiths, during one of the highest stages of educational and cultural achievement in the Muslim world.

The Crusades are well known and remembered as a war between Christianity and Islam for political kingdoms. Traditional studies of this history focus on the differences between the two sides, yet there were also similarities and positive moments of coexistence and cooperation. Both Christians and Muslims shared cultural ideals of chivalry, loyalty, bravery, and honor. In fact, the Muslim leader Saladin (Salah al-Din) was highly respected and admired by the Christians, especially Richard the Lionhearted, for his mercy, honor, and bravery. Likewise, Saint Francis of Assisi won the respect of the Muslims he came to convert, for his example of piety and reverence. Some treaties were also concluded in the 13th century between Christians and Muslims who granted Christians free access to sacred places then reoccupied by Islam. Saint Francis met Salah al-Din's nephew Sultan al-Malik al-Kamil in 1219, leading the Sultan to grant freedom of worship to his more than 30,000 Christian prisoners when hostilities were suspended, as well as the choice of returning to their own countries or fighting in his armies.

THE MODERN DEBATE

In recent years, many Muslims, attributing the failures of their societies to an excessive dependence on and dominance by Western governments, values and culture, reject secular governments and conservative religious establishments, holding them responsible for the long period of decline and demoralization. Thus, the resurgence of Islam and of Muslim identity has swept across much of the Muslim world.[1] A somewhat similar process occurred in Christianity during the Christian Reformation of 15th and 16th centuries. Many in Europe, shocked by the failure of their rulers to resolve the economic and social ills of the time and the decline and corruption of the orthodox Church, pushed for a return to the foundations of the faith. They emphasized a relearning and reappropriation of God's intentions for human civilizations and an insistence that God's order for society be followed as a means of reviving Christian civilization. Similarly, at the turn of the century, Pope Leo XIII condemned American-style pluralism and voluntarism as patterns for adoption by the church (*Longinqua Oceani,* 1895). He critiqued both American society and its economic doctrines (*Rerum Novarum,* 1891) because of unrestricted economic competition and the excesses of capitalism that grew out of it. It was not until the 1960s and the Second Vatican Council that Catholicism officially accepted religious pluralism.

ISLAM AND THE WEST: A CLASH OF CIVILIZATIONS?

In a controversial 1993 article, "The Clash of Civilizations?" Samuel Huntington warned that a "clash of civilizations will dominate global politics."[2] Many in the Muslim world saw this important American academic and opinion-maker, who had also held a prominent position in government, as articulating what they always thought was the West's attitude towards Islam. If some academics and government officials were quick to distance themselves from Huntington's position, the sales of his subsequent book, its translation into many languages, and the sheer number of international conferences and publications that addressed the question demonstrated that there was "a market" for "clash." The attacks of September 11 and the global threat of bin Laden and al-Qaʿida have resurrected

---

[1] For analyses of the Islamic resurgence and its impact see, John L. Esposito, *The Islamic Threat: Myth or Reality?,* 3rd ed., New York: Oxford University Press, 1999; Esposito, *Islam and Politics,* 4th ed., Syracuse NY: Syracuse University Press, 1998; and James P. Piscatori and Dale F. Eickelman, *Muslim Politics,* Princeton NJ: Princeton University Press, 1997.

[2] Samuel P. Huntington, "The Clash of Civilizations?" *Foreign Affairs* (Summer 1993), pp. 22, 39.

a knee-jerk resort to "the clash of civilizations" for an easy answer to the question, "Why do they hate us?"

Huntington, like many others today, characterized Islam and the West as age-old enemies: "Conflict along the fault line between Western and Islamic civilizations has been going on for 1300 years."[3] He interpreted resistance to secular Western models of development as necessarily hostile to human rights and progress: "Western ideas of individualism, liberalism, constitutionalism, human rights, equality, liberty, the rule of law, democracy, free markets, the separation of church and state, often have little resonance in Islamic [and other] ... cultures."[4]

In his 1997 follow-up book, Huntington concluded that "Islam's borders are bloody and so are its innards."[5] His blanket condemnation went beyond Islamic fundamentalism to Islam itself: "The underlying problem for the West is not Islamic fundamentalism. It is Islam, a different civilization whose people are convinced of the superiority of their culture, and are obsessed with the inferiority of their power."[6] Though Huntington has now significantly refined his position, September 11 unleashed new "updated" versions of an "Islamic threat" as many found it more expedient to fall back on convenient stereotypes of a monolithic Islam, an historic clash of civilizations, and a conflict between Islam and modernity, rather than examine the complex political, military, economic and social causes of terrorism.

Proponents of a clash cite bin Laden and al-Qa'ida as clear indicators of an unbridgeable gulf between two very different worlds. Similarly, the declared war of religious extremists and terrorists against entrenched Muslim governments and the West—all in the name of Islam—are also cited as proof that Islam is incompatible with democracy. However, while the actions of extremist groups and of authoritarian governments, religious and non-religious, reinforce this perception of a clash of civilizations, the facts on the ground present a more complex picture.

Neither the Muslim world nor the West is monolithic. Common sources of identity (language, faith, history, culture) yield when national or

---

3 Ibid., p.31.   4 Ibid., p.40.

5 Samuel P. Huntington, *The Clash of Civilizations and the Remaking of World Order*, (New York: Simon & Schuster, 1997), p.258.

6 Ibid., p.217.

regional interests are at stake. While some Muslims, as in the Iranian Revolution, have achieved a transient unity in the face of a common enemy, their solidarity quickly dissipates once danger subsides and competing interests again prevail. The evidence that there is no monolithic Islam is abundant. The inability of Arab nationalism/socialism, Saudi Arabia's pan-Islam, or Iran's Islamic Republic revolution to unite and mobilize the Arab and Muslim worlds, the competition and conflict between countries like Egypt, Libya, Sudan, and Saudi Arabia, the disintegration of the Arab (Iraq and the Gulf states) coalition against Iran after the Iran-Iraq war, and the subsequent Iraqi invasion of Kuwait and divisions in the Muslim world evident in the Gulf War of 1991 are but a few examples. Bin Laden's failure to effectively mobilize the vast majority of the 1.2 billion Muslims in the Islamic world or the majority of religious leaders in his unholy war despite his global terrorist network is a reminder that Muslims, like every global religious community, are indeed diverse. As Islamic history makes abundantly clear, mainstream Islam, in law and theology as well as in practice, in the end has always rejected or marginalized extremists and terrorists, from the radical groups of the past like Kharijites and Assassins, to contemporary radical movements like al-Qa'ida.

A WAR AGAINST GLOBAL TERRORISM OR AGAINST ISLAM?

In the aftermath of the September 11 attacks, President George Walker Bush and many policymakers were careful to emphasize that America was waging a war against global terrorism, not against Islam. Bush visited a major mosque in Washington and held meetings with Muslim leaders reinforcing his respect for Islam and the need to distinguish between the religion of Islam and the actions of terrorists. However, America's pursuit and prosecution internationally and domestically of its broad-based war against terrorism and the rhetoric and policies of the administration that have accompanied it, have convinced many Muslims that the war is indeed a war against Islam and Muslims.

Despite the fact that Bush and the Pentagon apologized for the early use of the terms Crusade and "Infinite Justice", months later, the code name "the Green Front" was employed for raids against Muslim organizations and homes in Northern Virginia and Georgia that were suspected of laundering funds that went to "terrorist" groups, reopening questions about the real attitude and motives of the administration. The propensity of President Bush and his administration to condemn Palestinian terrorism but not equally decry Israel's brutality, violence and terror enraged many who daily watch the Israeli armies "cleansing" cities and towns in the West Bank and Gaza.

The unfolding and trajectory of the war against terrorism has convinced many in the Muslim world that this is a war against Islam and Muslims. Several factors have reinforced this perception and belief, contributing significantly to a widespread anger and anti-Americanism that cuts across Muslim societies: the broadening of the American-led military campaign's scope beyond Afghanistan, the use of the term "axis of evil," and the continued "pro-Israel" policy during the current crisis and carnage on the part of the Bush administration and Congress.

Initially, the Bush administration declared that the purpose of the military campaign was to bring Osama bin Laden and al-Qa'ida to justice. When the Taliban refused to surrender bin Laden and warned that they would militarily resist American forces, the war was widened to include the overthrow of the Taliban. The widespread and extensive bombing of Afghanistan with its civilian casualties, followed by the pursuit of second fronts in the Philippines, Yemen, and Pakistan and the designation of Iraq, Iran and Syria as an axis of evil have been capstoned by the Bush administration's policy in Palestine/Israel. The failure to acknowledge and condemn Ariel Sharon's provocation of the second intifada through his visit to the Temple Mount, and the Israeli sustained invasion and devastation of Palestinian cities and villages in its war against "Palestinian terrorism", has fed a rage that has been witnessed across the Muslim world. The lack of parity in rhetoric and policy as the Bush administration criticized and held Arafat fully accountable for suicide bombings, but praised Sharon as a man of peace, reinforced the popular perception of a Bush-Sharon, American-Israeli alliance.

At the same time, the American media's coverage and editorials often reveal glaring contrasts with those of Europe and the Arab and Muslim world. The differences between programming on the BBC or al-Jazeera versus CNN and Fox News, the sharp contrast between headlines and coverage of Jenin, Nablus, and Bethlehem as well as assessments of the Bush administration in *The New York Times, Wall Street Journal, The Washington Post* and their counterparts in Europe is glaring. Moreover, the depth and breadth of media bias is reflected in editorials, op-eds and articles of commentators such as Bernard Lewis, Daniel Pipes, Charles Krauthammer, William Safire, Steven Emerson, Judith Miller, Martin Kramer, A. M. Rosenethal, William Kristol, George Will, Martin Peretz, Morton Zuckerman, Norman Podhoretz and others in publications like the *Wall Street Journal, The New York Times, The Washington Post, The New York Post, The New Republic, The Weekly Standard,* and *National Review.*[7] However different, they all tie the war on terrorism and an anti-Islam rhetoric to an uncritical, pro-Israel position.[8] As a result, the Palestinians are painted consistently as the brutal aggressors and the Israelis as innocent victims, despite Israel's vastly disproportionate firepower and the far greater number of Palestinian deaths and injuries.

The American media has quite rightly highlighted the horrific impact of suicide bombings on innocent Israeli civilians and children, but fails to provide equal coverage and images of the brutality and terror, deaths and casualties experienced by Palestinian civilians. Articles underscore the growth of anti-Semitism, but are silent about a comparable growth of anti-Arabism and anti-Islamic sentiment. Arafat is portrayed as responsible for acts of terrorism, but Sharon's current and past (Shatila and Sabra) record is ignored. There is no balance in underscoring the failures of both Arafat and Sharon; no balance in depicting both Palestinians and Israelis as warriors as well as victims. At the same time, the alliance between the Christian Right and Republican neo-conservatives who espouse a theological/ideological pro-Israel, Zionist agenda exacerbates the situation. Their calls for the targeting of "terrorist" states from Libya and Sudan to Iran, Iraq and Syria seemingly confirms advocates of a widespread "conspiracy" against Islam.

[7] See for example, Bernard Lewis, "The Roots of Muslim Rage," *The Atlantic*, September 1990, "The Revolt of Islam," *The New Yorker*, November 19, 2001, "What Went Wrong," *The Atlantic*, January 2002; William Safire, "4 Secular Questions," *The New York Times*, March 25, 2002; Daniel Pipes, "The New Global Threat," *Jerusalem Post*, April 11, 2001 and "The Danger Within: Militant Islam in America," *Commentary*, November 2001; for a brief critique with quotations from Pipes' writings, see "Who is Daniel Pipes," http://www.cair-net.org/misc/people/daniel_pipes.html; and Charles Krauthammer, "We Can't Blow It Again," *Washington Post*, Friday, April 19, 2002.

[8] Eric Alterman, "Media War," *The Nation*.

The resultant image of America and American foreign policy is increasingly that of an "imperial" America, whose overwhelming military and political power is used unilaterally, disproportionately and indiscriminately in a war not just against global terrorism and religious extremists, but also against Islam and the Muslim world. The failure of the American administration to practice a parity of rhetoric and politics in Palestine-Israel, India-Pakistan, Russia-Chechnya feeds anti-American sentiment among the mainstream as well as the hatred of America among militant extremists. Across the political spectrum there is a growing tendency to believe that a clash of civilizations is on the horizon, provoked by America as well as al-Qaʿida and other extremists.

AMERICAN FOREIGN POLICY IN THE MUSLIM WORLD

After September 11, slogans like a clash of civilizations, a war between the civilized world and terrorists or against fundamentalists who hate Western democracy, capitalism, and freedom; or a war against "evil" and "merchants of death" were common, emphasizing a white and black world that obscures the deeper realities and long-term issues that exist.[9] Similarly, belief that overwhelming force brought a quick victory in Afghanistan and is an effective answer has distracted from the need to address the nature and causes of real and future threats. Other bin Ladens exist as do the political and economic conditions that they can exploit to recruit new soldiers for their unholy wars.[10]

Osama bin Laden, like the secular Saddam Hussein and the Ayatollah Khomeini before him, cleverly identified specific grievances against Muslim regimes and America that are shared across a broad spectrum of Muslims, most of whom are not extremists. He then used religious texts and doctrines to justify his jihad of violence and terrorism. Anti-Americanism is driven not only by the blind hatred of terrorists, but also by a broader-based anger and frustration with American foreign policy among

---

[9] This section is drawn from my *Unholy War: Terror in the Name of Islam* (New York: Oxford University press, 2002), ch.4.

[10] For a discussion of the attacks of September 11, 2001, their roots, relationship to Islam and U.S. foreign policy, see John L. Esposito, *Unholy War: Terror in the Name of Islam* (New York: Oxford University Press, 2002) and Peter L. Bergen, *Holy War Inc.: Inside the Secret World of Osama Bin Laden* (New York: Free Press, 2002).

many in Arab and Muslim societies: government officials, diplomats, the military, businessmen, professionals, intellectuals, and journalists. Many admire the fundamental principles and values (political participation, human rights, accountability, basic freedoms of speech, thought, the press) of the West. But they also believe that a double standard exists; these American principles and values are applied selectively or not at all when it comes to the Muslim world.

Part of the problem Americans have had in understanding anti-Americanism is the failure to recognize that Arabs and the broader Muslim world sees more than Americans see. In recent years, America had become less international-minded and more preoccupied with domestic issues. Many members of Congress saw no reason to travel abroad; a prominent congressional leader freely quipped that he had been to Europe once and saw no reason to return. Major American networks and newspapers have cut back on the number of foreign bureaus and correspondents. Domestic news coverage expanded at the expense of American public awareness of international affairs. In contrast with the past, today many in the Muslim world are no longer dependent on CNN and the BBC for news of the world. International Arab and Muslim publications and media provide daily coverage of foreign affairs. Families in the Muslim world sit glued to their television sets, watching daily coverage on Al-Jazeera which gives them live news in vivid color from Palestine/Israel, Iraq, Chechnya, and Kashmir. Many see America's espousal of self-determination, democratization, and human rights as disinguous in light of its foreign policies. With the exception perhaps of Kosovo, America's recent interventions abroad, in Kuwait and Iraq in the Gulf war and in Somalia, are seen as driven solely by national interest rather than American principles.

While the average American sees one side of the latest explosive headline event such as suicide bombings in Israel, they are not bombarded daily with the sight of Israeli violence and terror in the West Bank and Gaza, the disproportionate firepower, the number of Palestinian deaths and casualties, the use of American weapons including F16s and Apache helicopters provided to Israel and used against Palestinians, including civilians, in the occupied territories. America's relationship with Israel has proved to be a lightning rod. While some in the West downplay or deny the significance of the Palestinian issue, surveys continue to verify its importance to Muslims globally. A survey in Spring 2001 of five Arab states (Egypt, Saudi Arabia, the United Arab Emirates, Kuwait and Lebanon), demonstrated that the "majority in all five countries said that the Palestinian issue was "the single most important issue to them personally."[11] In a Zogby International poll of American Muslims in November/December 2001, 84% believed that the US should support a Palestinian state, 70% believed that it should reduce financial support to Israel.[12]

America's long record of relatively uncritical support of Israel—expressed in its levels of military and economic aid to Israel, its voting record in the United Nations, official statements by American administrations and government officials, and votes by Congress (often opposed by administrations in the past) to move the American embassy from Tel Aviv to Jerusalem, in direct contravention of long-standing UN resolutions—are seen by many in the Muslim world as proof of American hypocrisy.

Other critical foreign policy issues include the impact of sanctions on more than a half million innocent Iraqi children (with little direct effect on Saddam Hussein) and sanctions against Pakistan, but failure to hold India and Israel to similar standards for their nuclear programs. The moral will so evident in Kosovo is seen as totally absent in US policy in the Chechnya and Kashmiri conflicts. A native-born American convert to Islam, Ivy League educated and a former government consultant, spoke with a frustration shared by many Muslims: "Every informed Muslim would point to America's bizarre complicity in the genocidal destruction of Chechnya, its tacit support of India's incredibly brutal occupation of Kashmir, its passivity in the ethnic cleansing of Bosnia, and even America's insistence on zero casualties in stopping the ethnic cleansing of Kosovo. These are hot spots in the so-called "ring of fire" around the edge of the Muslim world, where Muslims are throwing off the shackles of old empires."[13]

The war against global terrorism has been taken as a green light for

[11] Shibley Telhami, "Defeating Terror: Confront Supply and Demand," *Middle East Insight*," Nov.-Dec. 2001, Vol. XVI, No.5, p.7.

[12] "American Muslim Poll," (Washington, D.C.: Project MAPS, Georgetown University, 2001). p.7.

[13] Robert Crane, "Re-thinking America's Mission: The Role of Islam," *American Journal of Islamic Social Sciences*, (Fall/Winter), 2001.

some authoritarian regimes in the Muslim world, particularly in Central Asia, to further limit the rule of law and civil society or repress non-violent opposition. Many governments use the danger of "Islamic fundamentalism" as an excuse for authoritarian responses and policies, labeling all Islamic movements, extremist as well as moderate (whom they characterize as wolves in sheep's clothing), as a threat. Many Muslim and Western governments oppose any Islamic candidates' participation in elections, fearing that they will hijack elections. These fears often obscure the fact that many governments themselves have proven non-democratic or authoritarian track records.

American, as well as European, responses must remain proportionate, from military strikes and foreign policy to domestic security measures and anti-terrorism legislation. A reexamination, and where necessary, reformulation of US foreign policy will be necessary to effectively limit and contain global terrorism. Short-term policies that are necessitated by national interest and security must be balanced by long term policies and incentives that pressure our allies in the Muslim world into promoting a gradual and progressive process of broader political participation, power sharing, and human rights. Failure to do so will simply perpetuate the culture and values of authoritarianism, secular as well as religious, and feed anti-Americanism. If foreign policy issues are not addressed effectively, they will continue to provide a breeding ground for hatred and radicalism, the rise of extremist movements, and recruits for the bin Ladens of the world.

CONCLUSION: COEXISTENCE OR CONFLICT?

The political, as well as religious, challenge in today's increasingly global, interdependent world is to recognize not only our competing interests, but also our common interests. America's policy toward Japan or Saudi Arabia is not based primarily upon a sense of shared culture, religion, or civilization, but upon common political and economic interests. Cooperation can result from common religious and ethnic backgrounds; however, more often it comes from the recognition of similar or shared interests.

A clash of civilizations can become the clarion call that justifies aggression and warfare. However, future global threats will be due less to a clash of "civilizations" than a clash of interests, political, economic and military. For indeed, the followers of the three great monotheistic faiths share much in common. While there are distinctive differences of doctrine, law, institutions, and values between Judaism, Christianity, and Islam, there are also a host of similarities. They all see themselves as Children of Abraham, are monotheists, believe in prophethood and divine revelation, have a concept of moral responsibility and accountability. This shared perspective has been recognized in recent years by the notion of a Judeo/Christian tradition, a concept that is slowly being extended by some who speak of a Judeo/Christian/Islamic tradition.

Historic clashes and violent confrontations have occurred, but they do not represent the total picture. Positive interaction and influence have also taken place. Islamic civilization was indebted to the West for many of the sources that enabled it to borrow, translate and then to develop its own high civilization that made remarkable contributions in philosophy, the sciences and technology, while the West went into eclipse in the Dark Ages. The West in turn reclaimed a renovated philosophical and scientific heritage from Islamic civilization, retranslating and re-appropriating that knowledge, which then became the foundation for its Renaissance.

In the modern period, Muslims have freely appropriated the accomplishments of science and technology. In many ways, they face a period of reexamination, reformation, and revitalization. Like the Reformation in the West, it is a process not only of intellectual ferment and religious debate, but also of religious and political unrest and violence.

Today it is critical to distinguish between the "hijacking" of Islam by extremists and mainstream Islam, in order to appreciate that all members of the international community—Muslims and non-Muslims alike—are in one way or another caught in the current confrontation between the civilized world and global terrorism.

The continued tendency of many to see Islam and events in the Muslim world only through explosive headlines hinders the ability to distinguish between the religion of Islam and the actions of extremists who hijack Islamic discourse and belief to justify their acts of terrorism. It reinforces the tendency to equate Islamic fundamentalism and terrorism with all Islamic movements, political and social, non-violent and violent. Yet, a deadly radical minority does exist; they have wrought havoc primarily on their own societies from Egypt to the southern Philippines. Osama bin Laden and others appeal to some through real as well as imagined injustices and prey on the oppressed, alienated, and marginalized sectors of society. The short-term military response to bring the terrorists to justice must also be balanced by long-term policy that focuses on the core issues that breed radicalism and extremism.

Muslims today face critical choices. If Western powers need to rethink, reassess their policies, mainstream Muslims worldwide will need to more aggressively address the threat to Islam from religious extremists. Governments that rely upon authoritarian rule, security forces and repression will have to open up their political systems, build and strengthen civil society, discriminate between free speech with its expression in mainstream opposition and a violent extremism that must be crushed and contained. Societies that limit freedom of thought and expression produce a sense of alienation and powerlessness that often results in radicalization and extremism. Formidable religious obstacles must be overcome: the ultra conservatism of many (though not all) ulama; the more puritanical militant exclusivist brands of Islam; the curriculum and training in those madrasas and universities that perpetuate a "theology of hate," the beliefs of militants who reject not only non-Muslims, but also other Muslims who do not believe as they do.

Relations between the Muslim world and the West will require a joint effort, a process of constructive engagement, dialogue, self-criticism and change. The extremists aside, the bulk of criticism of Western, and particularly American policy, comes from those who judge the West by its failure to live up to its principles and values. Regardless of cultural differences, Muslims and Christians share common religious/civilizational principles, values and aspirations: belief in God and His prophets, revelation, moral responsibility and accountability, the sanctity of life, the value of the family, a desire for economic prosperity, access to education, technology, peace and security, social justice, political participation, freedom and human rights. An increasing number of Muslims, like non-Muslims, are concerned about the excesses of modernity and globalization: a secularism that instead of denying privilege to any one faith in order to protect the rights of all its citizens, is anti-religious in its identity and values; an emphasis on individual rights and freedoms that is not balanced by an equal concern for the public good; a free market capitalism that is not balanced by the common good; a process of globalization that threatens to create a new form of western, especially American, economic and cultural hegemony.

Post September 11 challenges governments, policymakers, religious leaders, the media and the general public to all play both critical and constructive roles in the war against global terrorism. The process will have to be a joint partnership which emphasizes the beliefs, values and interests that we share in common; addresses more constructively our differences and grievances; and builds a future based upon the recognition that all face a common enemy, the threat of global terrorism, which can only be effectively contained and eliminated through a recognition of mutual interest and the use of multilateral alliances, strategies and action.

12 | Jihad as Perpetual War

ZAID SHAKIR

O NE OF THE FUNDAMENTAL ideas underlying the argument of those who advocate a clash of civilizations between Islam and the West[1] is the thesis that Islam is a religion that advocates perpetual warfare. This warfare, in their formulation, is what Muslims know as Jihad. In his provocative book, *Islam Unveiled*, Robert Spencer unequivocally states:

> The Jihad that aims to increase the size of the *dar al-Islam* at the expense of the *dar al-harb* is not a conventional war that begins at a certain point and ends at another. Jihad is a "permanent war" that excludes the idea of peace but authorizes temporary truces related to the political situation (muhadana).[2]

Other Western writers and ideologues go further by linking the idea of Jihad to an effort by Muslims to obtain global domination. For example, Daniel Pipes, writing in the November edition of *Commentary*, states:

> In pre-modern times, jihad meant mainly one thing among Sunni Muslims, then as now the Islamic majority. It meant the legal, compulsory, communal effort to expand the territories ruled by Muslims (known in Arabic as dar al-Islam) at the expense of territories ruled by non-Muslims (dar al-harb). In this prevailing conception, the purpose of Jihad is political, not

---

[1] Such a "clash" has been popularized by Sam Huntington in his 1993 essay and subsequent book, *The Clash of Civilizations*. See Samuel Huntington, "The Clash of Civilizations?" *Foreign Affairs*, vol. 72, no.3 (Summer 1993).

[2] Robert Spencer, *Islam Unveiled: Disturbing Questions About the World's Fastest Growing Faith* (San Francisco: Encounter Books, 2002), p.145.

religious. It aims not so much to spread the Islamic faith as to extend sovereign Muslim power (though the former has often followed the latter). The goal is boldly offensive, and its ultimate intent is nothing less than Muslim domination over the entire world.[3]

As the pre-modern world never came totally under the sway of Islam, Jihad, in the formulation described by Pipes, meant permanent war. Pipes does not see modernity mitigating this pre-modern tendency in Jihad, for he goes on to say:

> In brief, jihad in the raw remains a powerful force in the Muslim world, and this goes far to explain the immense appeal of a figure like Osama bin Laden in the immediate aftermath of September 11, 2001.[4]

It is significant that Spencer, Pipes, and others buttress their arguments with formulations and concepts associated with classical Islamic political theory. However, their understanding presupposes a single, narrow reading of the Islamic tradition, based on certain ideologically determined parameters, which limit their ability to accommodate an alternative reading of the tradition. For example, the often-cited division of the world into *dar al-harb* and *dar al-Islam* fits well with attempts to explain the inevitability of a clash between Islam and the West. However, it does not really give us an idea of the nuances and complexities of those terms, nor the diverse ways in which Muslim thinkers, over an extended period of time, defined and actually applied them.

The purpose of this article is to show that Jihad, even in its classical formulation, does not present a scheme of perpetual warfare. A failure on the part of Western ideologues and policymakers to recognize this fact will lead to tragic misunderstandings that create the possibility for catastrophic wars, which could render the Islamic heartland an uninhabitable waste, and greatly increase the likelihood of attacks against the United States and her interests abroad.

In discussing the perpetual warfare thesis I will focus on Qur'an 9:5[5]

---

[3] Daniel Pipes, "Jihad and the Professors," *Commentary* vol. 114, no.4, (November 2002) p.19.

[4] Ibid., p.20.

[5] This verse reads, "But when the sacred months have passed, slay the polytheists wherever you find them, take them captive, besiege them, and lie in ambush for them everywhere."

because of its centrality in that conceptualization, and Qur'an 9:29[6] because of its implications for Muslim-Christian relations. I will further divide this article into two parts, one dealing with the textual foundations of the perpetual war thesis, the other dealing with its contemporary implications.

I. THE PERPETUAL WARFARE THESIS: TEXTUAL FOUNDATIONS

One of the proofs buttressing the case of those Muslims[7] and non-Muslims who claim that Islam advances a theory of perpetual warfare, is Qur'an 9:5, a verse sometimes referred to as the "Verse of the Sword." This verse is said to abrogate all of the verses advocating restraint, compassion, peaceful preaching, mutual respect, and coexistence between Muslims and non-Muslims. Hence, many Western writers cite this verse to justify a state of permanent war between Muslims and non-Muslims. There are also numerous classical Muslim exegetes who explain the verse in a way that

[6] This verse reads, "Fight against those People of the Book [Jews and Christians] who do not believe in Allah nor the Last Day; those who forbid not that which Allah and His Messenger have forbidden; those who do not accept the Religion of Truth, until they pay the tribute out of hand, with all due humility."

[7] In modern times, it is difficult to find many Muslims who advocate the idea that Jihad embodies a scheme of indiscriminate, perpetual warfare. This is why I distinguish between classical Muslim exegetes and modern radicals. For example, bin Laden's infamous 1998 "fatwa" advocated the indiscriminate killing of Americans and their allies, and not all "infidels." For a translation of the most virulent passages of that document, see Bernard Lewis, "License to Kill: Osama bin Laden's Declaration of Jihad," *Foreign Affairs* vol.77, no.6 (November–December 1998), pp.14–19. A more textually grounded, if distorted, modern-day Muslim interpretation of Jihad, an interpretation which moves closer to the idea of permanent war, is that of Abd al-Salaam Faraj, *al-Farida al-Gha'iba*, trans. Johannes J. G. Jansen, *The Neglected Duty: The Creed of Sadat's Assassins and Islamic Resurgence in the Middle East* (New York: Macmillan, 1986). Both Faraj and bin Laden have been influenced by the writings of Sayyid Qutb, the Egyptian thinker whose seminal writings on Jihad and Muslim/non-Muslim relations have influenced many contemporary Islamic radicals. Qutb's radical interpretation of Islamic doctrine can be found in his exegesis of the Qur'an, *Fi Dhilal al-Qur'an*, (Cairo, Egypt: Dar al-Shuruq, 1996). His views on Jihad have been most cogently stated in *Ma'alam fi al-Tariq*, translated as *Milestones* (Delhi, India: Markazi Maktaba Islami, 1988). This small treatise sets forth the clearest modern-day Muslim statement of the Jihad as "perpetual war" thesis. Qutb's writings exerted a powerful influence on a generation of Islamic thinkers and activists in the 1970s and 1980s. Their importance, therefore, cannot be minimized. However, with the revival of traditional learning in many Muslim societies, the spread of the same among converts during the 1990s, and the strength of the apolitical, anti-Jihad branch of the Salafi movement—the followers of Nasir al-Din al-Albani, Qutb's influence is clearly on the wane among today's Muslim youth.

supports this perpetual war thesis.[8] However, a closer examination of this verse reveals that this is not how the vast majority of exegetes have understood it.

In properly understanding the "Verse of the Sword," one must place it in context. This verse is part of a series of verses, located at the beginning of the ninth chapter of the Qur'an, dealing with the polytheists. The first of these verses begins with the statement, "[This is] a declaration of immunity from Allah and His Messenger to those polytheists with whom you have made pacts."[9] In the subsequent discussion of this declaration, many mitigating conditions, which argue against the idea of a perpetual, unrelenting war against non-Muslims, are mentioned.

First of all, many of the classical exegetes explain that these verses do not apply to Jews and Christians. Their discussion of the verses in question center on relations with the polytheists, to the exclusion of the "People of the Book." For example, Imam al-Qurtubi (d.671 AH), renowned for his exposition on the legal implications of the Qur'anic text, states, concerning the verse in question:

> [...] it is permissible to [understand] that the expression "polytheists" does not deal with Jews and Christians (*Ahl al-Kitab*).[10]

This opinion is reinforced by the interpretation of a related Prophetic tradition, "I have been ordered to fight the people until they testify that there is no God but God ..."[11] Imam Nawawi (d.676 AH) mentions in his commentary on this tradition:

> Al-Khattabi says, "It is well-known that what is intended here are the people of idolatry, not the people of the Book (Jews and Christians).[12]

Among contemporary exegetes, Dr. Mustafa al-Bugha says, commenting on the term *Naas* (people), which occurs in this tradition, "They are the

---

[8] See for example, Ibn Juzayy al-Kalbi, *al-Tashil li'Ulum al-Tanzil*, (Beirut, Lebanon: Dar al-Arqam, no date) vol.1, pp.21–22, for a forthright presentation of this idea.

[9] Al-Qur'an 9:1.

[10] Muhammad Ibn Ahmad al-Qurtubi, *al-Jami' li Ahkam al-Qur'an*, (Beirut, Lebanon: Dar al-Fikr, 1987) vol.8, p.72.

[11] Versions of this Hadith are related by al-Bukhari #1399, 1457, 2946; Muslim #124–128; Abu Dawud #1556, 1557; al-Tirmidhi #2607; and al-Nasa'i #2442, 3091–3093.

[12] Al-Imam Muhyiddin Al-Nawawi, *al-Minhaj: Sharh Sahih Muslim,* (Beirut, Lebanon: Dar al-Ma'rifah, 1998) vol.1, p.156.

worshipers of idols and the polytheists."[13] Imam Abu Hanifa, Imam Ahmad, and most contemporary scholars, are of the opinion that the polytheists who are to be indiscriminately fought are those living in the Arabian Peninsula.[14] As that area has been free from polytheism since the earliest days of Islam, according to their opinion, the order is now a dead letter.

Just as we can argue that the people who are to be fought against are not an unrestricted class, based on a classical understanding of the "Verse of the Sword," there are also considerations governing when the restricted classes can be fought. In the verse preceding the "Verse of the Sword," we read:

> [...] except those you have convened a treaty with from the polytheists; when they have not breached any of its conditions, nor supported anyone in aggression against you, complete the terms of the treaty.[15]

Imam al-Qurtubi says concerning this verse, "Even if the terms of the covenant are for more than four months."[16] This condition and others mentioned in the verses following the "Verse of the Sword," led Abu Bakr ibn al-'Arabi (d.543 AH), the great Maliki exegete and jurist, to conclude:

> It is clear that the intended meaning of the verse is to kill those polytheists who are waging war against you.[17]

In other words, fighting them is conditional on their aggression against the Muslim community. This position, the permissibility to fight in order to repulse aggression, is the view of the majority of the Sunni Muslim legal schools as has been explained in great detail by Dr. Muhammad Sa'id Ramadan al-Buti in his valuable discussion of the rationale for Jihad.[18]

---

[13] Dr. Mustafa al-Bugha and Muhyiddin Mistu, *al-Wafi: Fi Sharh al-Arba'in al-Nawawiyy*, (Damascus, Syria: Dar al-'Ulum al-Insaniyya, n.d.), p.47.

[14] For a summary of the jurists' views as to the lawfulness of unrestricted warfare against the polytheists of the Arabian Peninsula, see Dr. Muhammad Khayr Haykal, *al-Jihad w'al-Qital fii al-Siyasa al-Shar'iyya* (Beirut, Lebanon: Dar al-Bayadir, 1996), pp. 1456–1457.

[15] Al-Qur'an, 9:4.

[16] Al-Qurtubi, vol.8, p.71.

[17] Abu Bakr Muhammad Ibn al-'Arabi, *Ahkam al-Qur'an* (Beirut, Lebanon: Dar al-Fikr, n.d.), vol. 3, p. 406.

[18] See Muhammad Sa'id Ramadan al-Buti, *al-Jihad fii al-Islam*, (Beirut, Lebanon: Dar al-Fikr, 1997) for an insightful discussion of the rulings and rationale for warfare in Islam. Unfortunately, no English translation is available to date.

Another argument against the indiscriminate application of the "Verse of the Sword" is the view of many classical exegetes and jurists that it is abrogated by the verse:

> Then, when you encounter the disbelievers in battle, smite their necks; after you have routed them, bind (the prisoners) tightly. Then set them free or ransom them [...][19]

The point to be made here is that if an indiscriminate, unconditional order has been given to kill the non-Muslims, how can one have a choice to free or ransom them?

Imam al-Qurtubi mentions that al-Dahhak, 'Ata, and others are of the opinion that the above-mentioned verse [47:4] abrogates the "Verse of the Sword." Al-Thawri relates from Juwaybir, that al-Dahhak said:

> [The verse,] "Slay the polytheists wherever you find them..." is abrogated by the verse, "Then set them free or ransom them [...]"[20]

Imam al-Tabari (d.310 AH), the dean of all classical Qur'anic exegetes, reaches the following conclusion concerning this latter verse, after mentioning the proofs of those who consider that it abrogates or is abrogated by the "Verse of the Sword":

> The correct opinion in this discussion, as far as we are concerned, is that this verse [47:4] is effective, it has not been abrogated. This is because the description of what constitutes an abrogating or an abrogated [verse], which has been mentioned in more than one place in this book of ours, occurs when it is not possible to join the two conflicting rulings advanced by the verses, or there is convincing proof that one of the rulings abrogates the other. [In this case] it isn't farfetched to say that a choice has been given to the Messenger of Allah, peace and blessings of Allah upon him, and those charged with the affairs of the community after him, between liberating, ransoming, or executing [the combatant non-Muslims].[21]

Hence, Imam al-Tabari holds that the soundest opinion is to join between the two verses. This opinion serves as the basis for the sort of flexibility

---

[19] Al-Qur'an, 47:4.
[20] Al-Qurtubi, vol.16, p.227.
[21] Al-Tabari, *Tafsir al-Tabari* (Beirut, Lebanon: Dar al-Kutub al'Ilmiyya, 1997), vol. 11, p.307.

and moderation that has governed the policy of the Muslim community towards non-Muslims for much of its history. This attitude is supported by other verses in the Qur'an, all of which argue against the idea of indiscriminate or perpetual warfare against non-Muslims. Among them are the following:

> "Almighty God does not forbid you to be kind and equitable to those disbelievers who have not made war on your religion, nor driven you from your homes. Almighty God loves those who are equitable."[22]

> "If they [the enemy forces] incline towards peace, then you should so incline, and place your trust in Almighty God."[23]

> "Fight in the Way of Almighty God those who fight you, but do not initiate hostilities. Almighty God loves not the aggressors."[24]

Our discussion to this point has focused on Qur'an 9:5 because of its centrality in the argument of the advocates of the perpetual war thesis. Here we wish to discuss some issues which arise from Qur'an 9:29. This verse is critical for Muslims in determining the parameters of our relationship with Jews and Christians. Unfortunately, this verse has been misunderstood by some Muslims and used to advance a theory of constant warfare between Muslims, and Jews and Christians. Sayyid Qutb, in his commentary on this verse advocates such warfare.[25] Dr. Sherman Jackson has examined some of the methodological flaws of Qutb's argument in his valuable article, "Jihad in the Modern World".[26] Jackson raises issues relating to alternative Qur'anic verses which mitigate the harsh tone of Qur'an 9:29, as well as historical developments which force Muslims to reconsider the prevailing legal implications of the verse. Those developments center on the evolution of an international political regime, which has made peace the norm governing international relations. This situation is in opposition to pre-modern times when war prevailed.

Even a superficial reading of Qur'an 9:29 reveals that it cannot be the basis for a scheme that advocates perpetual war. Such a reading clearly

---

[22] Al-Qur'an, 60:8.   [23] Al-Qur'an, 8:61.   [24] Al-Qur'an, 2:190.

[25] See Qutb, *Fii Dhilal al-Qur'an*, 3: 1619–1650.

[26] See in this regard, Sherman A. Jackson, "Jihad in the Modern World," *The Journal of Islamic Law and Culture*, vol.7, no.1 (Spring/Summer 2002), pp.22–24.

indicates that fighting the People of the Book is conditional on their refusal to pay a nominal tribute, *al-Jizya*, in exchange for protection by the Muslim authorities and exemption from military service. Despite the nominal nature of that tribute, there are those, Muslim and non-Muslim, who seek to use the verse as the basis for a scheme which totally humiliates Jews and Christians living in the Islamic realm. An examination of exegetical sources reveals that attempts to present this verse as the basis for such humiliation are disingenuous. Such attempts are based on the interpretation of the term, *wa hum saghirun*, as meaning "utterly subdued."[27] However, classical exegetes differed on the meaning of this term. Imam al-Tabari mentions several sayings in that regard, among them:

> "The legitimate interpreters differ as to the meaning of the word, "*al-Sighar,*" which Almighty God means at this point [*wa hum saghirun*]. Some of them say that he [the Jew or Christian] pays it [the tribute] standing while the recipient is seated." And, "Others say [it means] that they bring it themselves, walking, even if they dislike this." He also mentions, "Some say that its mere payment is humbling."[28]

All of these interpretations mentioned by al-Tabari, and others,[29] belie the idea that the *Jizya* is a tribute designed to "utterly subdue," or totally humiliate Jews and Christians living in the Islamic realm. Rather, the humility is to be manifested at the time of actually paying the tribute, and not in debasing or demeaning treatment afterwards. The accuracy of this conclusion is born out by the fact that the expression "*wa hum saghirun*" is an adverbial clause describing the state of those paying the tribute at the actual instance of payment. For this reason, I have translated the relevant passage in this verse, "[…] until they pay the tribute out of hand, with all due humility.[30]

These exegetical understandings were reflected in the writings of the jurists. For example, the scholars agree that anything which would be deemed offensive to a Muslim is forbidden to visit upon a protected Jew or Christian. Anything that would demean, belittle, or oppress a protected

---

[27] This translation of the term, *wa hum saghirun*, is found in *The Holy Qur'an: With English Translation* (Istanbul, Turkey: Ilmi Nesriyat, 1996), p.190.

[28] Al-Tabari, vol. 6, pp. 350.

[29] See for example, Ibn al-'Arabi, vol.2, pp. 479–480.

[30] See our translation of the entire verse in note #6, above.

non-Muslim is strictly forbidden.[31] This prohibition emanates from the Prophetic Tradition, "As for one who oppresses a protected non-Muslim, or belittles him, or burdens him above his capability [if he employees him], or takes anything from him against his will, I will be his disputant on the Day of Resurrection."[32] It is even forbidden to address him with such terms as "nonbeliever."[33]

Furthermore, the tribute is not universally applicable. For example, it is not to be paid by women, children, unemployed men, those nursing lengthy illnesses, the terminally ill, the blind, the elderly, or bondsmen. In modern times, jurists are in agreement that the tribute mentioned in Qur'an 9:29 can be applied nominally as the type of taxes modern states levy against the generality of their citizenry. This is based on the precedent of 'Umar ibn al-Khattab in his dealings with Bani Taghlib ibn Wa'il. When that Christian Arab tribe protested against the tribute as demeaning, 'Umar accepted it from them, nominally, in the same manner the poor due was taken from Muslims.[34]

A full exposition of this subject would be quite lengthy, as there are many aspects of the issue I have not explored. Before moving to the second part of this article, I wish to examine one final issue, as it has direct bearing on the situation confronting Muslims currently. It also presents an Islamic teaching that mitigates against the permanence of warfare in Islam. This issue is associated with one of the foundational Islamic legal principles, "Harm is to be removed."[35] This principle is based on the prophetic tradition, "There is no facilitating or reciprocating harm."[36] One of the implications of this principle is giving preference to warding off harm over securing a benefit. Hence, even though Jihad has been legislated for Muslims, in circumstances where its prosecution threatens widespread

---

[31] For a discussion of this issue see Dr. Muhammad Khayr Haykal, *al-Jihad w'al-Qital fii al-Siyasa al-Shar'iyya* (Beirut, Lebanon: Dar al-Bayariq, 1996), pp.1467–1470.

[32] Abu Dawud al-Sajistani, *Sunan Abu Dawud* (Riyadh, Saudi Arabia: Dar al-Salaam, 1999), p.447, #3052.

[33] Haykal, op. cit., p.1469.

[34] Abu Bakr al-Bayhaqi, *al-Sunan al-Kubra* (Beirut, Lebanon: Dar al-Kutub al-'Ilmiyya, 1994), p. 315, #18,645.

[35] For a discussion of the meaning, textual foundation, and application of this principle see 'Ali Ahmad al-Nadawi, *al-Qawa'id al-Fiqhiyya* (Damascus, Syria: Dar al-Qalam, 2000), pp.287–293.

[36] This tradition is included by Imam Nawawi in his *al-Arba'in*, see al-Bugha, *al-Wafi*, p.239.

harm to the Muslim community, it should be left. Al-Khatib al-Shirbini states in *Mughni al-Muhtaj*:

> If the non-Muslim forces are at least double the Muslim force [...] and if we feel that we will be annihilated with no chance of victory, it is incumbent upon us to leave [off war].[37]

The current state of the Muslims clearly indicates that at this critical juncture in our history, we should be thinking deeply about the implications of warfare, in light of this jurisprudential principle. The increasing destructiveness of modern military technology and the growing gap between the West and the Muslim world are creating a situation where it is becoming increasingly difficult to achieve any of the objectives that underlie Islamic law through armed conflict. While Muslim nations may well be able to resist, and possibly repulse armed aggression from the West, the price associated with such resistance has to be carefully assessed, and alternative strategies of resistance considered. We will return to this issue in the second part of this article.

II. CONTEMPORARY IMPLICATIONS OF THE PERPETUAL WAR THESIS

The above discussion should make it clear that Islam, even in its classical formulation, has never advocated a theory of perpetual, indiscriminate warfare. Attempts to present Islam as the new communism, a system locked in a life and death struggle with the West, while making for good ideology, are fundamentally flawed, and could lead to disastrous consequences for both the United States and the Muslim world.

In the aftermath of the Cold War, elements of this country's foreign policy establishment have been searching for an enemy menacing enough to justify a huge and wasteful military budget. Throughout the 1990s rogue states and international terrorism emerged as the most pressing threats to US global interests. These two threats came to be epitomized by Taliban-dominated Afghanistan, the ultimate rogue state; and Osama bin Laden, the ultimate terrorist.

---

[37] Al-Khatib al-Shirbini, *Mughni al-Muhtaj* (Beirut, Lebanon: Dar al-Marifa, 1997), vol.4, p.226.

However, neither was considered a systemic threat, which could rationalize defense budgets exceeding 300 billion dollars annually. China was the only international actor whose stature could even remotely justify such spending. That being the case, confusion prevailed in the defense establishment, with all departments preparing for inevitable budget cuts and restructuring. When Osama bin Laden was implicated in the attacks on New York and the Pentagon, a powerful incentive was presented to establishment ideologues to find an underlying motivation that could explain the inevitable appearance of future bin Ladens. Hence, the "Jihad as perpetual war thesis." A perpetual threat to America would mean perpetual preparedness, and perpetually large defense budgets to fight Bush's "war that would last a lifetime."

The Pentagon's *Quadrennial Defense Review Report,* which was prepared to describe China as the greatest strategic threat to America's international interests prior to September 11, 2001, was subsequently changed by the administration to present

[...] a scruffy band of terrorists—desperate fanatics who exist in tiny numbers and in many places—[as] their principal enemies for the indeterminate future.[38]

Gabriel Kolko and others rightfully dismiss the threat posed to US interests by radical Islamic groups.[39] The inherent weakness of those groups was illustrated by the ease with which the Saudi and Egyptian regimes were able to repulse the challenge of bin Laden's al-Qaʿida and Ayman al-Dhawahiri's Jihad Islami respectively, during the mid-1990s.[40]

---

[38] Gabriel Kolko, *Another Century of War,* (New York, NY: The New Press, 2002) p.127.

[39] For an insightful, balanced assessment of the threat posed by radical and other Islamic groups, see John L. Esposito, *The Islamic Threat: Myth or Reality,* (New York, Oxford: Oxford University Press, 1992). Especially useful is the final chapter, "Islamic Fundamentalism and the West."

[40] Attempts to overstate the strategic threat posed by al-Qaʿida are disingenuous and dangerous. Although the threat of random acts of terrorism against American targets is quite real, that threat existed before September 11, 2001, as illustrated by the embassy bombings in Africa, and the attack on the USS Cole. However, as a result of increased American vigilance, such attacks are far less likely today. Clearly, military aggression is no way to combat small group terrorism. One must note that it was military aggression, specifically the Gulf War, which turned bin Laden, a former ally, against the United States. Virtually all accounts of bin Laden's life mention the Gulf War as a critical turning point. For a fairly objective, concise treatment of the evolution of bin Laden's war against America see Gilles Kepel, *Jihad: The Trail of Political Islam* (Cambridge, Massachusetts: Belknap/The Harvard University Press, 2002), pp.313–322.

Despite the innate weakness of such groups, America can do little to destroy them, owing to their diffuse nature. Her military machine has been designed to confront the large, standing, fixed-piece army of the former Soviet Union. What she will probably do is engage in jingoistic campaigns such as the recent Afghanistan War, which while ostensibly undertaken to confront the evil of "terrorism," only add to the desperation and suffering of ordinary Muslims.

These campaigns will likely bring immediate military victories, but long-term political disasters. They will help to create the conditions that will swell the ranks of radical Islamic groups, and engender a deep anti-Americanism throughout the Muslim world, making the realization of American interests in the region, without the use of direct force, or increasingly venal and ruthless proxy regimes, virtually impossible. Unable to resist through conventional means, Muslim radicals are likely to resort to increasingly irrational terrorist attacks, attacks which are nearly impossible to predict or effectively combat.

As the growing anti-war movement indicates, the American public does not desire such wars. Additionally, the draconian measures being taken by our government in the name of combating terrorism are leading to increasingly bold criticisms of America's post 9/11 strategic posture. This trend is illustrated by the emergence of the powerful movement protesting an invasion of Iraq which emerged even before the first troops landed.

Such wars are also undesirable to ordinary Muslims. As for the extreme radical elements within Muslim ranks, it is time for them to realize that inflammatory rhetoric, delusional visions and terrorist acts are no substitute for a realistic, pragmatic strategy of empowerment. Just as the radical Islamic groups had no viable deterrent to American air power in Afghanistan, they possess no credible deterrent to the nuclear warheads, which have been turned away from their original targets in the former Soviet Union, and redirected towards the major population centers of the Muslim world. In addition to those weapons, a new generation of tactical nuclear warheads is being developed for use in battles that will ultimately be fought in the Islamic heartland, along with conventional devises of unproven destructiveness, such as massive fuel-air explosive devices, electromagnetic weapons, particle-beam devices, and stun gases which can temporarily incapacitate the population of entire towns.

We have seen the devastating effect of nearly 200 tons of depleted uranium used on armor piercing projectiles during the 1991 Gulf War.[41] Many areas of the Iraqi ecosystem have been contaminated for generations to come. Similar environmental damage has been caused by tons of incinerated chemical and biological agents, as well as spilled and incinerated crude oil and petrochemical derivatives. Unless the reigning climate of irrational confrontation is reversed, we can realistically anticipate similar ecological disasters, and their associated human costs, as well the possibility of a direct nuclear attack against the defenseless populations of the Muslim World. Mr. Bush has already threatened such an attack.

Changing the current political climate will require a thorough reassessment of all of its ideological premises. Rejecting the "Islam as permanent warfare" thesis is a big step in the right direction. An additional step would involve a total rethinking of our contemporary security paradigm. The current American policy of violent confrontation, vilification, and isolation will only increase the socioeconomic polarization, environmental destruction, and militarization, which will combine to produce further instability and violence in the global system, especially in the Muslim world. Such tactics are part of a failed paradigm, as the tragedy of September 11, 2001 has made painfully clear. If America acts with courage, wisdom, and vision, she can begin restructuring the international system in ways that truly enhance our collective security. Her failure to do so could mean another century of increasingly deadly wars, wars that will have no real winners.[42]

---

[41] For a thorough, if frightening, exposé of the origins and dangers of depleted uranium weapons, including their connection to Gulf War Syndrome, see International Action Center, *Metal of Dishonor, Depleted Uranium: How the Pentagon Radiates Soldiers and Civilians with DU Weapons* (New York, NY: Depleted Uranium Project International Action Center, 1997).

[42] For an informed critique of the contemporary global security paradigm, and the outlines of an alternative arrangement, see Paul Rogers, *Losing Control: Global Security in the Twenty-first Century,* (London: Pluto Press, 2000).

13 | Tradition or Extradition? The Threat to Muslim-Americans

ABDAL HAKIM MURAD

Is AMERICAN ISLAM inevitable? Until recently we scarcely asked the question. We assumed that the demography of the East, and the expanding economies of the West, made nothing so certain as continued Muslim immigration to the United States, and the progressive entrenchment of Muslim believers in the diverse American socio-economic reality.

The rise of al-Qaʻida has now placed that assurance in question. An ever-increasing number of scholars and politicians in the West are voicing their doubts about the Muslim presence. Citing the Yale academic Lamin Sanneh, the right-wing English journalist Melanie Phillips suggests that the time has come to think again about Muslim immigration to the West.[1] Sanneh, whose views on Islam's reluctance to adjust to the claims of citizenship in non-Muslim states seem very congenial to right-wing theorists, is here being used to reinforce the agenda that is increasingly recommended on the far right across Europe, with electrifying effects on the polls.

Cooler heads, such as John Esposito and James Morris, reject the alarmism of Sanneh and Phillips. Contrary to stereotypes, they insist, Islam has usually been good at accommodating itself to minority status. The story of Islam in traditional China, where it served the emperors so

---

[1] Melanie Phillips, 'How the West was lost', *The Spectator*, 11 May 2002. Speaking to an Anglican conference, Sanneh remarked: 'It is only a thin secular wall that prevents the Islamic tide from sweeping over the west [...] Islam might be called a religion that has almost no questions and no answers [...] That revelation is externalised and fossilized. Islam is a set of immutable divine laws [...] Islam is a religious imperialism [..., but] God delights in our freedom and not in our enslavement.' (www.latimer.org.nz, accessed on 3 April 2003.) The replication of traditional anti-Semitic language is striking; see note 5 below.

faithfully that it was recognized as one of the semi-official religions of the Chinese state, represented the norm rather than the exception. Minority status is nothing new for Islam, and around the boundaries of the Islamic world, Muslims have consistently shown themselves to be good citizens in contexts a good deal less multiculturalist than our own.[2] The Hanafi school of Islamic law is particularly insistent on the sacrosanct nature of the covenant of *aman* (safe-conduct) which Muslim minorities enter into with non-Muslim governments. It is forbidden, even in times of war, for Muslims living under those governments to commit crimes against non-Muslims, even when those powers are at war with Muslim states.[3] The jurists note that Ja'far, the Prophet's cousin, had no objection to serving in the army of a Christian king.[4]

The anti-Dreyfusard charge against the Muslim presence, however, knows nothing of this. In consequence, where a hundred years ago the cultivated Western public problematized Jews, it is now Muslims who are feeling the pressure. Anti-Semites once baited the Jews as an alien, Oriental intrusion into white, Christian lands, a Semitic people whose loyalty to its own Law would always render its loyalty to King and Country dubious. Christianity, on this Victorian view, recognized a due division between religion and state; while the Semitic Other could not. There was little wonder in this. The Christian, as heir to the Hellenic vision of St Paul, was free in the spirit. The Semitic Jew was bound to the Law. He could hence never progress or become reconciled to the value of Gentile compatriots. Ultimately, his aim was to subvert, dominate, and possess.[5]

---

[2] John Esposito, *The Islamic Threat: Myth or Reality?* 3rd edition (New York, 1999), pp.233–40; James Morris, 'The Unique Opportunities and Challenges Facing American Muslims in the New Century,' *The American Muslim*, vol. 12 (2002), pp.17–26. For Chinese Muslim integration see Sachiko Murata, *Chinese Gleams of Sufi Light: Wai-Tai-yü's Great Learning of the Pure and Real and Liu Chih's Displaying the Concealment of the Real Realm* (Albany, 2000); P.D. Buell, 'Saiyid Ajall (1211–1279)', in E. de Rachewiltz, Hok-lam Chan, Hsiao Ch'i-ch'ing, and P.W. Geier (eds), *In the service of the Khan: eminent personalities of the early Mongol-Yüan period (1200–1300)* (Wiesbaden, 1993), pp.466-79. For the theory see Tim Winter, 'Some thoughts on the formation of British Muslim identity', *Encounters* 8 (2002), pp.3–26; Khaled Abou el-Fadl, 'Striking a Balance: Islamic Legal Discourses on Muslim Minorities', in Yvonne Yazbeck Haddad and John L. Esposito (eds.), *Muslims on the Americanization Path?* (Oxford, 2000).

[3] Shams al-Din al-Sarakhsi, *al-Mabsut* (Cairo, 1324 AH), X, p.88; cf. Abou el-Fadl, p.59.

[4] Sarakhsi, X, p.98.

[5] Rosemary Ruether, *Faith and Fratricide: The Theological Roots of Anti-Semitism* (London, 1975), p.241 and *passim*. Modern studies of European Fascism increasingly identify classical readings of St

Few in the West seem to have spotted this similarity. One of the great ironies of the present crisis is that many of the most outspoken defenders of the State of Israel are implicitly affirming anti-Semitic categories in the way they deny the value of Islam. Pim Fortuyn, the Dutch anti-immigration politician who proposed the closure of Holland's mosques, published his book *Against the Islamisation of our Culture* to celebrate the fiftieth anniversary of the creation of Israel. Yet his book is filled with characterizations of the new Muslim presence that fit perfectly the categories of anti-Semitism. The Muslim Other is irrational. He mistreats his women. He obeys primitive dietary laws. He is driven by the Law, not the Spirit. He must, therefore, be always the same, a single phenomenon, incapable of reform. His intentions are not to enrich his country of adoption, but to overcome it for the sake of a transnational religious enterprise of domination and contempt.[6]

We are, in a sense, the New Jews. An odd transposition has taken place, with one religious community ducking from beneath a Christian yoke, which then found Muslim shoulders to rest on.[7] We have little time or inclination to contemplate the irony of this strange alteration, however; since we cannot ignore the fate of the prejudice's earlier victims, and its current prospects. The road from Auschwitz to Srebrenica was not such

---

Paul as one strand in its composition. For Nazi enthusiasm for Paul, see, for instance, Frank Thielman, *From Plight to Solution: A Jewish Framework for Understanding Paul's View of the Law in Galatians and Romans* (Leiden, 1989), pp.6–9. For the still inadequately addressed tragedy of Lutheran theological support for Nazism, see Robert P. Ericksen, *Theologians under Hitler: Gerhard Kittel, Paul Althaus and Emmanuel Hirsch* (New Haven, 1985); p.67 for the Jews' 'rigid legalism'; p.68 for the universalism of Christianity as opposed to the text-based particularism of the Semite; p.163 for 'Christianity as the only religion based upon a free, personal, individual relationship to God'; p.165 for the separation of faith from politics; etc. Cf. also Robert P. Ericksen and Susannah Heschel (eds.), *Betrayal: German Churches and the Holocaust* (Minneapolis, 1999), for instance p.16, for those who contrasted the 'religion of the heart' with 'the religion of the Pharisees', which 'consisted almost exclusively in observances'. The work of Thielman, Longenecker, Parkes and others has done much to blunt this traditional polarisation; as yet, however, the old categorisations are still regularly applied to the 'other Semites,' with serious political consequences. Compare Serbian nationalist scholars of Islam, who consider it 'totalitarian': Michael Sells, *The Bridge Betrayed: Religion and Genocide in Bosnia* (Berkeley and London, 1996), 202, to which Sells replies: 'If the term "totalitarian" is to be applied to Islam because the religion is not restricted to private life, then it must also be applied to Halakhic Judaism'.

[6] For Fortuyn, see Angus Roxburgh, *Preachers of Hate: The Rise of the Far Right* (London, 2002), pp.158–78; Andrew Osborn in *The Guardian*, 9 July 2002.

[7] Cf. Nick Ryan, *Homeland: Into a World of Hate* (Edinburgh, 2003), p.294: "'Is Islam a greater threat than international Judaism – especially after 11 September?' [...] "The enemy is changing," he says.' (Interview with Christian Worch, German neo-Nazi leader.)

a crooked one; and the new rightist politicians in the West are surely positioned somewhere along that road.

Given that al-Qa'ida, or its surrogates, have massively reinforced this new chauvinism, it is depressing that its roots and possible entailments have yet to be assessed by most Muslim advocates in the West. But we need to look it in the eyes. We are hated by very many people; and cannot discount the possibility that this hatred will spill over into immigration filters, mosque closures, the prohibition of *hijab* in schools, and a generalized demonising of Muslims that makes the risk of rioting or state repression against us uncomfortably great. Liberalism, as the Weimar Republic discovered, can be a fragile ideology.

Nevertheless, the charge requires a frank response. Was our immigration purely economic? Or did we arrive to take tactical advantage of liberal press laws in order to launch a subversive internationalist agenda that will be profoundly damaging to our hosts? Are we Americans, or Canadians, or Britons, simply by virtue of holding a passport and finding employment? Or is this our emotional home?

Traditional Islam has been expert in adoption and adaptation. The new anti-Semitism makes not the slightest headway against it. It is also manifestly the case that moderate reformists have produced many American Muslim communities that are sincerely American, and speak frankly against extremism. Yet it needs also to be recognized that a growing number of scriptural-literalist community leaders, particularly those funded by Middle Eastern states where the language of sermons is violently anti-American, are sceptical of the kind of versatility offered by traditional Islam or by the reformers. For them, we will always be a kind of diaspora, with roots in an Arab elsewhere.

An inference needs to be squarely faced. Those whose belongingness to their adopted countries is only about economics cannot blame the host societies for regarding them with dislike and suspicion. For if we are suspicious of non-Muslims in Muslim majority countries who fail to acclimatise themselves to the ambient values and sense of collective purpose of their countries of citizenship, then it is unreasonable that we should demand that they behave differently when it is we who are the minority. A country that accepts migrants, however conspicuously economic their primary motives, has the right to expect that they engage in some form of cultural migration as well. No Muslim would deny that multicultural-ism must always have some limits.

It is time to realise that if we are here purely to enhance our earning power, then our sojourn may prove short-lived. It is annoying that the new kind of sermonizers who are loudest in their demonizing of Western coun-tries are often the slowest to grasp that those countries might turn out not to tolerate them after all. The greatest irony of our situation might just be that our radicals end up on the road to the airport, astonished at the dis-covery that their low opinion of the West turned out to be correct.

A major shift in our self-definition is therefore urgently required. This may be hard for the older generation, most of which is embedded either in regional folklorisms which have no clear future here, or in a Move-ment Islam of various hues. But we need some deep rethinking among the new generation, that minority which has survived assimilation in the schools, and knows enough of the virtues and vices of Western secular society to take stock of where we stand, and decide on the best course of action for our community. It is this new generation that is called upon to demonstrate Islam's ability to extend its traditional capacities for courte-ous acculturation to the new context of the West, and to reject the radi-cal Manichean agenda, supported by the extremists on both sides, which presents Muslim minorities as nothing more than resentful, scheming archipelagos of Middle Eastern difference.

Like all 'hyphenated Americans', US Muslims should be alert to the longstanding ambiguity of a country which used Ellis Island not only to welcome immigrants, but also to deport them when they proved ideolo-gically unsuitable.[8] Current Islamophobic hostilities are not so different from the popular American response to events as distant as the 1886 Hay-market bomb outrage,[9] or the assassination of President McKinley by 'a ragged, unwashed, long-haired, wild-eyed fiend'.[10] The resident alien, and

7 Cf. Nick Ryan, *Homeland: Into a World of Hate* (Edinburgh, 2003), p.294: "'Is Islam a greater threat than international Judaism—especially after 11 September?" […] "The enemy is changing," he says.' (Interview with Christian Worch, German neo-Nazi leader.)

8 William Preston Jr., *Aliens and Dissenters: Federal Suppression of Radicals 1903–1933* (Cambridge MA, 1963), p.190.

9 Malwyn A. Jones, *The Limits of Liberty: American History 1607–1992* (Oxford and New York, se-cond edition 1995), p.323.

10 Preston, op. cit., p.26.

the naturalized American with the foreign accent and appearance who was implicitly in solidarity with murky European comrades, furnished for much of American history the lightning-rod for a host of suspicions. Anarchism and anarcho-syndicalism, culminating in the Red Scare of 1919, quickly triggered a host of restrictive laws and inquisitorial procedures, including summary deportation of aliens and the denial of access to legal counsel until a very late stage of the judicial process. Two years after McKinley's assassination, the 1903 Immigration Act applied ideological filters to immigration applicants for the first time. For their part, radicals such as the socialist leader William Haywood made matters worse by insisting that 'no Socialist can be a law-abiding citizen', and refusing to condemn violent action against governmental or plutocratic targets.[11] In 1906, a new Naturalization Act obliged candidates to swear that they were not anarchists, while the Bureau of Naturalization pronounced that 'As long as the advocates of these malignant and un-American doctrines remain aliens, they may be deported and their gospels may be overthrown at their inception, but once they succeed in obtaining their citizenship, this method of purging our country becomes more difficult, if not impossible.'[12] The 'treasonable ingrates' who had obtained citizenship defended themselves on habeas corpus grounds, only to be thwarted by the use of military rather than civil detention.[13] In 1917, over a thousand were rounded up and deported to a remote stockade in New Mexico.[14]

Anarcho-syndicalism lost its edge, but the underlying energies of American nativism were undiminished. The Ku Klux Klan continued to demand a white, Protestant normalcy in the Southern states, occasionally targeting Arabs as well as Jews, Catholics and African-Americans.[15] And the same New Deal bureaucrats who had resolved many of the resentments of the labour movement were soon rounding up the Japanese-American population amid the confusion and xenophobia that followed the outbreak of war with Japan. Again, existing chauvinisms made this politically straightforward. Long beforehand, the mayor of San Francisco had

[11] Ibid., p.49. [12] Ibid.

[13] Ibid., p.106. The restrictions against Communist immigration were not finally lifted until 1990 (Jones, op. cit., 628).

[14] Preston, op. cit., p.93.

[15] See David M. Chalmers, *Hooded Americanism: The History of the Ku Klux Klan* (Durham, 1987), p.71, for the expulsions of Syrians and Lebanese from a town in Georgia in the 1920s.

announced that 'the Chinese and Japanese are not bona fide citizens. They are not the stuff of which American citizens can be made […] They will not assimilate with us and their social life is different to ours.'[16] After Pearl Harbor, the bank accounts of American citizens of Japanese descent were frozen, and detention camps were set up, with anomalous legal procedures ensuring that appeals against the sentencing were held long after the incarceration began. Replying to liberal protests against the FBI's draconian methods, Chief Justice Harlan Stone explained that 'because racial discriminations are in most circumstances irrelevant and therefore prohibited, it by no means follows that, in dealing with the perils of war, Congress and the Executive are wholly prohibited from taking into account those facts […] which may in fact place citizens of one ancestry in a different category.'[17]

After the war, the nativist inquisition again exhausted itself, only to be revived by the anti-Communist mood of the 1950s. The Emergency Detention Act of 1950 was deliberately modelled on Roosevelt's anti-Japanese measures, taking advantage of the fact that the Supreme Court had already ruled that these had not infringed the Constitution.[18] Again, the nation watched the establishment of detention camps, and the reactivation of the principle of holding hearings after, rather then prior to, incarceration.

What Richard Freeland describes as 'cycles of repression in American history'[19] surfaced again at the end of the 1970s, with the rise of Islamic militancy in the Middle East and nervousness about naturalized and alien individuals of Middle Eastern origin within the United States. Although the Emergency Detention Act had been shamefacedly repealed in 1971, and official contrition for the Japanese-American detentions was now longstanding, the Carter administration considered interning Iranians as a result of the 1979 Tehran hostage crisis.[20]

The events of 11 September triggered a new and particularly vehement wave of repression. Shortly before, one observer had predicted that 'an

---

[16]   Roger Daniels, *Prisoners without Trial: Japanese Americans in World War II* (NY, 1993), p.9.

[17]   Ibid., p.60.

[18]   Ibid., p.110.

[19]   Richard M. Freeland, *The Truman Doctrine and the Origins of McCarthyism: Foreign Policy, Domestic Politics, and Internal Security, 1946–1948* (New York, 1972), p.4.

[20]   Daniels, op. cit., p.112.

event of catastrophic terrorism will bring with it the danger of precipi-
tous action that is detrimental to other social values, such as civil liberties.'[21] The immediately resulting legislation, including the Patriot Act
and the creation of a Department of Homeland Security, empowered
by a remarkably broad definition of domestic terrorism which may be
invoked by FBI investigators armed with new powers of search and
surveillance, has been built on genuine fear of further 'Islamic' acts of
terrorism. History suggests, however, that behind this fear lie much older
themes in American nativism, including biblically-based denunciations
of 'foreign' creeds, racial insecurities, and polemics against the allegedly
high birthrates of the suspect population. As a result, in the words of the
Center for Constitutional Rights,

> In the weeks after September 11th, hundreds or perhaps thousands of indi-
> viduals were rounded up as suspected terrorists [...] They were held with-
> out criminal charges, and often with no access to an attorney. [...] The
> ordeal many endured was harrowing and counterproductive. There have
> been numerous reports of beatings, and many more of less serious mis-
> treatment.[22]

Faced with this incipient inquisition, the community must face the
realisation that the future of Islam in an instinctively nativist land will be
a genuinely American future, if it is to happen at all. As the 'war against
terrorism', with all its clumsy, pixelated violence, and cultural simpli-
fications, gathers momentum, it is likely that there will be further events
and atrocities which will render the current social and psychological
marginality of the community still more precarious. Unless American
Muslims can locate for themselves, and populate, a spiritual and cultural
space which can recognisably be called American, and develop theological and social tools for identifying and thwarting local extremism, they
will increasingly be the target of nativist and implicitly anti-Semitic discourses, with incalculable consequences.

Regrettably—and this is one of its most telling failures—our community leadership has invested much energy in Islamic education, but has

---

[21] Ashton B. Carter and William J. Perry, *Preventive Defense: A New Security Strategy for America*
(Washington, 1999), p.156.

[22] Center for Constitutional Rights Fact Sheet: *Beyond September 11th: balancing security and liberty interests* (New York, 2002).

spent little time studying American culture to locate the multiple elements within it which are worthy of Muslim respect. Too many of the extremist activists dismiss their new compatriots as promiscuous drunkards, or as fundamentalist fanatics. Movement Islam, with its often vehement dislike of the West on grounds that often in practice seem more tribal than spiritual, and rooted in various utopian projects that seldom seem to work even on their own terms, can seem little better. All too frequently it provides ammunition to chauvinists allied to the stance of Daniel Pipes, for whom all 'Islamists' are a fifth column to be viewed with unblinking, baleful suspicion.

The new generation urgently needs to take several courageous steps. Firstly, it needs to acknowledge that furiously anti-Western readings of Islam are unlikely to serve Muslims in the hazardous context of modern America. It is already clear to many that Mawdudi and Qutb were not writing for 21st century Muslim minorities, but for a mid-twentieth century struggle against secular oppression and corruption in majority Muslim lands. They themselves would probably be startled to learn that their books were being pressed on utterly different communities, fifty years on. For too long much of the leadership has read their texts as normative guides; yet our other, less ideological, readings of our tradition are readily available to those with a knowledge of Muslim civilization. As Sachiko Murata notes:

> The fact that so many interpretations of Islam have now been narrowed down to fit into ideological frameworks is simply a reflection of modern Muslims' ignorance of the Islamic tradition and their sense of impotence in the face of the impersonal forces of modernity. It says nothing about the rich resources of the tradition itself.[23]

As well as 'de-ideologizing' Islam, we need to turn again to the religion's founding story for guidance on the correct conduct of guests. An insulting guest will not be tolerated indefinitely even by the most courteous of hosts; and pulpit broadsides against Western culture have to be seen as dangerously unwise. A measured, concerned critique of social dissolution, unacceptable beliefs, or destructive foreign policies will always be a required component of Muslim discourse, but wild denunciations

---

[23] Murata, op. cit., p.7.

of Great Satan's or global Crusader Conspiracies are, for Muslims here, not only dangerous, but are also discourteous—scarcely a lesser sin. This must be made absolutely clear to organisations which offer our communities funding from totalitarian states.

Imam al-Ghazali provides us with some precious lessons on the conduct of the courteous guest. He cites the saying that 'part of humility before God is to be satisfied with an inferior sitting-place.' The guest should greet those he is sitting beside, even if he should privately be uncomfortable with them. He should not dominate the conversation, or loudly criticise others at the feast, or allow himself to be untidy. Ghazali also tells us that he should not keep looking at the kitchen door, which would imply that he is primarily present for the food. It is hard to avoid thinking of this when one contemplates the loud demands of many Muslims, particularly in Europe, for financial payouts from the state. If we wish to be tolerated and respected, one of our first responsibilities is surely to seek employment, and avoid reliance on the charity of our hosts. Reliance on affirmative-action policies, or outright sloth, are likely to provoke a backlash.[24]

Some hardline scholars of the Hanbali persuasion took a narrow view of the duty of guests. Imam Ahmad himself said that if a guest sees a kohl-stick with a silver handle, he should leave the house at once, on the grounds that it is a place of luxurious indulgence. Yet for Imam al-Ghazali, and for the great majority of scholars, one should always give one's host the benefit of the doubt.[25] And in the West, our neighbours usually fall into the category of *ahl al-kitab*, for whom certain things are permissible that we would condemn among Muslims. Resentment, contempt, hypercriticism, all these vices are discourteous and inappropriate, particularly when used to disguise one's dissatisfaction with oneself, or with one's own community's position in the world.

The refugee, or migrant, is therefore subject to the high standards that Islam, with its Arabian roots, demands of the guest. Discourtesy is dishonour. And nowhere in the Prophetic biography do we find this principle more nobly expressed than in the episode of the First Hijra. Here, the

---

[24] The recent revival in KKK fortunes may be partly the consequence of affirmative action policies (Chalmers, op. cit., p.435).

[25] Abu Hamid al-Ghazali, *Ihya' 'Ulum al-Din* (Cairo, 1347 AH), II, pp.11–15.

first Muslim asylum-seekers stand before the Emperor of Abyssinia to explain why they should be allowed to stay. Among them were Uthman and Ruqaiyya, and Ja'far and Asma', all young people famous for their physical beauty. Umm Salama, another eyewitness, narrates the respect with which the Muslims attended upon the Christian king. They would not compromise their faith, but they were reverent and respectful to the beliefs of an earlier dispensation. Their choice of the annunciation story from the Qur'an was inspired, showing the Christians present that the Muslim scripture itself is not utterly alien, but is beautiful, dignified, and contains much in common with Christian belief. Stressing what they held in common with their hosts, they made a hugely favourable impression, and their security in the land was assured.[26]

Today, we seem less inclined to use the Chapter of Mary as the basis for our self-presentation to the host community. Instead, we create lobby groups that adopt provocatively loud criticisms of American policy, thereby closing the door to any possibility that they might be heard. Many of our sermons pay little attention to the positive qualities in our neighbours, but instead recite dire warnings of the consequences to our souls of becoming 'like Americans'. Again, the danger is that the cumulative image given by angry American Muslims will result in our being treated as cuckoos in the nest, stripped of rights, and even ejected altogether. In the long term, the choice is between deportment, and deportation.

Faced with this new nativist inquisition, American Muslim communities need a new agenda. This need not be sought in an Islamic liberalism. Liberalism in religion has a habit of leading to the attenuation of faith, and its resources for dealing with extremism are severely limited. Instead, the surest option seems to be a return to the spirit of our tradition, and quarry it for resources that will enable us to regain the Companions' capacity for courteous conviviality.

One step forward will be the realisation that Islamic civilisation was a providential success story. Salafist and modernist agendas which present medieval Islam as little more than obscurantism or as wicked deviation from scripture will leave us orphaned from the evolving and magnificent story of Muslim civilisation. If we accept that classical Islam was a

---

[26] See e.g., Ibn Ishaq, *Sira*, tr. A. Guillaume as *The Life of Muhammad* (Oxford, 1955), pp.146–154; the annunciation is described in Qur'an, chapter 19.

deviant reading of our scriptures, we surrender to the claims of a certain type of Christian evangelical Orientalism, which claims that the glories of Muslim civilisation arose despite, not because of, the Qur'an. We are called to be the continuation of a magnificent story, not a footnote to its first chapter.

A recovery of our sense of pride in Islam's cultural achievements will allow us to reactivate a principle that has hardly been touched by most Muslim communities in the West, namely the obligation to witness. It is evident that *da'wa* is our primary duty as a Muslim minority; indeed, al-Mawardi considered it a valid reason for taking up residence outside the House of Islam;[27] and it is no less evident that this becomes difficult if we abandon tradition in order to insist on rigorist and narrow readings of the Shari'a. Our neighbours will not heed our invitation unless we can show that there is some common ground, that we have something worth having, and, even more significantly, that we are worth joining. Radical and literalist Islamic agendas frequently seem to be advocated by unsmiling zealots, whose tension, arrogance and misery are all too legible on their faces. Few reasonable people will consider the religious claims made by individuals who seem to have been made miserable and desperate by those claims. More usually, they will be repelled, and retreat into negative chauvinism.

The face is the believer's greatest argument. True religion lights up the face; false religion fills it with insecurity, rage and suspicion. This is perceptible not only to insiders, but to anyone who maintains some connection with unsullied primordial human nature. The early conversions to Islam often took place among populations that had no access to the language of the Muslims who now lived among them; but they were no less profound in consequence. Religion is ultimately a matter of personal transformation, and no amount of missionary work will persuade people—with the occasional exception of the disturbed and the desperate—unless our own transformation is complete enough to produce a transformation in others.[28]

27 Abou el-Fadl, op. cit., p.49.
28 For the continuity between classical and modern patterns of conversion to Islam, see my 'Conversion as Nostalgia: Some Experiences of Islam,' in Martyn Percy (ed.), *Previous Convictions: Conversion in the Real World* (London, 2000), pp.93–111.

Rigorism, discourtesy and narrow-mindedness, the tedious refuges of the spiritually inadequate and the culturally outgunned, end up reinforcing the negative attitudes that they claim to repudiate. Conversely, a reactivation of the Prophetic virtue of *rifq*, of gentleness, which the hadith tells us 'never enters a thing without adorning it',[29] will make us welcome rather than suspected, loved and admired rather than despised as a community of resentful failures.

Again, the story of the Migration to Abyssinia is paradigmatic. Here is the plea of the first Muslim asylum-seekers to be faced with deportation:

> [Our Prophet] commanded us to speak the truth, be faithful to our engagements, mindful of the ties of kinship and kindly hospitality, and to refrain from crimes and bloodshed. He forbade us to commit abominations and to speak lies, and to devour the property of orphans, to vilify chaste women. [...] Thereupon our people attacked us, treated us harshly [...] When they got the better of us, treated us unjustly and circumscribed our lives, and came between us and our religion, we came to your country, having chosen you above all others. Here we have been happy in your protection, and we hope that we shall not be treated unjustly while we are with you, O King.' [...] Then the Negus said: 'Of a truth, this and what Jesus brought have come from the same niche. You two may go, for by God, I will never give them up to them, and they shall not be betrayed.'[30]

The early Muslims retained warm memories of the Christians of Abyssinia. More generally, we look in vain in the scriptures for a polemic against Christian life. While unimpressed by Byzantine rule, the Companions refused to demonize the Byzantine citizenry. In one account, 'Amr ibn al-'As praised them as follows:

> They have four qualities. They are the most forbearing of people during tribulations. They are the swiftest to recover after a disaster. They are the best at returning to the fray after having fled. And they are the best to paupers, orphans and the weak.[31]

The strength implied by this humility deserves to be emulated, to

---

[29] Muslim, Birr, 78; cf. Qur'an, 3:159: 'Had you been harsh and hard of heart they would have scattered from around you.'

[30] Ibn Ishaq (Guillaume), pp.151–2.

[31] Muslim, Fitan, 10.

replace the insecure self-indulgence of hatred and self-exculpation. It will not come easily until we reconnect with the religion's history of spirituality. No other religious community in history has produced the number and calibre of saints generated by Islam. Jalal al-Din Rumi has now become America's best-selling poet,[32] an extraordinary victory for Islamic civilisation and the integrity of its spiritual life which our communities are scarcely aware of. Our spirituality is the crowning glory of our history, and the guarantor of the transformative power of our art, literature, and personal conduct. Once we have relearned the traditional Islamic science of the spirit, we can hope to produce, as great Muslim souls did in the past, enduring monuments of literature, art and architecture which will proclaim to our neighbours the quality of our souls, and our ability to enrich America.

The task may seem daunting; but the new generation produces more and more Muslims eager to reinvigorate Islam in a way that will make it the great religious success story of modern America, rather than the plaintive sick man of the religious milieu that it currently seems to be. Increasingly our young people want passionately to be Muslims and to celebrate their uniquely rich heritage, but in a way that does not link them to the desperate radical agendas now being marketed in a growing minority of the mosques. As those young people assume positions of leadership in their communities, and proclaim a form of Islam that is culturally rich and full of confidence in divine providence, Islam will surely take its place as a respected feature on America's religious landscape, and begin the process of integration here that it has so successfully accomplished in countless other cultures throughout its history, and which is a condition for its continuing existence in a potentially hostile place.

[32] Alexandra Marks, *Christian Science Monitor*, November 25, 1997.

14 | Piety, Persuasion and Politics: Deoband's Model of Social Activism

BARBARA METCALF

WHEN THE AFGHAN Taliban emerged into the international spotlight at the end of the twentieth century, no image was more central than what seemed to be their rigid and repressive control of individual behavior, justified in the name of Islam. They set standards of dress and public behavior that were particularly extreme in relation to women—limiting their movement in public space and their employment outside the home. They enforced their decrees through public corporal punishment. Their image was further damaged, particularly after the bombings of the East African American embassies in 1998, when they emerged as the "hosts" of Osama bin Laden and other "Arab Afghans" associated with him.[1]

Many commentators described the Taliban by generic, catch-all phrases like "fanatic," "medieval," and "fundamentalist."[2] The Taliban identified themselves, however, as part of a Sunni school of thought that had its origins in the late nineteenth century colonial period of India's history, a school named after the small, country town northeast of Delhi, Deoband, where the original *madrasa* or seminary of the movement was founded in 1867. Many of the Taliban had, indeed, studied in Deobandi

[1] I am grateful to Muhammad Khalid Masud, Academic Director, and Peter van der Veer, Co-director, who invited me to give the annual lecture of the Institute for the Study of Islam in the Modern World, Leiden University, 23 November 2001. This essay is based on the lecture I gave on that occasion.

[2] An example of the typically imprecise discussion of "deobandism" is: "a sect that propagates ... a belief that has inspired modern revivals of Islamic fundamentalism." John F. Burns, "Adding Demands, Afghan Leaders Show Little Willingness to Give Up Bin Laden." *The New York Times*, 19 September 2001.

schools, but one spokesman for the movement, in its final months went so far as to declare "Every Afghan is a Deobandi."[3] This comment may be disconcerting to those familiar with the school in its Indian environment where its *ulama*—those learned in traditional subjects and typically addressed as "mawlana"—were not directly engaged in politics and were primarily occupied in teaching and providing both practical and spiritual guidance to their followers. (The comment might be disconcerting as well, moreover, since it was suggestive of a regime shaped by ideals more than reality, given, for example, the substantial Shi'a element in the Afghan population).

Another movement linked to Deoband came to international attention at the same time, an apolitical, quietest movement of internal grassroots missionary renewal, the *Tablighi Jama'at*. It gained some notoriety when it appeared that a young American who had joined the Taliban first went to Pakistan through the encouragement of a Tablighi Jama'at missionary.[4] This movement was intriguing, in part by the very fact that is was so little known, yet with no formal organization or paid staff, it sustained networks of participants that stretched around the globe.

The variety of these movements is in itself instructive: clearly, all Islamic activism is not alike, and each of these movements deserves attention on its own. Together, however, for all their variety, these Deoband movements were, in fact, alike in one crucial regard that set them apart from other well-known Islamic movements. What they shared was an overriding emphasis on encouraging a range of ritual and personal behavioral practices linked to worship, dress, and everyday behavior. These were deemed central to Shari'a—divinely ordained morality and practices, as understood in this case by measuring current practice against textual standards and traditions of *Hanafi* reasoning. The anthropologist Olivier Roy calls such movements "neo-fundamentalist" to distinguish them from what can be seen as a different set of Islamic movements, often called

3 Conversation with "the ambassador at large" of the Taliban, Rahmatullah Hashemi, Berkeley, CA, 6 March 2001, in the course of his tour through the Middle East, Europe, and the United States.

4 See for example " A Long, Strange Trip to the Taliban" In *Newsweek*, 17 December 2001, and Don Lattin and Kevin Fagan, "John Walker's Curious Quest: Still a Mystery How the Young Marin County Convert to Islam Made the Transition from Spiritual Scholar to Taliban Soldier." *San Francisco Chronicle*, 13 December 2001.

"Islamist."[5] Limited, as he puts it, to "mere implementation of the Shari'a" in matters of ritual, dress, and behavior, "neo-fundamentalist" movements are distinguishable from Islamist parties primarily because, unlike them, they have neither a systematic ideology nor global political agenda. A more precise label for them is, perhaps, "traditionalist" because of their continuity with earlier institutions, above all those associated with the seminaries and with the ulama in general.

The contrasting Islamist movements include the Muslim Brothers in Egypt and other Arab countries, and the *Jama'at-i Islami* in the Indian sub-continent, as well as many thinkers involved in the Iranian revolution. All these constructed ideological systems and systematically built models for distinctive polities that challenged what they saw as the alternative systems: nationalism, capitalism, and Marxism.[6] Participants were western educated, not seminary educated. They were engineers and others with technical training, lawyers, doctors, and university professors, and, generally speaking, they had little respect for the traditionally educated ulama. These "Islamist" movements sought to "do" modernity in ways that simultaneously asserted the cultural pride of the subjects and avoided the "black" side of western modernity. Many of the Jihad movements that arose in Afghanistan in opposition to the Soviets were heirs of Islamist thought (although over time they also moved to define their Islamic politics primarily as encouragement of a narrow range of Islamic practices and symbols).[7] Participants in militant movements, including bin Laden's al-Qa'ida, often belonged to extremist, break-away factions of Islamist parties.

What is perhaps most striking about the Deoband-type movements is the extent to which politics is an empty "box," filled expediently and

[5] Olivier Roy, "Has Islamism a Future in Afghanistan?" In William Maley, ed. *Fundamentalism Reborn? Afghanistan and the Taliban*. (New York: NYU Press, 1998, pp.199–211.) p.208.

[6] Here I differ from Salman Rushdie who uses the term too broadly: "These Islamists [here he speaks of "radical political movements"]—we must get used to this word, "Islamists," meaning those who are engaged upon such political projects, and learn to distinguish it from the more general and politically neutral "Muslim"—include ... the Taliban. " Salman Rushdie, "Yes, This is About Islam." *The New York Times*, 2 November 2001.

[7] The Jamiyyat-i Islami was formed by Burhanuddin Rabbani and others who had studied at Al Azhar; the Hezb-i Islami of Gulbuddin Hekmatyar was more influenced by the Pakistani Jama'at-i Islami. On the original movements, see Seyyid Vali Nasr, *The Vanguard of the Islamic Revolution: The Jama'at-i Islami of Pakistan*. (Berkeley: University of California Press, 1994) and Richard Mitchell, *The Society of the Muslim Brothers* (London, Oxford University Press, 1969).

pragmatically depending on what seems to work best in any given situation. Islam is often spoken of as "a complete way of life"—arguably a modernist and misleading distinction from other historical religious traditions—so that political life must be informed by Islamic principles. In fact, as these movements illustrate, virtually any strategy is accepted that allows the goal of encouraging what are defined as core, Shari'a-based individual practice, coupled with a range of mundane goals that may or may not be explicit—from protection of life and property, to social honor and political power, to the dignity that comes from pious adherence to what are taken as divine commands. Indeed, these movements often work well in the context of secular regimes where they can pursue their emphasis on disseminating adherence to correct practice with relative freedom.

Secondly, the movements illustrate another important corrective. A great deal is written about modern Muslim societies being consumed with antipathy toward America, American values, and American international political activities. No one, especially after September 11 2001 would deny that that anger exists. However, anger may well be very specific, for example directed at American intervention abroad and not at American "freedom" or "values" in general. Moreover, Islamic movements like the ones discussed here may have many goals and offer a range of social, moral, and spiritual satisfactions that are positive and not merely a reactionary rejection of modernity or "the West." Quite simply, these movements may, in the end, have much less to do with "us" than is often thought. In all their complexity, the Deobandi movements serve as an example of one important model of contemporary Islamic thought and action, a major example of what can be called "traditionalist" Islamic activism.

THE DARU'L-'ULUM AND "CULTURAL STRENGTHENING"

The origin of the Deobandi school of thought is literally a school, a madrasa or seminary, founded in the late nineteenth century at the height of colonial rule in the Delhi region of northern India.[8] Indeed, the

---

[8]   See my *Islamic Revival in British India: Deoband 1860–1900* (Princeton: Princeton U.P., 1982).

key institution of the movement would prove to be the seminary. The madrasa does not appear to have been a major institution in the pre-colonial period. Instead, those who wished to be specialists in the great classic disciplines studied through Arabic—Qur'an, Qur'anic recitation and interpretation, *hadith*, jurisprudential reasoning based on these holy sources, and ancillary sciences like logic, rhetoric, and grammar—would sit at the feet of one or more teachers, traveling often from place to place, seeking not a degree but a certificate of completion of particular books and studies. The modern madrasa, in contrast, as a formal institution, organized by classes, offering a sequential curriculum, staffed by a paid faculty, and supported by charitable campaigns, was a product of the colonial period and the result of familiarity with European educational institutions. The founders of the school gained support by utilizing all manner of new technologies from printing presses to the post office to railroads as they turned from reliance on increasingly-constrained princely patronage to popularly based contributions. Deoband spun off some two-dozen other seminaries across the sub-continent by the end of the nineteenth century.[9]

Boys who came to the school were provided their basic necessities. They lived modestly, and were expected to adhere to a serious schedule of discipline. They did not learn English or other "modern" subjects. They did use Urdu as a lingua franca, enhancing links among students from Bengal to Central Asia to the south. The ulama who founded this school were above all specialists in Prophetic hadith, the narratives which constitute the Prophet Muhammad's sayings and practices which serve either directly or analogously to guide every aspect of moral behavior. Their lives were meant to embody their teachings. Through the giving of fatawa, they responded to inquiries with advisory opinions to guide their followers as well. By the end of the nineteenth century, Deoband formalized the position of a Chief Mufti at the school. Increasingly, the Deobandi fatawa, like the *fatawa* of other groups, were disseminated through print. Fatawa were judgments, attempts to fit sanctioned precedent to present circumstances, and it was well accepted that there could be differences of opinion

---

[9] For an evocative picture of the education of an 'alim that, despite the Shi'a setting, resonates broadly with the kind of education briefly described here, see Roy P. Mottahedeh, The *Mantle of the Prophet: Religion and Politics in Iran* (New York : Simon and Schuster, 1985).

about what was correct. The core of Islamic Law is not rigid but profoundly contextual.

Focus on hadith was not only central to the desire to live in external conformity to certain behavioral patterns. It also was a route to cultivating, through practice, love and devotion to the Prophet Muhammad, and through the bonds of Sufism, to those guides and elders who were his heirs in chains of initiation that stretched back through time. Many of the teachers at Deoband shared Sufi bonds and many students sought initiation into the charisma-filled relationship of discipleship. The Deobandis cherished stories about the Sufis. They practiced the disciplines and meditations that opened them to what was typically imagined as a relationship that developed from one focused on their teacher, to one engaged with the Prophet, and, ultimately, with the divine. The bonds among students and teachers in this largely male world were profound and enduring, based on shared experience, commitments, and affection.

The "ulama" as a class were new in the modern period, much as the madrasas that produced them were. There of course had been learned people in Mughal times, but the emergence of a distinctive class, one that over time became professionalized (for example with "degrees" recognized by state authorities) was very new. The role of the ulama was distinctive as well. Instead of being trained, as the learned had been in the past, for specific state functions, in such areas as the judiciary, these scholars went out to take up positions as teachers themselves, writers, debaters with rival Muslims and non-Muslims, publishers in the expanding vernacular marketplace, prayer leaders and guardians at mosques and shrines.

The Deobandis were "reformists" in a way that, with broad strokes, was shared across a whole range of Muslim, Sikh, and Hindu movements in the colonial period. Characteristic across the board were movements that assessed worldly powerlessness and looked to earlier periods or pristine texts as a source of cultural pride and a possible roadmap to resurgence. Armed with their studies of hadith, the Deobandis, for example, deplored a range of customary celebrations and practices, including what they regarded as excesses at saints' tombs, elaborate lifecycle celebrations, and practices attributed to the influence of the Shi'a.

There were rival Islamic reformist schools in the quest for true Islamic

practice. One group, the *Ahl-i Hadith*, for example, in their extreme opposition to such practices as visiting the Prophet's grave, rivaled that of the
Arabians typically labeled "Wahhabi." The "Wahhabis" were followers of
an iconoclastic late 18th century reform movement associated with tribal
unification, who were to find renewed vigor in internal political competition within Arabia in the 1920s.[10] From colonial times until today, it is
worth noting, the label "Wahhabi" is often used to discredit any reformist
or politically active Islamic group. Another group that emerged in these
same years was popularly known as "Barelwi," and although engaged in the
same process of measuring current practice against hadith, it was more
open to many customary practices. They called the others "Wahhabi."
These orientations—"Deobandi," "Barelwi" or "Ahl-i Hadith"—would
come to define sectarian divisions among Sunni Muslims of South Asian
background to the present. Thus, ulama, mosques, and a wide range of
political, educational, and missionary movements were known by these
labels at the end of the twentieth century, both within the South Asian
countries of India, Pakistan, and Bangladesh, as well as in places like
Britain where South Asian populations settled.[11] Beginning in the colonial
era, the ulama competed in public life to show themselves as the spokes-
men or defenders of "Islam" to their fellow Muslims. This was a new understanding of Islam, as a corporate identity in competition with others,
and it created a new role in public life for religious leaders.

That role in the colonial period was not overtly political. The brutal

---

[10] For a comparative view of the contexts of such movements see William R. Roff, "Islamic Movements: One or Many?" in William R. Roff, ed., *Islam and the Political Economy of Meaning*. London:
Croom Helm and Berkeley: University of California Press, 1987, pp.31–52.

[11] For a general background to all these movements see Metcalf 1982 op. cit. On the "Barelwis"
(who call themselves Ahlu's- Sunnat wa'l-Jama'at in order to assert that they are true Muslims, not a
sect), see Usha Sanyal, *Devotional Islam and Politics in British India: Ahmad Riza Khan Barelwi and His
Movement, 1870–1920* (Delhi: Oxford University Press, 1996). For the experience of religious ins-
titutions in Pakistan, see Jamal Malik, *Colonization of Islam : Dissolution of Traditional Institutions in
Pakistan* (New Delhi: Manohar, 1996) and Muhammad Qasim Zaman, "Religious Education and the
Rhetoric of Reform: The Madrasa in British India and Pakistan" in *Comparative Studies in Society and
History* 41:2 (April 1999) pp.294–323 and "Sectarianism in Pakistan: The Radicalization of Shi'i and
Sunni Identities" in *Modern Asian Studies* 32:3 (July 1998) pp.689–716 as well as his forthcoming
monograph from Princeton University Press. For the religious institutions of South Asian Muslims
in Europe and North America, see Philip Lewis, *Islamic Britain: Religion, Politics and Identity among
British Muslims* (London: I. B. Tauris, 1994) and Barbara D. Metcalf, ed., *Making Muslim Space in
North America and Europe* (Berkeley: University of California Press, 1995).

repression of the so-called Mutiny of 1857 against the British had fallen very hard on north Indian Muslims. In the aftermath, the ulama, not surprisingly, adopted a stance of apolitical quietism. As the Indian nationalist movement became a mass movement after World War I, the Deobandi leadership did something of an "about face". They were never a political party as such, but, organized as the Association of the ulama of India (*Jamiat ulama-i Hind*), they threw in their lot with Gandhi and the Indian National Congress in opposition to British rule. Deobandi histories written before 1920 insisted that the ulama did not participate in the anti-colonial rebellion of 1857; those written after, give "freedom-fighters" pride of place. Like much of the orthodox Jewish leadership in the case of the Zionist movement, most Deobandis opposed the creation of what in 1947 would become the independent state of Pakistan—a separate state for Muslims to be led by a westernized, secular leadership.[12] They preferred operating in an officially secular context, apart from the government, in pursuit of their own goals.

Despite a serious dispute over control of the institution in the early 1980s, Deoband at the end of the twentieth century continued to thrive with over 3000 students enrolled, although in the mid-1990s the Government of India terminated visas that allowed foreign students to enroll. The seminary's web page displayed a monumental marble mosque, still being built and intended to accomodate more than 30,000 worshippers. Links provided further information in English, Hindi, Arabic, and Urdu.[13] Visitors to the school reported remarkable continuity in the content and mode of teaching characteristic of the school,[14] and the web page itself

---

[12] Yohanan Friedmann, "The Attitude of the Jam'iyyat-i ulama'-i Hind to the Indian National Movement and the Establishment of Pakistan" in Gabriel Baer, ed., The *Ulama in Modern History*. (Jerusalem: Israeli Oriental Society, Asian and African Studies, VII, 1971, pp.157–83).

[13] http://www.darululoom-deoband.com. The estimate of numbers to be accommodated in the mosque is in Rahul Bedi, "Taliban Ideology Lives on in India," On-line *Asia Times* (12 December 2001; www.atimes.com/ind-pak/CL12Df01.html).

[14] Many journalists traveled to Deoband in late 2001 in order to report on the source of Taliban religious training. See, for example, Luke Harding, "Out of India," *The Guardian* 2 November 2001; Kartikeya Sharma, "Scholar's Getaway," *The Week* (www.the-week.com/21jul01/life; Michael Fathers, "At the Birthplace of the Taliban", *Time Magazine* (21 September 2001 reprinted on www.foil.org/resources/9-11/Fathers010921-Deoband.) On 29 December 2001 the search engine "Google" listed approximately 2500 sites for "Deoband," many of them reporting on the links of the school to the Taliban.

stressed its enduring role: the training "of Ulama, Shaikhs, traditionists, jurisconsults, authors and experts." Its network of schools, moreover, were "stars of this very solar system by the light of which every nook and corner of the religious and academic life of the Muslims of the sub-continent is radiant." Among these, presumably, would be the humble Deobandi madrasas along the Pakistan-Afghan frontier and in southern Afghanistan, which were the original Taliban base.[15] But within India at least, the ulama of Deoband continued their pre-independence pattern: they did not become a political party and they justified political co-operation with non-Muslims as the best way to protect Muslim interests. "Freedom Fight" is one of the web site's links. For "millions of Muslim families," the web site continues … [their] inferiority complex was removed …".

TABLIGHI JAMAʿAT

The *Tablighi Jamaʿat* was an offshoot of the Deoband movement. In some ways, it represented an intensification of the original Deobandi commitment to individual regeneration apart from any explicit political program. All reform movements strike some balance between looking to individual regeneration on the one hand and intervention from above on the other. The *Tablighis* put their weight wholly at the end of reshaping individual lives. They were similar in this regard to an organization—to pick a familiar example—like Alcoholics Anonymous, which began about the same period, in its rejection of progressive era government politics in favor of individual bootstraps. And like AA, the heart of Tablighi Jamaʿat strategy was the belief that the best way to learn is to teach and encourage others.

Always closely tied to men with traditional learning and the holiness of Sufis, Tablighi Jamaʿat nonetheless took its impetus from a desire to move dissemination of Islamic teachings away from the madrasa, the heart of Deobandi activity, to inviting "lay" Muslims, high and low, learned and illiterate, to share the obligation of enjoining others to faithful practice. It also differed from the original movement because it eschewed debate with other Muslims over jurisprudential niceties and resultant details of

[15] The Madrasa Haqqania in Akhora Khatak trained the core Taliban leadership. See Jeffrey Goldberg, "Jihad U.: The Education of a Holy Warrior." *The New York Times Magazine* 25 June 2000.

practice. The movement began in the late 1920s, when Mawlana Muhammad Ilyas Kandhlawi (d.1944), whose family had long associations with Deoband and its sister school in Saharanpur, Mazaahiru'l-'Ulum, sought a way to reach peasants who were nominal Muslims being targeted by a Hindu conversion movement.

Mawlana Ilyas' efforts took place in an atmosphere of religious violence and the beginnings of mass political organization. His strategy was to persuade Muslims that they themselves, however little book learning they had, could go out in groups, approaching even the ulama, to remind them to fulfill their fundamental ritual obligations. Participants were assured of divine blessing for this effort, and they understood that through the experiences of moving outside their normal everyday enmeshments and pressures, in the company of likeminded people bent on spending their time together in scrupulous adherence to Islamic behavior, they themselves would emerge with new accomplishments, dignity, and spiritual blessing. Tablighis not only eschewed debate, but also emulated cherished stories, recalling Prophetic hadith, of withdrawing from any physical attack, an experience mission groups periodically encountered. No word resonates more in Tablighi reports of their experiences than *sukun*, the "peace" they experience as a foretaste of the paradise they believe their efforts (jihad) in this path of Allah help merit.

A pattern emerged of calling participants to spend one night a week, one weekend a month, 40 continuous days a year, and ultimately 120 days at least once in their lives engaged in tabligh missions. Women would work among other women or travel, occasionally, with their men folk on longer tours.[16] Although Tablighis in principle preferred to use any mosque as their base while traveling, over time specific mosques throughout the world have come to be known as "Tablighi mosques." Periodic convocations also came to be held. With no formal bureaucracy or membership records, it is hard to calculate the number of participants over time, but at the end of the twentieth century, annual meetings of perhaps

---

[16] See my "Women and Men in a Contemporary Pietist Movement: The Case of the Tablighi Jama'at," in *Appropriating Gender: Women's Activism and Politicized Religion in South Asia.* edited. Amrita Basu and Patricia Jeffery. (New York: Routledge, 1998, pp.107–121) and reprinted in re-titled volume: *Resisting the Sacred and the Secular: Women's Activism and Politicised Religion in South Asia.* (Delhi: Kali for Women, 1999).

two million people would congregate for three-day meetings in Raiwind, Pakistan and Tungi, Bangladesh; large regional meetings were regularly held in India; and other convocations took place in North America and Europe, for example in Dewsbury, site of a major seminary associated with Tablighi activities in the north of England. These convocations were considered moments of intense blessings. They also gave evidence of the vast numbers touched by the movement.

Even though there are publications specific to the movement, above all those associated with Mawlana Muhammad Zakariyya Kandhlawi (d.1982) of the Mazaahiru'l-'Ulum madrasa at Saharanpur, the emphasis in the movement was not at all on book learning but rather on face-to-face, or "heart-to-heart," communication.[17] Their cherished books included topically-arranged Prophetic traditions, used as a stimulus to everyday behavior. In invoking and embodying those traditions, participants felt themselves part of dense networks of Muslims, both dead and alive, and aspired to reliving the Prophet's own time when he too was part of a faithful few among a population sunk in ignorance. Participation thus gave meaning and purpose to every day life. It is important to see that participation in such a movement, often explained as a response to the failure of the corrupt, underdeveloped, or alienating societies in which Muslims perhaps find themselves, in fact offered a positive, modern solution to people who were geographically and socially mobile. Participants in principle made a "life style" choice; they found a stance of cultural dignity; they opted for a highly disciplined life of sacrifice; they found a moral community of mutual acceptance and purpose. That community would be re-invented and reformed in the course of missions, and re-placed if participants themselves relocated. Other contemporary Islamic movements of the ulama or, indeed, of Sufi brotherhoods, provided many of the same satisfactions.

As noted above, the original Deobandis were both ulama and Sufis, offering "a composite" form of religious leadership. Indeed Pnina Werbner has recently argued that the fact that Muslims in South Asia (in contrast to some other parts of the Muslim world) have not had to choose

---

[17] I discuss the movement's publications in "Living Hadith in the Tablighi Jama'at." *The Journal of Asian Studies* 52, 3 (1993): pp.584–608.

between Sufism and a learned, often reformist, leadership in the modern period, accounts for the vitality of Sufism and, indeed, for the continued role of the ulama.[18] Tablighis continued to offer the ulama a respected role. The place of Sufism was more complex. Although what were seen as deviant customs around holy men were discouraged, Sufism in no sense disappeared. Indeed, among Tablighis, the holiness associated with the Sufi Pir was in many ways defused into the charismatic body of the *jama'at*, so that the missionary group itself became a channel for divine intervention. The kind of story typically told about a saint—overcoming ordeals, being blessed with divine illumination, triumphantly encountering temporal authority—was in fact often told about a group engaged in a mission. Thus, as in the initial Deoband movement and in many other Sufi and sectarian movements in modern South Asia, it was not necessary to choose between the devotional power of Sufism and the conviction of reformist imitation of prophetic teaching.

Participants in tablighi activities define their efforts as jihad. This word is, of course, widely translated as "holy war", but its root meaning is "effort" or "struggle." Following Prophetic hadith, jihad may be classified as "the greater jihad," the inner struggle to discipline and moral purification that a person exerts upon the individual self, or as "the lesser jihad" of militancy or violence. For both kinds of jihad, the focus transcends the nation state to a global *umma*. Tablighis use the same discourse of jihad as do those engaged in militant action. Their leaders are amirs; their outings are "sorties" or "patrols;" the merit for actions are exponentially multiplied as they are during a military campaign; a person who dies in the course of tabligh is a *shahid*, or martyr. Finally, the obligation to mission is not negotiable: on fulfilling it hinges nothing less than one's own ultimate fate at the Day of Judgment. Both militants and Tablighis, moreover, stress the obligation of the individual believer, not (in the case of mission) the ulama, nor (in the case of militancy) the state.[19] One of the fundamental characteristics of the reform movements of the colonial

[18] See her forthcoming study of the regional Sufi brotherhood of Zindapir (*Pilgrims of Love: The Anthropology of a Global Sufi Cult*, Bloomington: Indiana University Press, 2002). This study also exemplifies the positive accommodation to contemporary life offered by a transnational Sufi movement. The author explicitly distinguishes herself from those who explain Islamic religious movements as a reaction to frustration and failure.

period and after, was a diffusion of leadership and authority, a kind of "laicization," evident here.

The key difference in the two kinds of jihad is, of course, that one is the jihad of personal purification, the other of warfare. In the words of an annual meeting organizer at Raiwind, "Islam is in the world to guide people, not to kill them. We want to show the world the correct Islam."[20] As noted above, the oft-told tales of the movement are ones of meeting opposition, even violence, and of unfailingly withdrawing from conflict—and of so gaining divine intervention and blessing. Effectively by this focus, as in the original Deoband movement, religion in practice became a matter of personal, private life, separate from politics. This division, albeit untheorized, has worked well in the context of a wide variety of state structures including the modern liberal state. The Sufi tradition, moreover, here as elsewhere, always engages with, but imagines itself morally above, worldly power. This attitude further encourages an apolitical or detached stance toward government.

THE TALIBAN AND THEIR TEACHERS, THE *JAMIAT ULEMA-I-ISLAM* (JUI)

In the final years of colonial rule, a minority group among the Deobandi ulama dissented from support for the secular state and the privatization of religion espoused by the Indian nationalist movement. They organized, instead, as the Jamiat Ulema-i-Islam to support the Muslim League and the demand for a separate Muslim state. In independent Pakistan after 1947 they became a minor political party led by ulama and a voice in the on-going debate over the nature of the Pakistani state. Should it be the secular state presumably intended by its founders, or a state meant to be shaped in accordance with Islam? The JUI has never had more than minute popular support, and the content of the party's programs over the

---

[19] A little noted aspect of Osama bin Laden's leadership was his claim to authority, despite his lack of a traditional education, to issue fatawa. His call to make jihad incumbent on all Muslims deployed a technical distinction of Islamic legal thought, saying that jihad was an individual duty, *farz 'ain*, rather than a duty on some subset of the umma (e.g. political leaders, soldiers), *farz kifaya*.

[20] Tempest Rone, "Huge Gathering of Moderate Muslims in Pakistan." *San Francisco Chronicle*, 3 November 2001. Also, Mawlana Zubair-ul-Hassan: "[The Holy Prophet] said it is not bravery to kill the non-believers but to preach [to] them is the real task." Quote in "Tableeghi Ijtima Concludes," *The Frontier Post* (Peshawar), 5 November 2001, (www.frontierpost.com.pk).

years, it is probably fair to say, has been a fairly simplistic call for the primacy of Islam in public life.[21]

Like other Pakistani parties, the JUI has been subject to factional splits coalescing around personalities more than issues, and there were perhaps a half-dozen factions and reorganizations over its first half century.[22] The JUI struck alliances with any party that would win them influence. In the 1970s, for example, they allied with a Pashtun regionalist party in opposition to Bhutto's Pakistan People's Party (PPP), a party that was, in principle, socialist. In the mid 1990s, in contrast, they allied with that same PPP, now led by Bhutto's Harvard and Oxford educated daughter. Its ulama were given to *realpolitik* with a vengeance and, like just about every party in Pakistan, not shielded from corruption, in this case because they were clerics. Their most famous leader at one point, for example, was referred to as "Mawlana Diesel" because of his reputed involvement in fuel smuggling earlier in the 1990s.[23] When the JUI was excluded from power, its Islamic rhetoric became a language of opposition, often invoking a discourse of "democracy" and "rights."

At the same time, the ulama of the JUI were engaged with the madrasas that furthered Deobandi teachings. From the 1980s on, the number of seminaries in Pakistan soared, used as a tool of conservative influence by the military dictator Ziaul Haq (in power 1977–1988), who was, in fact, particularly sympathetic to the Deobandi approach. The seminaries were not only a resource in domestic politics, but at times found themselves engaged in a kind of "surrogate" competition between Saudis and Iranians, as each patronized religious institutions likely to support their side.[24] It was in this atmosphere of politics and education that the origin of the Taliban is to be found.

The surge in the number of madrasas in the 1980s coincided with the

---

[21] Seyyid Vali Reza Nasr, op. cit., makes the important argument that it is by welcoming Islamist parties into the democratic process, as happened in Pakistan in the mid 1980s, that they become politically moderates.

[22] See Sayyid A. S. Pirzada, *The Politics of the Jamiat Ulema-i-Islam Pakistan 1971–77* (Karachi: Oxford University Press, 2000).

[23] The target of this is Fazlur Rahman, head of the JUI (F). See Rick Bragg, "A Pro-Taliban Rally Draws Angry Thousands in Pakistan, Then Melts Away." *The New York Times*, 6 October 2001.

[24] See Vali R. Nasr, "International Politics, Domestic Imperatives, and Identity Mobilization: Sectarianism in Pakistan, 1979–98" (*Comparative Politics* 32:2 [January 2000] pp.171–190).

influx of some three million Afghan refugees, for whose boys the madrasas located along the frontier frequently provided the only available education. One school in particular, the Madrasa Haqqaniya, in Akhora Khatak near Peshawar, trained many of the top Taliban leaders. These sometime students (*talib*; pl. *taliban*) were shaped by many of the core Deobandi reformist causes, all of which were further encouraged by Arab volunteers in Afghanistan. These causes, as noted above, included rigorous concern with fulfilling rituals; opposition to custom-laden ceremonies like weddings and pilgrimage to shrines, along with practices associated with the Shi'a minority; and a focus on seclusion of women as a central symbol of a morally ordered society. Theirs was, according to Ahmed Rashid, a long time observer, "an extreme form of Deobandism, which was being preached by Pakistani Islamic parties in Afghan refugee camps in Pakistan."[25] This focus on a fairly narrow range of Shari'a law, which emphasized personal behavior and ritual, was something the Taliban shared with other Deobandi movements, even while the severity of the Taliban approach made them unique.

The Taliban emerged as a local power in Afghanistan starting in 1994, because they were able to provide protection and stability in a context of warlordism, plunder, and corruption. They found ready support from elements within the Pakistani state, which welcomed an ally likely to protect trade routes to Central Asia and to provide a friendly buffer on the frontier. Similarly, the Taliban also appeared in the mid-1990s to serve a range of US interests, above all in securing a route for an oil pipeline to the Central Asian oilfields outside Iranian control. The Taliban, on their part, like their teachers, were not ideologically driven as they determined whom they were willing to work with as allies and supporters. Indeed, the scholar Olivier Roy suggests that while they could not be manipulated easily—for example in relation to issues related to women—they were profoundly expedient when it came to securing a power base. They worked with the Pakistani state, the United States, and anti-Shi'a or not, he argues, they would have dealt with Iran had it served their advantage.[26]

The United States' interest in the Taliban shifted away from them,

[25] Rashid is the definitive source for the history of the Taliban. Ahmed Rashid, *Taliban: Militant Islam, Oil and Fundamentalism in Central Asia*. (New Haven: Yale University Press, 2000), p.88.
[26] Roy, op. cit., p.211.

however, first, because of what were seen as human rights abuses in relation to women, and second, because the East African embassy bombings
in August 1998 were linked to the presence of terrorist activists within
Taliban-controlled areas, with Osama bin Laden as their most visible
supporter. That alliance would, after the World Trade Center bombing
of September 11 2001, be the Taliban's undoing. Bin Laden's charisma,
his access to wealth, and his networks had been invaluable to the Taliban in
achieving their success, and his anti-Americanism found fertile soil
among the Taliban already inclined to disapproval of "the West." There
is an irony in the fact that links to him brought them down, since the
Taliban's driving force at core had not been abhorrence of Western culture, but the specific goal of prevailing within Afghanistan, and in so
doing, fostering Islamic behavior.

The Taliban, for all their extremism and the anomaly of their rise to
power on the basis of dual levels of support from Pakistan and Arabs,
nonetheless throw into relief an important dimension of Deobandi strategy in the school's early years and later. None of the Deobandi movements has a theoretical stance in relation to political life. They either
expediently embrace the political culture of their time and place, or withdraw from politics completely. For the Taliban, that meant engaging with
the emerging ethnic polarities in the country and seeking allies wherever
they could find them.[27] For the JUI, it meant playing the game of *realpolitik* of Pakistani political life. For the Deobandis in India and the Tablighi
Jama'at, it meant fostering benign relations with existing regimes—necessary even in the latter case to receive permits for meetings, travel visas,
and protection.

DEOBANDIS, TALIBS, AND TABLIGHIS

Deobandis, Talibs, and Tablighis demonstrate pragmatic responses to the
varying environments in which they find themselves. The Taliban surely
represent an exceptional case both in their rigor—criticized for example
in relation to women even by leading ulama of the JUI—and in the deal

---

[27] The phrase "ethnic polarization" is Olivier Roy's. He uses this phrase to suggest that ethnic loyalties are complex and fluid, not ideologized. He further argues that these loyalties have shaped all
parties in the Afghan competitions of recent years.

they struck with Arab extremists, who were like them in embracing Islamic rituals and social norms, but so unlike them in their vision of global jihad. Even the Taliban, arguably, had moderate voices, as well as pragmatism in their alliances that might one day have made their society more acceptable in terms of international standards had that possibility not been foreclosed by the attacks of September 11 and the American "war on terrorism."[28]

The other Deobandi movements—the JUH in India, the JUI in Pakistan, Tablighi Jama'at everywhere—although they tend to see the world in black and white, in fact all have played a largely moderate role by participating in or accepting on-going political regimes. The recent exceptions were some students and teachers in the madrasas of Pakistan, as well as Pakistanis in other walks of life, who were drawn to the heady rhetoric of demonizing America and Jews on the one hand, and imagining the triumph of global Islam on the other, symbolized by the jihad in Afghanistan.[29] Deobandi madrasas on the Pakistani frontier at the turn of the twenty-first century periodically closed to allow their students to support Taliban efforts.[30]

The historical pattern launched by the Deoband ulama, nevertheless, for the most part treated political life on a primarily secular basis, typically, *de facto* if not *de jure*, identifying religion with the private sphere, and in that sphere fostering Islamic teachings and interpretations that proved widely influential. Aside from Deoband's enduring influence, it exemplifies a pattern, represented in general terms in a range of Islamic

---

[28] Hashemi, for example, attempted to establish common ground with his foreign interlocutors in the spring of 2001 (see note 3, above). He emphasized the desperate conditions inside his country, both the crisis of public order characterized by warlordism following the Soviet withdrawal in the early 1990s and the immediate extreme conditions produced by drought and famine, as partial explanation for the regime's severe policies. He insisted that the regime favored public employment and education for women, but in the conditions of the time needed "to protect" them. He tried to show that the destruction of the Bamian Buddhas was understandable – if perhaps irrational, he almost suggested— as a reaction to offers of international aid to preserve antiquities rather than to avert starvation and disease.

[29] For a sensitive analysis of the tension between the lure of this rhetoric and actual moderation in behavior on the part of most British Muslims, see Pnina Werbner, "The Predicament of Diaspora and Millenial Islam." *Times Higher Education Supplement*, 14 December 2001. The argument is suggestive for the behavior of many Muslims in a place like Pakistan as well.

[30] See Thomas L. Friedman, "In Pakistan, It's Jihad 101." *The New York Times*, 13 November 2001 and Jeffrey Goldberg, "Jihad U.: The Education of a Holy Warrior." *The New York Times Magazine*, 25 June 2000.

movements outside South Asia as well, of a pattern of "traditionalist" cultural renewal on the one hand coupled with political adaptability on the other. This tradition, seen over time and across a wide geographical area, illustrates the fact that there are widespread patterns of Islamic apoliticism that foster a modus vivendi with democratic and liberal traditions. It also demonstrates, most notably in the teaching and missionary dimensions of their activities, that the goals and satisfactions that come from participation in Islamic movements may well have little to do with opposition or resistance to non-Muslims or "the West." Their own debates or concerns may well focus on other Muslims, an internal, and not an external "Other" at all.[31] And what they offer participants may be the fulfillment of desires for individual empowerment, transcendent meaning, and moral sociality that do not engage directly with national or global political life at all.

As for political life, recently the commentator Nicholas Lemann has argued that particularly in contexts of weak or non-existent states, alliances typically reflect estimates of who will prevail, not who is "right." As Lemann puts it, "in the real world people choose to join not one side of a great clash of civilizations but what looks like the winning team in their village."[32] The JUI would seem almost a textbook case of this kind of argument. In the fragmented, factionalized world of Pakistan's gasping democracy, the winning side seems to be whatever party—regional interest, secular, or Islamic—offers some leverage. In the aftermath of the terrorist attacks of September 11, along with the Jamaat-i Islami, the JUI was at the forefront of anti-American protest. Were they motivated, given their support base among Pashtuns along the Afghan border, by the expectation that the "winning team" would be transnational Islamic militants (and their funding sources), and, in the end, that they would gain the support of the presumed majority of Pakistanis who do not support

---

[31] Mixed in with sites addressing current political issues among those noted in note 5 above, are sites that primarily transfer the materials of polemical pamphlets to the web. Thus, a site posting "Barelwi" perspectives excerpts Deobandi fatawa to show that they are guilty of the very insolence toward the Prophet that they condemn—the kind of condemnation current a hundred years ago. See www.schinan.com/jhangi. A particularly elaborate site, intended to show that Ahl-i Hadith beliefs alone are true, reviews the errors of many other groups, with a dozen and a half linked pages challenging issues of "Tableegi-Jama'at." See www.salaf.indiaaceess.com/tableegi-jamaat.

[32] Nicholas Leman, "What Terrorists Want." *The New Yorker*, 29 October 2001 (pp.36–41), p.39.

religious parties but do resent American foreign policy? As for the Deobandis in India, sometimes the winning team seemed to be the British colonial power, sometimes the Indian National Congress, sometimes other parties.

Tablighi Jama'at is particularly striking in regard to its accommodationist strategy, since it implicitly fosters the privatization of religion associated with the modern liberal state. Political leaders of all stripes in Pakistan and Bangladesh, at least since the mid-1980s, have invariably appeared at the annual convocations and been welcomed accordingly. Some observers and political figures claim that the movement in fact is covertly political; others claim, that it is a first stage on the way to militancy. This argument is particularly made in Pakistan since the majority of Tabligh participants there belong to the frontier province adjoining Afghanistan. All of this is, however, speculation. What is clear is that the formally apolitical missionary tours, gatherings in local mosques and homes, and annual gatherings continue to be the routine of the movement, one that clearly offers meaning and dignity to many who participate. In the many goals fostered by these movements, social, psychological, moral, and spiritual, as well as in the political strategies adopted with such virtuosity—movements, in the end, turn out to be less distinctive than either they or outsiders often assume they are.

15 | Fanaticism and its Manifestations in Muslim Societies

M. HASHIM KAMALI

I. INTRODUCTORY REMARKS

FANATICISM IS PRIMARILY a religious phenomenon which is probably as old as religion itself. It is not confined to any particular religion, nor even to religion as such, certainly not to Islam nor to its Shari'a. We learn from history that the further back we look into the Middle Ages, the stronger and more pervasive are the manifestations of fanaticism we find in almost all communities and religions. Mankind has evidently not found a satisfactory solution to the problem, for it has continued its presence into modern times, and acquired new dimensions which may be attributed to a variety of causes. For one thing, due to mass communications, fanaticism can no longer be contained within geographical boundaries. Mass dislocation of populations, the rising tide of secularism and triumphant materialism may be said to have evoked imbalanced responses often verging on fanaticism. These developments have also exposed the individual to uncertainty and disillusionment and a consequent urge for security and reassurance—which religion may seem to promise. One can refer to other causes that might in one way or another explain the phenomenon.

The attempt I have made in the following pages to identify the causes and manifestations of fanaticism may be seen as an initial step in the search for better and more refined methods of dealing with the problem. When it is realized that the causes and manifestations of fanaticism, are not constant, but that they are liable to change in conjunction with other variables, then it becomes evident that a strategy that might have been good at a certain point of time may no longer be adequate under a different set of circumstances. We must therefore stress the need for sustained effort and the awareness that the problem can only be tackled, contained, and minimized over a period of time.

Some of the familiar themes of contemporary fanaticism are a recourse to violence in demanding for the establishment of an Islamic State; restrictions on women's liberty and participation in public life, and the enforcement of *hudud* punishments (crimes in Islamic law that require the enforcement of corporal punishment, such as theft, robbery etc). There is also a persistent emphasis on specific behaviors and on dress, which may be added to the list. But beyond these, one does not find many actual plans or ideas for original reform. The proposed establishment of the Islamic State is also more in the nature of a demand which is not supported by a properly articulated or well-defined plan that might specify the details of a particular model.

This essay is presented in six sections and a conclusion. A brief discussion of the relevant English and Arabic terminology in section two is followed by a general characterization of fanaticism in section three. The next section addresses the various manifestations of fanaticism, and is followed by a discussion of the causes of the phenomenon before us. The last section explores possible remedies for fanaticism and discusses strategies that would help in opening up a climate of communication and prospects for a better understanding of the issues involved.

II. NOTE ON TERMINOLOGY

Neither the *Encyclopedia of Islam* nor the *Encyclopedia of Religion*, nor in fact any of the other encyclopedias that I was able to consult, have recorded an entry for 'fanaticism'. The dictionaries describe 'fanaticism' as "the tendency to indulge in wild and extravagant notions, especially in religious matters." A fanatical person is thus characterized as one whose behavior is influenced by excessive and mistaken enthusiasm, especially in religious matters. 'Religious maniac' and 'unreasoning enthusiast' are the other descriptions of a fanatic.[1] Fanatics are thus portrayed as emotionally unstable

---

[1] The *Oxford English Dictionary*, 2nd ed., vol. V, p. 712. The other two encyclopedias that I checked are the *Encyclopedia of Religion and Ethics* and the *Encyclopedia Britannica*, neither of which have a listing for 'fanaticism'.

individuals who allow themselves to be "hurried away by their fancy and feelings, to the adoption not only of wild enthusiastic views, but also of inordinate and not infrequently persecuting measures."[2]

The Arabic equivalents of 'fanaticism' are *al-ta'assub* which is descri-bed as 'being zealous or a zealot in religion'.[3] Other equivalent Arabic words are *al-ghuluw* (excessiveness, extremism), *al-tashdid* (exceedingly restrictive) and *al-tatarruf* (moving to the farthest point) all signifying a tendency that is away from what is deemed moderate and balanced.[4]

'Fundamentalism' (Arabic equivalent: *al-usuliyya*) has its origins in Christian theological thought and it is often associated with evangelism and "the literal exposition of all the affirmations and attitudes of the Bible and the militant exposure of all non-Biblical affirmation and attitudes".[5] It is this element of militancy which distinguishes fundamen-talism from other forms of revivalist movements. A fundamentalist was, in other words, ready to stand up for the faith and defend it against modernist theologies, secular humanism and the like.[6] The western media in general, and the American media in particular, has used "funda-mentalism" in reference to Islam almost synonymously with its emotion-ally loaded equivalents: 'fanaticism', 'extremism' and even 'terrorism'. The latest additions to this list are 'Islamism' and 'Islamist', which hardly represent an improvement. This usage, whether of fundamentalism or Islamism is anomalous in so far as it ignores totally the inherently positive meaning of these words, in that adherence to the fundamentals of Islam, or to Islam itself, is not only central to Islamic faith and dogma, but also that many modern Muslim thinkers have seen a return to the fun-damentals of Islam, and purifying Islam from spurious accretions, as the surest hope of gain-ing liberation from internal and external bondage and some of the disturbing realities of life in contemporary Muslim societies.[7]

[2] *Encyclopedia of Religion and Ethics*, vol. 4

[3] E.W. Lane, *Arabic-English Lexicon*, vol. 5 p.2058.

[4] Cf. Aisha B. Lemu, *Laxity, Moderation and Extremism in Islam*, occasional papers 5, International Institute of Islamic Thought, Herndon VA and London, 1993, p.6.

[5] Cf. George W. Dollar, *A History of Fundamentalism in America*, Greenville: Bob Jones University Press, 1973, p.xv.

[6] Cf. Riffat Hassan, "The Burgeoning of Islamic Fundamentalism: Toward an Understanding of the Phenomenon," in ed. Norman J. Cohen, *The Fundamentalist Phenomenon*, William B. Eerdsman Publishing Co. 1990, p.23.

[7] Cf. Fazlur Rahman, *Islam and Modernity: Transformation of an Intellectual Tradition*, Chicago: University of Chicago Press, 1982, pp.5–8.

This fact, important as it is in understanding Islam and the development of Islamic thought, has received scant attention in the West, which continues to assume that the term 'fundamentalism' can have no meaning for Muslims other than the one assigned to it by them. The Arabic equivalents of fundamentalism and fundamentalist (*usuliyya, usuliyyun*) are not used in the Arabic media. The word 'radical' although not Arabic in origin is often used as an equivalent. The phrase *al-radicaliyya al-Islamiyya,* for example, is often used in contradistinction with *al-ihya' al-Islami* (Islamic revivalism) and *al-sahwa al-Islamiyya* (Islamic awakening).[8] Hasan al-Banna, the founder of the Muslim Brotherhood (*Ikhwan al-Muslimin*) described his mission as a *salafiyya* (lit. ancestral), a "Qur'anic, Muhammadan, Islamic society which follows the way of the Noble Qur'an, takes the path of the Great Prophets, does not deviate from what has come down to us in God's Book, His Messenger's Sunna (sayings, practices, actions and living habit of the Prophet) and the conduct of the venerable forefathers."[9] The Egyptian media began to use such terms as Islamic radicals and 'extremist religious groups' in the time of Sadat, initially with the purpose of distinguishing these from the *salafiyya* of the Muslim Brotherhood. These and other phrases such as 'terrorist religious groups' were used in reference to militant groups when they resorted to criminal violence and assassination of their opponents.

III. A GENERAL CHARACTERIZATION OF FANATICISM

Fanaticism is a complex phenomenon and we need to know its various manifestations and causes in order to understand what it is. Since fanaticism is inherently emotive and also relative, some may be inclined to include unrelated things within its scope. The words 'fanatics' and 'extremists' in this essay refer, on the whole, to people who follow a right cause, or one which finds support, wholly or partially, in valid precedent,

---

[8] For a discussion on the use of these and similar Arabic terms see Louis J. Cantori's article in Arabic, "*Al-Muhafazah wa'l taqaddum fi Misr: al-Ihya' al-Islami,*" in *Qira'at siyasiyya* (an Arabic periodical published by World & Islam Studies Enterprise, Tampa Florida) vol.3, no.2, 1413/1993, p.8ff; note also the title of Yusuf al-Qaradawi's book *Al-Sahwa al-Islamiyya* (Islamic Awakening).

[9] Hasan al-Banna's letter to the newspaper *al-Misri,* 26 July 1938 quoted in Abdel Azim Ramadan, "Fundamentalist Influence in Egypt: The Strategies of the Muslim Brotherhood and the Takfir Groups," in eds. Martin A. Marry and R. S. Appleby, *Fundamentalisms and the State: Remaking Polities, Economies, and Militance* (The Fundamentalism Project) Chicago and London: University of Chicago Press 1993, p.152.

but who resort to wrong methods in order to obtain it. As for those who are engaged in falsehood in the first place, they are deviationists as from the start and are therefore not included under the term 'fanatics'. Having said this however, exaggeration and imbalance in the expression and articulation of ideas may generally be seen as a manifestation of fanaticism. Recourse to violence and a militant approach to the implementation of ideas is a strong indication of fanaticism, although not its prerequisite, because one can identify a fanatic as one who goes to excess even without resorting to violence. The mean test for fanaticism, as I elaborate below, is that of moderation and balance. However, it appears that none of these terms can be given exact definitions, although they can be described and identified. The difficulty over definition is not over any inherent complexity in the meaning of these terms; it is rather the relative and circumstantial contents of the terms that makes the attempt at comprehensive definitions prone to inaccuracy and possible error.

Fanaticism can best convey its meaning when it is visualized in conjunction with laxity and moderation. Laxity signifies a negligent attitude toward religion, whereas fanaticism is over-emphatic and restrictive at the other extreme. Both are reprehensible and negative in contradistinction to moderation, which is generally encouraged. An awareness of what is moderate is therefore necessary in order to give a meaning to the terms laxity and extremism. Moderation in Islam is distinguished by the following four characteristics: (a) An intermediate position that combines the interests of both continuity and change; (b) acknowledgment of what is changeable and what is not open to change; (c) avoidance of rigidity and stagnation on the one hand and of an open-ended elasticity that verges on deviation on the other; and (d) a holistic approach to the understanding of Islam that is all-encompassing and comprehensive.[10]

Moderation is recommended and desirable in Islam. There is a great emphasis on justice, moderation and balance in the Qur'an and Sunna, to the extent that Islam characterizes itself as a religion of moderation. The Qur'an also identifies the *umma* (Muslim community) as the *umma* of moderation and balance "*ummatan wasatan*" (al-Baqarah, 2:143). We also note that in a number of *ahadith* (pl. of hadith; saying of the Prophet) the

---

[10] Yusuf al-Qaradawi, *Islamic Awakening: Between Rejection and Extremism*, eng. trans. A. S. Al-Shaykh 'Ali, Riyad: International Islamic Publishing Houses, 2nd ed, 1412/1991, p.58.

Prophet, peace be on him, praises those who adopt a moderate approach to religion. On several occasions, the Prophet instructed the believers not to overburden themselves in worship and to observe moderation in its performance. Worship should be done with freshness of the heart, not as an exhausting routine carried out, in order to attain merit, in spite of fatigue. To prevent this, various provisions were laid down in the Qur'an and Sunna which grant concessions for the traveler and the sick, the elderly, the poor, and pregnant women in their observance of religious duties. The Prophet is reported to have said: "Beware of excessiveness in religion (*al-ghuluw fi'l-din*). People before you have perished as a result of such excessiveness." And we read in another hadith: "Ruined were those who indulged in hair-splitting details (*halak al-mutanatti'un*)."[11]

The word 'moderate' is sometimes taken to mean 'only half committed'. This is inaccurate because a moderate person may be, indeed should be, just as deeply committed to the principles of the faith as an extremist, however, they will differ in the way they fulfill their commitments; they differ in other words, in regard to the external manifestation of their commitments. For in regard to the essence of belief, the dogma of Islam and its basic values of truth and justice, the distinction between moderation and extremism is basically irrelevant. There is, in other words, no such thing as a 'moderate belief' that may be distinguished say from an "extremist belief" in God, or 'moderate truth' as opposed to 'extreme truth'. A hard and fast distinction between belief and conduct may be difficult to sustain. I still maintain, however, that moderation and extremism relate mainly to the externality of conduct and the approach that one takes to the practice of Islam, to the interpretation of its teachings and the way that one relates to other people and their adherence to Islamic values.

Al-Qaradawi has described extremism (or fanaticism) in religion as follows:

> Literally, extremism (*al-tatarruf*) means being situated at the farthest possible point from the centre. Figuratively, it indicates a similar remoteness in religion and thought as well as behavior. One of its main consequences

---

[11] Muslim b. Hajjaj al-Nishapuri, *Mukhtasar Sahih Muslim*, ed. Nassir al-Din al-Albani, 6th ed., Beirut: Al-Maktab al-Islami, 1407/1987, p.481; see also Yusuf al-Qaradawi, *Al-Sahwa al-Islamiyya, Bayn al-Juhud wa'l-Tatarruf*, 3rd ed., Doha: Kitab al-Umma, 1402/1982, p.25.

is exposure to danger and insecurity. Islam therefore recommends moderation and balance in everything: in belief, worship, conduct and legislation. Moderation and balance are not only general characteristics of Islam, they are fundamental principles.[12]

People's perceptions of such concepts as 'laxity', 'moderation', and 'fanaticism' are value-laden and tend to be influenced by such factors as personal piety, family background and social environment. For example, people brought up in a strict Muslim environment tend to regard any deviation with aversion and horror. At the other end of the spectrum are those whose background is so unislamic that they regard even minimal adherence to Islam as a kind of fanaticism. They express surprise at someone who prays five times a day, cast doubt on the status of what is clearly *haram* (forbidden) and even regard the Islamic dress style for women as an act of fanaticism. We may also add here that people tend to differ in their natural orientations and temperament. Within the natural boundaries of the religion, some take things easy and facilitate matters, others do not. This is also true of the Prophet's Companions, peace be upon them all. The famous Companion 'Abd Allah Ibn 'Abbas, for example, was inclined to facilitate religious matters, while 'Abd Allah Ibn 'Umar was more strict. However, this is not what we mean by fanaticism and it would be improper to accuse a person of fanaticism simply for having adopted, out of conviction perhaps, a hardline opinion of a certain scholar or *madhhab* (a school of law) which is supported by evidence, but I shall have more to say on this later.

IV. MANIFESTATIONS OF FANATICISM

Fanaticism shows itself in a variety of forms and it would be difficult to provide an exhaustive treatment of all the possible manifestations of this phenomenon, but we may still attempt a general picture of it as follows:

1. Bigotry and Intolerance

The fanatic is obstinately devoted to his own opinions and prejudices and lacks clarity of vision regarding the interests of other human beings, the purposes of Shari'a (Islamic law) or the circumstances of the age. Such a person does not allow opportunity for dialogue and expects others to

---

[12] Al-Qaradawi, *Islamic Awakening*, p. 21

comply with his views. He cannot tolerate differences of opinion and regards anyone who differs with him as an enemy or at best an unworthy and ignorant person. Agreement is possible when people hold moderate positions, but a bigot neither knows nor believes in moderation. The issue becomes more critical when such a person develops a tendency to coerce others, not necessarily physically, but by accusing them of *bid'a* (pernicious innovation), laxity, deviation and *kufr* (disbelief). Such intellectual terrorism is as horrifying as physical terrorism.[13] For an example, we may refer here to the *Jama'a al-Muslimin* organization of Egypt, also known as *al-Takfir wa'l-Hijra*, which was founded by Shukri Mustafa in the 1970s. This group became notorious after they kidnapped and then assassinated the Minister of Religious Endowments, al-Shaykh al-Dhahabi in July 1977.[14] They held the view that there must be a migration of the righteous elements of society who work for Islam and its Shari'a to a place suitable for this purpose. Shukri Mustafa called on his followers to desert non-Muslim places of worship (i.e. all mosques in Egypt not under the society's control). He called the Egyptian society a society of *jahiliyya* (atheism and ignorance) and therefore the abode of war. Shukri Mustafa embellished the idea of *takfir* (charging Muslims with disbelief) with the following assertions:

a. All sin is a kind of polytheism and an atrocious crime.
b. It is necessary to perform all the religious imperatives of Islam. If one is missed, the rest are of no avail.
c. Every Muslim who is reached by the call of the Society of the Muslims and does not join it is an infidel.
d. Infidels deserve death, whether singly or as a group.
e. It is not permissible to name any mosque as a mosque of God unless all those who pray there believe in God and the Day of Judgment, give *zakat* (wealth tax) and fear only God.[15]

---

[13] Cf. al-Qaradawi, *Islamic Awakening*, p.34.

[14] The Society of Muslims made al-Dhahabi's release conditional on the government's freeing of the Society's detainees. When the government showed signs of evasion, the Society killed al-Dhahabi.

[15] See Ramadan, "Fundamentalist Influence in Egypt: The Strategies of the Muslim Brotherhood and the Takfir Groups," p.158; Sami Zubaida, "The Quest for the Islamic State: Islamic Fundamentalism in Egypt and Iran," in *Studies in Religious Fundamentalism*, ed. Lionel Caplan, London: Macmillan Press, 1987, pp.39–40.

The Society also encouraged its members to avoid military conscription, and indicated their separation from the religious and social institutions of *jahili* society by such other practices as arranging their own marriages without the customary payment of *mahr* (dower) and other ceremonies. Some of their members physically emigrated to the mountains and caves of Upper Egypt where they engaged in physical training and worship.[16]

While the Society of Muslims declared all the people outside their group to be infidels, the *Jihad* group, the group responsible for the assassination of President Sadat, declared only the rulers to be infidels, while the ordinary people were Muslims. Their task therefore was to remove these rulers and restore the rule of God. Formed in Alexandria in 1975, the *Jihad* organization consisted primarily of students and it was led by an engineer, Ahmed Salih Amer. This was the first organization to bear the name *Jihad*, but the name was also adopted later by a succession of other organizations. An off-shoot of the original *Jihad* emerged in 1979 under the leadership of another engineer, Muhammad Abd al-Salam Faraj. This was also a *takfir* group, as Faraj believed that "since the state is ruled by the judgments of atheism, despite the fact that its members are Muslims, and since the laws which are raised over the Muslims today are the laws of atheism ... hence there is peace for the Muslim and *jihad* against the atheist state." They maintained that this *jihad* to establish an Islamic state was an obligation, and that the state should be the nucleus from which to reestablish the Islamic caliphate to unite all Muslims. Faraj maintained that these blasphemous rulers were responsible for oppression and colonialism in Islamic lands, so they must be eliminated.[17] Speaking against parliamentarism and reform, another member of this group stated that "these institutions are secular *jahiliyya* institutions arising from secular concepts found in a secular constitution, which must be erased from the face of the earth so that the structure of Islam may be built on it once again".[18] A leader of the Brotherhood in Asyut refused to associate with this kind of extremism which he referred to as "a hollow drum ... they have no base among the people ... Their credibility with

[16] Zubaida, op. cit., p.41.
[17] Ibid.
[18] Shamir Irshadi, quoted in Barry Rubin, *"Islamic Fundamentalism in Egyptian Politics"*, p.139.

the masses is zero and public opinion is always on the side of moderation".[19]

Bigotry and intolerance was also the hallmark of Iran's 'Devotees of Islam', *Fida'iyan-i Islam*, the first post World War II militant group of a small number of activists to include assassination as a major part of its activities. They considered the government and some of its members in particular, to be traitorous foreign agents, and felt that unbelieving foreign influences must be obliterated and true Islam restored. The early wrath of the group's founder, Nawab Safavi, was directed against the leading intellectual, Ahmad Kasravi, who had strongly criticized Shi'ism and clerical power as a source of moral and political corruption in Iran. Ruhollah Khomeini's first major published tract, the 1941 *Kashf al-Asrar* (*Uncovering of Secrets*) had been in part a counterattack on Kasravi and his followers. Safavi's disciples assassinated Kasravi in an open courtroom in 1946. The next clearly *Fida'iyan* assassination was of a former Prime Minister Abdul Husain Hazhir in 1949. Hazhir was tied both to foreigners and to the Baha'is. Even more sensational was the March 1951 assassination of the Prime Minister, General Ali Razmara, who was trying to negotiate a compromise with the British in the dispute over Iranian oil and was accused of having ties with the British and the Americans. Navvab Safavi and three other top leaders of *Fida'iyan* were then executed, after which the group went underground until the 1978–79 revolution. But despite some public support for their actions, the *Fida'iyan* never presented a well-worked out and coherent ideological position or a specific program for an Islamic government. They called for reversal of changes in the status of women that they considered unislamic. They did not reject monarchy in principle although they opposed Shah Muhammad Raza Pahlavi, and one of their followers was accused of a failed assassination attempt on the Shah in 1949.[20]

In the post-revolutionary period, especially from 1979 to 1984, the promotion and spread of "Islamic revolution" was a foreign policy goal of the Khomeini government, explicitly stated in the exhortation of Iran's Constitution "to perpetuate the revolution both at home and abroad."

[19] Ibid., p.137.
[20] For details see N. Keddie and F. Monian, "*Militancy and Religion in Contemporary Iran*," in E. Marty, *Fundamentalisms and the State*, p.514ff.

This was followed by a second phase beginning in 1984, when Iranian leaders appear to have realized the limited usefulness of aggressive policies and starting taking a more pragmatic approach to issues.[21]

One might think that discussing the *Takfir* and *Fida'iyan* rebels and assassins under the heading of fanaticism would be somewhat out of place. To use Islam as the basis, let alone the justification, for such violent views and conduct is, in my view, a serious violation of Islamic teachings. As far as the question of *takfir* is concerned, (charging a Muslim or a group of Muslims with *kufr*) this too is a very serious violation of Islamic teachings, as we read in the following hadith, "When a man calls his brother 'O *kafir*' (disbeliever) one of them is deserving of the charge. If the accusation is not true, it falls upon the person who uttered it in the first place."[22] A Muslim may not be declared a disbeliever or apostate when he says or does something which carries a mere probability of disbelief. According to Imam Abu Hanifa, if the utterance or conduct in question amounts to disbelief by ninety-nine per cent but to *iman* (affirmation of faith) by a mere one per cent, it would still not amount to *kufr*. There were instances, during the time of the caliph 'Ali bin Abu Talib, where the Kharijites indulged in excess and charged many of the leading Companions with *kufr*. Although the Kharijites were regarded as transgressors, yet the Caliph did not declare any of them *kafir*, instead he said that a person who seeks the truth and makes an error is never the same as one who seeks falsehood and then proceeds to commit it.[23]

2. Excessiveness and Exaggeration

The second manifestation of fanaticism is excessiveness and exaggeration in the observance of religion and the attempt to opt for more difficult choices and expect others to do likewise, notwithstanding clear evidence in the Qur'an and Sunna to the contrary. To quote just one of the several verses of the Qur'an on this theme, "Allah intends every facility for you.

---

[21] Ibid., p.523.

[22] Yahya b. Sharaf al-Nawawi, *Riyad al-Salihin*, ed. Muhammad Nassir al-Albani, 2nd edn., Beirut: Al-Maktab al-Islami, 1404/1984, Hadith 1741.

[23] Muhammad Abu Zahrah, *Al-Jarimah wa'l 'Uquba fi'l-Fiqh al-Islami*, Cairo: Dar al-Fikr al-'Arabi, n.d., p. 182. For further details on the Kharijites and also generally on the subject of *takfir* (charging a Muslim with disbelief) see M. H. Kamali, *Freedom of Expression in Islam*, Cambridge: The Islamic Text Society, 1997, p.186ff.

He does not want to put you in difficulty." (al-Baqarah, 2:185). It is also reported that "whenever the Prophet, peace be on him, was given a choice between two options, he always chose the easier unless it amounted to sin."[24] Evidence in the *hadith* further shows that the Prophet discouraged prayer leaders from lengthening the congregational prayers, so as to avoid hardship to the weak and the old and also to avoid discouraging people from attending the congregational prayers.[25]

It is excessive to ask the people to observe the supererogatory in the same way as they would observe the obligatory, or to hold them accountable for things which are reprehensible (*makruh*) as if they were forbidden (*haram*). Speaking from personal experience, al-Qaradawi wrote that one day an extremist told a man off who drank water while standing, and said that it was a deviation from the Sunna. The man was then told that if he were a true Muslim, he should induce vomiting to purify himself. At this point "I gently intervened and said that the matter does not deserve ... such condemnation or harshness ... The Prophet, peace be on him, in fact drank water while standing during his farewell pilgrimage."[26] One should only demand that people observe the clear injunctions of Islam and give them the option regarding the non-obligatory rules. When a Muslim observes the obligatory duties but slips into committing a minor deviation, he or she should not be readily dismissed and expelled, as it were, from the fold of Islam. The Qur'an has made clear that "Good deeds remove those that are evil" (Hud, 11:114; see also al-Nisa', 4: 31 to the same effect). People may slip on some occasions, but then this may be compensated for by the good works they might do. Al-Qaradawi is of the view that it is sufficient for a Muslim to support his conviction from one of the Islamic *madhahib* or with a reliable *ijtihad*, a ruling based on sound evidence from the Qur'an and Sunna.[27] This is basically a sound view and we can agree with it provided that the ruling or *ijtihad* at issue is also applied in an acceptable way, such that would appeal to moderation and takes into account the prevailing conditions of its time and place. I therefore submit that it is not enough simply to say that this

---

[24] Muslim, *Mukhtasar Sahih Muslim*, n.11, Hadith no.1546.

[25] See for details al-Qaradawi, *Islamic Awakening*, p. 34.

[26] Yusuf al-Qaradawi, *Al-Sahwa al-Islamiyya wa Humum al-Watan al-'Arabi wa'l-Islami*, Doha: Bank al-Taqwa, 1408/1988, p.42.

[27] Al-Qaradawi, *Islamic Awakening*, p.31

or that opinion/*ijtihad* has a valid evidential basis in the established *madhahib*, but that the way in which it is projected or applied is also tactful and takes into consideration the prevailing customs and sensitivities of the people.

As for the reference to the rulings of the established *madhahib*, we should add that there may also be considerable scope for selection, and if there is an easier ruling available, the more difficult one should not be advocated. We note, for example, that a great number of Muslim jurists have held that the woman's dress should cover the whole of her body except for her face and hands, a ruling which has its general evidential basis in the Qur'an and Hadith (Cf. al-Nur, 24:31). A number of prominent ulama have on the other hand held that both the hands and face should be covered and they too cite evidence from the sources. This latter view is advocated by many contemporary ulama in Saudi Arabia, Pakistan, India and the Gulf States. They call upon Muslim women to veil their faces and wear gloves. The question now arises: should a woman who agrees with this view and follows it be called a fanatic? And then if a man persuades his daughter or wife to follow the same, could we also call him a fanatic? Similar differences of opinion exist among the ulama pertaining to music, singing and photography etc. There may be different responses in the existing body of opinion on these issues. The mere fact that there is disagreement on a certain matter is itself indicative of flexibility which may leave room for interpretation. I agree with al-Qaradawi that we should not condemn anyone with 'extremism' if he follows one or the other of these interpretations out of conviction, especially in matters that may be said to be a question of personal preference that do not encroach on the rights of others. But if, on the other hand, we reach the conclusion that this harder choice has a negative effect on matters of public concern and is likely to affect others, then I submit that a stubborn insistence on what might be awkward and impractical or which may violate the spirit of harmony and cooperation should not be condoned. For example, if a government institution in a Muslim society has a compulsory uniform or a dress code which is customarily deemed acceptable and decent, I believe that under the present circumstances one should not insist on covering the face and hands.

It is of interest to note that something like a breakthrough has occurred in the Islamic gender positions in the works of leading Muslim scholars in at least three instances as follows: (a) The 1990 *fatwa* of the Egyptian scholar Yusuf al-Qaradawi in which he said that women could seek parliamentary offices, be judges, and issue *fatwas* with the same authority as men.[28] (b) In a paper entitled "Women in Islam and Muslim Society" which was publicly circulated in 1991, Hasan al-Turabi, the prominent Sudanese leader, endorsed unequivocally a fully participatory role for women in politics and in every other sphere of society and declared that traditional restrictions on women's freedoms had nothing to do with Islam. (c) In 1990 Abd al-Halim Abu Shaqqa published a four-volume work, *Tahrir al-Mar'ah fi 'Asr al-Risala* (women's liberation in the Prophetic era) that immediately became influential in setting new parameters for the gender debate. This was an exhaustive and all embracing review of all the primary Islamic texts on the issue.[29] But we note nevertheless that despite these developments, women's participation in the top decision-making bodies of Muslim activist organizations has generally been limited, except perhaps in the cases of Sudan and Tunisia.

3. Sternness

Another manifestation of fanaticism is sternness without due regard for considerations of time and place, which often lead to inconvenience and hardship. This is perhaps one of the most pervasive features of fanaticism and it can take a variety of forms; it is often practiced by individuals and groups both in majority Muslim communities and by Muslim minorities abroad. It is perhaps indicative of a sense of insecurity due to being in the midst of an unwelcoming majority that minority Muslim communities often concern themselves with minor issues and allow these to mar the climate of fraternity and cooperation among themselves. Al-Qaradawi recounts that when he went on a tour of North America, in one of the Islamic centers he visited, devout young Muslims, who belonged to particular Muslim groups, had initiated a great controversy over minor issues. Included in these were the fact that Muslims sat on chairs during Saturday and Sunday lectures in the mosque instead of sitting on the floor, that they

[28] Yusuf al-Qaradawi, *Fatawa al-Mu'asira*, vol. 2, Cairo: Dar al-Wafa, 1993, p.338.
[29] See for details Najib Ghadbian, "Islamists and women in the Arab world: From Reaction to Reform," *The American Journal of Islamic Social Sciences*, 12 (1995), p.29.

did not face the Ka'ba, and that those who attended wore shirts and trousers rather than loose outer covering. Added to this list was also the fact that they sat at dining tables to eat instead of sitting on the floor. There were also instances of causing difficulties for converts as well as newly committed Muslims in the application of Islamic rules often over subsidiary matters of dress and social etiquette. Al-Qaradawi added that in another Islamic center people were making a lot of fuss over the showing of a historical or educational film in the mosque, claiming that "mosques have been turned into movie theatres", but forgetting that the purpose of the mosque is to serve both the worldly and the spiritual interests of Muslims. During the time of the Prophet, the mosque was used for both religious and social activities. On one occasion the Prophet permitted a group of Abyssinians to sport with their spears in the middle of his mosque and he also allowed his wife, 'Aishah, to watch them.[30]

Husayn Amin has reported that he visited the Islamic Center in Houston, Texas, and had a conversation with the director of that centre, Yahya Khayri, who said that fanatics were in the majority in Texas and that the situation in Indiana was even worse. "Did you know that only last week they set fire to a mosque in Indianapolis because women were praying together with men? And that the authorities had ordered the closure of the Islamic Centre of Washington for an indefinite period because of a scuffle that broke out there between the resident Muslims".[31] Isn't it strange to see this sort of thing happening, Husayn Amin added, amidst a community of well-educated Muslim professionals such as doctors and engineers in America? The narrative continues: The next day while Husayn Amin was with the director at his office in Houston a young bearded man of about 30 came and complained that he saw "strange things happening in the mosque: there is no barrier between the male and female sections in the mosque, and women wore trousers while praying with men".[32] The complainant, who turned out to be an engineer from Cairo on a short visit to America, then added that women also spoke in the mosque so that strange men could hear their voices and that this violated the hadith that "the woman's voice is '*awrah*" (parts of the body that are not supposed to

---

[30] Al-Qaradawi, *Islamic Awakening*, pp.36–37.

[31] Husayn Ahmad Amin, *Tatbiq al-Shari'a al-Islamiyya*, Beirut: Dar al-Nahda al-'Arabiyya, 1405/ 1985, p.141.

[32] Ibid., p.144.

be exposed to others). Yahya Khayri was able to dispel this misinformation as it turned out that the man had only heard this from someone else and had not seen the hadith in any valid source.[33] Husayn Amin also wrote that he was once giving a lecture at the same mosque and the director had barely introduced him when a black-bearded man in a long white gown came up, snatched the microphone from the director and addressed the audience in the following words, "Shame upon you! Stand up and leave your chairs, ask Allah for forgiveness and sit on the floor, because you know well that neither the Prophet, peace be on him, nor his Companions ever sat on a chair in the mosque".[34]

This excessive and unwarranted emphasis on detail is also observed in majority Muslim communities where attention is focused on such things as dress and social mannerism and not on beneficial dialogue over important issues. As al-Qaradawi observed, there is excessive and unnecessary discussion over such things as growing a beard, wearing clothes of a certain length, moving of the finger during the recitation of *tashahhud* in prayer, and the taking of photographs, at a time when Muslims are being confronted with unrelenting challenges and hostilities both from within and outside.

This total disregard for prevailing circumstances is also observed in many Muslim countries over the demand for the implementation of Shari'a, and in this context attention is focused almost exclusively on the enforcement of hudud punishments. The hudud are often seen as the testing ground of Islam and its Shari'a, and the demand is simply to enforce the hudud without paying attention to the prevailing conditions of modern society and the need for a great deal of preparatory work before the hudud can be meaningfully implemented as a means of attaining justice. But if evidence shows that conditions are not right for the enforcement of hudud, to the extent that enforcing them is likely to lead to injustice, then one ought to see the issues involved in their proper perspective. The rising tide of secularism which has followed the colonial domination of governments and institutions in Muslim lands has brought about a situation in which a purely technical approach to the hudud would simply fail the purpose which they are meant to achieve.

---

[33] Ibid., p.147.
[34] Ibid., p.157.

The hudud should not be seen, under these circumstances, as the first step in the enforcement of Shari'a in isolation from the rest of the Shari'a. Rather it should be seen as the last step in the effort toward the Islamization of law and government in modern society. As a part of the Shari'a, the hudud were revealed, mostly in Sura al-Ma'idah, in the final stages of the revelation of the Qur'an. This is itself a telling example of how the Qur'an has envisaged the stages in which the hudud were to be implemented. And even then we note that the Prophet was not eager to enforce them. On the contrary, he advised that the hudud should be suppressed as far as possible prior to reporting and adjudication, and in all instances of doubt. It is well to remember too that law alone, let alone a particular law on punishments, is not enough to put back into place the whole moral and legal structure of Islam. "The call (*da'wa*) to Islam should not be reduced", wrote al-Qaradawi, "to the enforcement of a few punishments such as cutting off the hand of the thief and flogging the adulteress, the slanderer and the drunkard. Although these are part of Islam, they are neither the whole of Islam nor even the most important part of it".[35] Even a cursory look at the Qur'an would show that only in four instances does the Qur'an refer to specific punishments, but that there are over fifty *ayat* on justice. The relationship between the hudud and justice is one of the specific to the general and of the means to the end. If one had to be forced into making a choice between them, then it would be preferable to administer justice, even if it entailed an unavoidable compromise on specified punishments.

Graduality is one of the hallmarks of *Sunnat Allah* which is manifested in the advent of the Qur'an and the Prophet's sustained efforts to combat oppression and ignorance. The Qur'an was revealed over a period of twenty three years and much of it was addressed to the issues and realities of Arabian life. The Shari'a is now undoubtedly with us, but our alienation from it in the practicalities of life is undeniable. Have we succeeded, for example, in implementing the *zakah*, and in eliminating *riba* (usury) from our economy, and have we also succeeded in minimizing, let alone eliminating, modern society's tendency towards sexual promiscuity and its manifestations? If a poor man wants to borrow 1,000 ringgit or rials for his day to day living, or for the purpose of setting up a business

---

35 Al-Qaradawi, *Al-Sahwa*, p.86.

in order to earn a living, he would have little choice but to borrow on interest. To enforce the hadd punishment of theft under these circumstances, where the economic system leads to the enrichment of the few at the cost of crushing poverty of the many, as Mawdudi has observed "would amount to protecting the ill-gotten wealth of the exploiters".[36] One must surely avoid the prospect of sacrificing the overall objective of justice at the altar of technical conformity to specifics.

The fanatics are prone to exaggeration over the implementation of Shari'a and tend to indulge in nihilism when they dismiss the Islamic identity of their society altogether. Among the members of the Islamic Party of Malaysia (known as PAS), for example, there are those who give little credit to any group other than their own, and that includes the ruling party, the United Malay National Organization (UMNO), for their Islamic identity. PAS has insisted on the creation of an Islamic state and society based on the Qur'an and Sunna and a strict implementation of the hudud.[37] But as Muzaffar has rightly observed, "it has done very little analysis of the character and content of the new society it wants to create ... and it relies heavily on the theological injunctions of the past handed down from generation to generation through the medium of the ulama".[38] There is, after all, a common core of identity with Islam and its Shari'a in almost every Muslim society and many of the laws that are in force in the majority Muslim countries are not repugnant to the Shari'a. It is to some extent a matter of opinion, but it might be of interest to note Khalid's view of Egyptian law when he noted that "nine-tenths of the existing law is consistent with Islamic jurisprudence. The penal code needs only the legal punishments ... The civil and commercial laws will only need an additional provision excluding usury. I do not think this is difficult to achieve".[39] This is not an indulgent opinion as it compares well with the findings in Pakistan of the Council for Islamic

[36] S.A.A. Mawdudi, *The Islamic Law and Constitution*, Lahore: Islamic Publications Ltd. 1983, p.54.

[37] For a discussion of the hudud Bill of Kelantan 1993, and the demand particularly by PAS and the Government of Kelantan to enforce the *hudud* punishments, see M.H. Kamali, *Punishment in Islamic Law: An Enquiry into the Hudud Bill of Kelantan*, Kuala Lumpur: Ilmiah Publishers, 2000 Institute for Policy Research, 1995.

[38] Chandra Muzaffar, *Islamic Resurgence in Malaysia*, Kuala Lumpur: Penerbit Fajar Bakti, 1987, pp.57 and 59.

[39] Khalid Muhammad Khalid, quoted in Barry Rubin, *Islamic Fundamentalism in Egyptian Politics*, p.136.

Ideology that was entrusted, pursuant to Article (204) of the 1962 Constitution and Article (230) of the 1973 Constitution of Pakistan, with harmonizing the then existing laws of Pakistan with the principles of Islam. After several years of investigation and the careful survey of over 137 statutes that were enacted under the British rule between 1836 and 1906, the Council concluded that "97 Acts were found not to be in conflict with the injunctions of Islam as laid down in the Holy Qur'an and Sunnah". In 30 Acts, only odd provisions were found to be repugnant and the recommendation was that they should "be suitably amended". Eight Acts were to be repealed and only two needed major revision.[40]

It is doubtful however whether the extremists will listen to all of this and it would not be surprising at all if they dismissed such findings altogether. In other words, their demand for the implementation of Shari'a is at once arbitrary, prone to value judgment and utopian. Without wishing to engage in elaborate details, a glance at the history of government during the Umayyads, Abbasids and subsequent periods would show that the extent to which the applied laws of government conformed with the Shari'a varied on the whole by reference to the prevailing realities of the time.[41]

4. Lack of Patience

Still related to the above, the extremists are also prone to haste and have little patience for sustained work; they want quick solutions to issues which often prove to be unfeasible. The demand to establish an Islamic state is one of them and as we noted above, neither violence and assassination nor vitriolic boycott and condemnation have achieved that purpose. There is also the impatience to set right the conditions of society at large and the conduct of individuals that they regard to be deviationist. Muslim youths sometimes declare their readiness to sacrifice their lives for the cause of Islam, but what is often needed is not their lives but patient endeavor. Unfortunately very few show the inclination for steady self discipline and application in order to excel in knowledge and discovery

---

[40] Tanzilur Rahman, "Implementation of Shari'a in Pakistan", in S.M. Haider, ed. *Shari'ah and Legal Profession*, Lahore: Ferozsons, 1985, pp.56–59.

[41] For detail on the enforcement of *hudud* penalties, see my *Punishment in Islamic law*, n.38, pp. 112ff.

of truth. They seek instant victory, even martyrdom, and refuse to realize the importance of well-planned and well-considered strategies which often require perseverance over many long years. We need to cultivate a sense of realism and balance that is goal-oriented and constructive. Some people object to this, as they think that patient endeavor could go on forever without achieving its goal. Al-Qaradawi responds: "But, do you not, in the meantime, instruct an ignorant person, guide someone to the right path, or lead another to repent. This would be a tremendous achievement which brings us closer to our goal".[42] The Qur'an integrates this outlook in the following verse:

> And say: "Apply yourselves. Allah will soon observe your work, and (so will) His Messenger and the believers. And you will be brought back to the Knower of the unseen and the seen, then He will show you the truth of what you have done." (al-Tawbah, 9:105)

Many seem to have misunderstood the proper import of the following hadith on the subject of *hisba* (i.e., commanding good and forbidding evil).

> "If any of you sees something evil, he should set it right by his hand; if he is unable to do so, then by his tongue, and if he is unable to do even that, then (let him denounce it) in his mind. But this is the weakest form of faith."[43]

It is sometimes said that this hadith requires direct action and bold use of force to set things right. But those who are aware of the proper conditions of conducting hisba will know that hisba is only valid if one is convinced that he is likely to achieve the purpose he is trying to pursue, and also that he does not cause a greater evil in his attempt to prevent a lesser one.[44] We are aware that the Prophet conducted his mission among the pagans of Makkah for thirteen years and never attempted to use force. When some of his followers were tortured and killed, his response was to send others to a place of safety in Abyssinia. But we could never say that these responses indicated lack of faith or courage, on the

---

[42] Al-Qaradawi, *Islamic Awakening*, pp.145.

[43] Muslim, *Mukhtasar Sahih Muslim*, ed. Nasir al-Din al-Albani, Beirut: Dar al-Maktab al-Islami, 1404/1984, p.16, Hadith 34.

[44] See for detail on *hisba*, Kamali, *Freedom of Expression*, n.23, p.34ff.

contrary these were signs of wisdom and realism, as the Prophet knew that use of force at that time would have been suicidal to his cause. He was not in a position, in other words, to stop oppression "by his hand", but he continued preaching and became increasingly effective in inviting people to the right path.

5. Harshness towards others

Fanaticism also manifests itself in harshness and ill-mannered treat-ment of people, which is contrary to the teachings of Islam and tends to frighten people away rather than draw them closer. The standard Qur'anic guid-ance on *da'wa* is to "Invite (all) to the way of your Lord with wisdom and beautiful advice, and argue with them in ways that are best and most elegant" (al-Nahl, 16:125). The substance of this teaching is confirmed on several other occasions in the Qur'an (cf. 9:128; 3:159) and also in the Sunna of the Prophet who has said, for example, that "God loves kindness in all matters"; and "kindness beautify things, violence makes them ugly." Harshness cannot fail to distort *da'wa* (invitation) to the path of God simply because *da'wa* can only achieve its purpose when it penetrates the thoughts and feelings of people and this is impossible to achieve without appealing to their reason and conviction by gentle means.

Extremism hinders *da'wa* by causing unnecessary conflicts which often invite intervention from government authorities. Governments are natur-ally sensitive to instability and will readily impose restrictions to prevent any recurrence of it. Such restrictions do not fail to limit the freedom of serious *da'wa* organizations to carry out their programs. To give an exam-ple from Nigeria, Aisha Lemu cited the case of an extremist group which began visiting a girls' boarding school, taking advantage of the freedom of the Muslim students' society and other religious organizations, to conduct religious lectures at weekends. It soon became clear, however, that these enthusiasts had convinced some of the Muslim girls to refuse to attend classes in "*kufr* knowledge" and to instead leave school and get married. The school and local authorities and the parents became involved and the outcome of it all was an Education Ministry directive which banned outside preachers from holding lectures and functions in all government schools. The Muslim students' society as well as other reputable organi-zations were consequently obliged to suspend their programs, which were designed to enlighten the secondary school students about Islam. This is just one example of how the extremists' abuse of freedom can end up damaging everyone including themselves. Lemu added with regret that in recent decades so many governments in the Muslim world have imposed severe restrictions on religious education and *da'wa* activities.[45]

6. Suspicion and distrust

And lastly we add suspicion and distrust to our list of the manifestations of fanaticism. A fanatic tends to readily accuse people, pass quick judgment and jump to conclusions the moment he suspects them of something, without taking the trouble to investigate first. This is not only contrary to the accepted norm that people should be deemed innocent until proven guilty, but also violates the clear teachings of the Qur'an, which tells the believers "to avoid suspicion as much (as possible), for suspicion in some cases is sin" (al-Hujurat, 49:12). The Prophet has also warned us to "beware of suspicion, for suspicion may be totally unfounded and may amount to the worst form of lying …"[46] The spirit of fraternity in this message is taken a step further in another hadith where we read, "when you hear something that your brother might have said, give it the best interpretation until you can no longer find an explanation for it." Imam Ahmad Ibn Hanbal elaborated on this hadith and said to "find an excuse for him by saying may be he said, or may be he meant, such and such."[47]

One could cite many examples where suspicion seems to dominate the outlook of fanaticism: If you are not carrying a stick or not sitting on the floor while eating—although such things have nothing to do with the Sunna of the Prophet—the fanatic would be inclined to accuse you of disrespect for the Prophet. If a jurist (*faqih*) gives a *fatwa* which facilitates matters for Muslims, he is considered lax on principles; and if a preacher (*da'i*) tries to call people to Islam in a manner suitable to the spirit and style of the age, he or she is accused of patronizing western culture. Al-Qaradawi has identified suspicion as "the gravest shortcoming of contemporary extremists." Had they understood the Qur'an and Sunna, they would have discovered that both seek to foster confidence and trust

45 Lemu, n.4, p.30.
46 *Sahih Muslim, Kitab. al-birr wa'l-sillah. Bab al-nahy 'an al-tajassus.*
47 Shams al-Din 'Abd Allah b. Maflah al-Maqdisi, *Al-Adab al-Shar'iyya wa'l-Minah al-Mar'iyya,* Cairo: Matba'a al-Manar, 1348 A.H., I, 340.

in the mind and heart of every Muslim. Suspicion is the antithesis of affection and trust which Islam seeks to nurture among the believers and the fraternity of mankind.[48]

V. CAUSES OF FANATICISM

Fanaticism finds its origin in a variety of causes: national, international, socio-economic and historical, which may be outlined as follows:

1. One of the causes of fanaticism and its militant manifestations among Muslims of the twentieth century has been a profound personal and social dislocation experienced as a result of rapid modernization. Modern society has often been ill-equipped to meet the human needs created by these dislocations, which are occasioned by mass migration from rural to urban areas, by unsynchronized socio-economic and cultural transformations, failures in educational and welfare systems and ultimately by the collapse of long-held assumptions about the meaning and purpose of human existence. The experience of dislocation tends to foster a climate of insecurity and crisis. People's hunger for material goods, in this situation, is matched by a thirst for spiritual reassurance and fulfillment. It seems that these needs invoke powerful and often unbalanced responses that offer the promise of fulfillment. Religion has represented itself as the bearer of that promise. Religious activists of recent decades have occupied themselves with defining, restoring and reinforcing the bases of personal and communal identity that were shaken or destroyed by modern dislocations. The sense of insecurity that is heightened by this situation also reinforces the need, on the part of the individual, especially among the underprivileged strata of society, to seek reassurance by associating with others who might have had similar experiences, and consequently have the tendency to a somewhat exaggerated adherence to group structure and leadership. People are united in their common experience of disillusionment or dislocation, bound together, as it were, in sacred community to follow the will of those who offer the promise of relieving them of their predicament. The ability of such associations to inspire heroism and self-sacrifice stems in part from the belief in personal salvation and immortality, which gives their leaders

[48] Al-Qaradawi, *Islamic Awakening*, n.10, p.42.

an important psychological advantage in mobilizing people for danger-ous assignments.[49]

Not all of the people who are involved in extremist religious move-ments, or who benefit from them, are devout. Indeed radical and militant associations in every tradition attract their share of charlatans and mani-pulators, who cloak themselves in religious orthodoxy for the sake of political or financial gain. Religious extremism often exploits economic and social discontent more skillfully and readily than it taps religious idealism. Yet we also note that militant religious associations are not just socio-political protest movements sugarcoated with religious pieties. There are undoubtedly people and leaders who genuinely believe in and live by their religious principles. Ironically though, the likelihood of these people ascending to the rank of fiery leaders who incite the masses is small indeed.

2. It is generally agreed that the Arab defeat in the 1967 war with Israel was the moment of truth for Nasserism and the secularist ideology of Pan-Arab nationalism in the Middle East, and as such was the moment when the radical Islamic critics of this ideology began to seize the moral and political initiative from Arab nationalist regimes.[50] The anger and disillusionment of the Muslim masses that followed the 1967 defeat created a fertile ground for militant activities in Arab countries and elsewhere. Militant extremism has consequently increased over the years. In a world marked by military defeats, confusion over identity, and economic hard-ship, the extremist call on the believers to take their destiny into their own hands, instead of leaving it to discredited rulers, strikes an impressionable note. As a Muslim Brotherhood leader, Shaykh Salih Abu Isma'il, pointed out that "Egypt has been living on promises since the July 1952 revolution and gaining nothing but disappointment". He then put down all "our economic hardships, military weakness and social unrest to the absence of the Shari'a".[51] Referring to Nasser's 1952 revolution, a leading Egyptian magazine noted in its editorial article that "the success of the revolution

---

[49] Cf. Martin E. Marty, "Remaking the State: The Limits of the Fundamentalist Imagination," in ed. E. Marty, *Fundamentalisms and the State*, n.9, p.620ff.

[50] See for details Hugh Roberts, "From Radical Mission to Equivocal Ambition: The Expansion and Manipulation of Algerian Islamism," in eds. Martin A. Marry and R. S. Appleby, *Accounting For Fundamentalisms: The Dynamic Character of Movements* (The Fundamentalism Project) Chicago and London: The University of Chicago Press 1993, p.438ff.

was due to the social class that turned to it. After the 1967 defeat, attitudes of the middle class turned to introversion, withdrawal, and silent political protest, which came to form the basis of the political rejectionist religious groups".[52] The Soviet military aggression for over a decade in Afghanistan (1979–1992) and the ensuing resistance and guerrilla warfare that it generated added greater claims to validity and a new dimension to the activities of Islamic militant groups. Continued unrest in Algeria and parts of the former Soviet republics, and of course persistent turmoil in Palestine and Bosnia all tended to generate new pressures and enhanced the scope and diversity of militant extremism on the global scene.

The Iranian revolution of 1979 had a tremendous impact in Muslim countries, especially the Arab world. Individuals and groups that were already inclined to Islamic affiliations and anti-government activities in their home countries drew fresh inspiration and strength from the victory of militant Islamic opposition to the Shah's regime. Here was an Islamic revolution which was populist and anti-imperialist and served to demonstrate to many that the deep-rooted values of religion and culture could not be overridden by modernization, which was to be seen as no more than a superficial veneer. With all the fascinations and fears that the Islamic revolution of Iran held for its fans and foes, it did not represent, as one commentator wrote "a starting point of political Islam, which has a long history in the modern world, nor the political/sociological prototype of Islamic political movements elsewhere." This was mainly a function of the institutional framework, historical and cultural differences, and not just the contrast between Sunni and Shi'a Islam, that are observed in individual Muslim countries and communities.[53]

3. Fanaticism is also stimulated by political oppression practiced by rulers and governments bent on imposing alien ideologies and values on their people. Because of their heavy reliance on police methods, such rulers do not enjoy popular support nor indeed the confidence that this can generate and are therefore dependent on foreign patronage. Foreign governments and nationals are increasingly allowed to pursue their self-

[51] Cited in Barry Rubin, ed., *Islamic Fundamentalism in Egyptian Politics*, New York: St. Martin's Press, 1990, p. 7.

[52] Ruz al-Yusuf, "*Al-Mujtama'at al-Islamiyyah*—Islamic Societies", Sept. 28, 1981.

[53] Sami Zubaida, "Islamic Fundamentalism in Egypt and Iran", n. 15 p. 28.

seeking interests to the extent that they dominate national policies and generate resentment, extremism and violence.[54] A vivid example of this was the case of Iran under the Shah's regime which for decades relied on oppressive police methods and became increasingly dependent on foreign support. Frequent torture and execution of political prisoners contributed to the wide-spread discontent. The United States replaced Britain as the main outside supporter of the Shah. American advisors and personnel were then ubiquitously present in Iran, and the Iranian economy was dominated by American interests, a factor which angered the Iranian public and invoked violent responses that eventually dislodged both the regime and its foreign allies. To bring the point home further, the Shah's downfall was followed by the hostage taking drama of the US embassy personnel in Iran and the chain reaction of violence that followed had worldwide repercussions, far beyond the national boundaries of Iran.

It may be instructive to make a brief reference here to Caliph 'Ali bin Abu Talib's response to the Kharijite provocations. The Caliph was confronted with rebellion and aggression as the Kharijites had challenged the legitimacy of his leadership and went as far as to declare him and many of the leading Companions infidels; they also validated aggression with regard to the lives and properties of Muslims who refused to join their ranks. But the Caliph did not fight the Kharijites until they embarked on violence and killed Khabbab b. Al-Aratt. From this, Abu Zahrah has drawn the conclusion that it is not lawful for the Imam to fight the rebels (*ahl al-baghy*) for mere differences of opinion until they break the peace and embark on violence.[55] The ulema of the *madhahib* have held different views and most of them validate war on rebels who directly challenge the leadership of the legitimate imam, or who present an imminent threat to peace and order in the community.[56]

4. Intellectual shallowness and lack of insight into the general objectives, spirit and essence of religion are probably some of the most pervasive causes of fanaticism. There is a tendency on the part of the extremists to claim knowledge of Islam and its Shari'a, but in reality their outlook tends

---

[54] Cf. Al-Qaradawi, n. 10 p.49ff; Lemu, n.4 p.15.

[55] Muhammad Abu Zahrah, *Al-Jarimah wa'l-'Uqubah fi'l-Fiqh al-Islami*, Cairo: Dar al-Fikr al-'Arabi, n.d. p.172.

[56] See for details, Kamali, *Freedom of Expression*, n. 23 p. 190 ff.

to be parochial and severely limited by a variety of constraints. They tend to be literalist and rigid in their approach, often at the expense of the higher objectives and purposes of Islam. These *neo-Zahirites*, to borrow al-Qaradawi's phrase, have seen it as their role and mission to adhere to the letter of the text at the expense of its spirit, and the result is, of course, a mechanical application of rules in isolation from their causes and rationale. Centuries ago, the Zahiriya school of thought took a similarly literalist approach to the Shari'a and eventually lost ground and this is also the most likely predicament that awaits the contemporary fanatics of Islam. To give an example, according to the ruling of a hadith, women should not travel alone without a *mahram* (a close male relative), a ruling which served a useful purpose to ensure that traveling women were protected against physical and moral danger. However, the conditions of modern society, such as dependency on full time employment for both men and women, the decline of extended family living at close quarters, and the high cost of travel may now make it prohibitive, in some cases at least, for a woman to travel with a family escort. A woman may be escorted to an airport, boarded on a plane and met upon arrival at the other end, without there even being an opportunity for her to have privacy in the company of men. Now to insist on a literal application of the hadith in this situation, while turning a blind eye to the change of circumstances and the underlying rationale of the hadith, tends to amount to a misreading of that hadith, which should be avoided. But the religious fanatic is more likely to insist on the literal application of the text and remain unreceptive to rational argumentation of this kind.[57]

This emphasis on external conformity, often at the expense of the more basic values of Islam, has unfortunately become a general feature of the Islamic movements of our time. The phenomenon that we see is a manifestation of the intellectual hollowness that is associated with indiscriminate imitation or *taqlid*. With reference to Malaysia, for example, the now defunct movement of Dar al-Arqam, which acquired considerable fame and influence before its decline in 1994—was noted for the fact that "its members eat Arab-style. Arqam males wear Arab-style green robes and turbans, and Arqam females are in purdah most of the time".[58] One of the problems noted of Arqam was its "uncritical attachment to ideas,

---

[57] Al-Qaradawi, n.10 p.52.

values and life-styles from the past … and also its inability to harness scientific knowledge … Arqam has given little or no attention to scientific research".[59] Included among the reasons for the eventual downfall of Arqam was its exaggerated claims, amounting to distortion of Islam itself. The claim, for example, that their leader Shaykh Suhaimi met with the Prophet and received "the *Aurad* from him in the holy Ka'bah". The reference here is to a controversial book by the Arqam leader, Ashaari Muhammad, entitled *Aurad Muhammadiah*, wherein it is also claimed that Shaykh Suhaimi is not dead, but has disappeared only to emerge later as the Mahdi. The Arqam followers claimed that the success of the Dar al-Arqam movement was due to the blessings of *Aurad Muhammadiah*.[60]

Speaking of the excessive zeal of "the fanatics who wish to practice Islam in an unreasonable manner", Dr. Mahathir wrote that they "make Islam a burden, cruel and a stumbling block to the well-being of Muslims".[61] Dr. Mahathir added that Islam is not an irrational religion which simply dismisses a change of circumstances and their effect on the teachings of religion: "It is some *fiqh* scholars and fanatic interpreters in Islam who are irrational".[62] Anwar Ibrahim has similarly observed that "moderation and pragmatism warrant that extreme emotions be kept under tight rein". While recognizing "the legitimate rights of victims of oppression and persecution" to use whatever means available to liberate themselves, Anwar Ibrahim noted nevertheless that "passion must give way to sobriety. For if it were otherwise, it would be a sure-fire formula for destruction and violence."[63]

During the lifetime of the Prophet, women were allowed to attend the mosque for congregational prayers. The position was, however, changed later by the Prophet's widow 'A'ishah, who ruled against women's attendance at the mosque on the basis that women needed to be protected against corruption. "Were the Prophet alive himself", said 'A'ishah, "he would have ruled likewise." Once again there is a total change of circumstances and we have before us a situation that warrants a recourse to the

---

58 Muzaffar, *Islamic Resurgence in Malaysia*, n.36, p.47.   59 Ibid., p.47.

60 See for further detail Kamali, *Freedom of Expression in Islam*, n.23, p.275.

61 Dr. Mahathir Mohamad, "Islam Guarantees Justice for All Citizens", in ed. Rose Ismail, *Hudud in Malaysia*, Kuala Lumpur: Sisters in Islam, 1995, p.72.

62 Ibid., p.73.

63 Anwar Ibrahim, *The Asian Renaissance*, Singapore: Times Books International, 1996, p.114.

basic rationale and purpose of the rule, rather than a literal reading of it. The change of circumstances has brought us face to face with the fact that women need to be active outside the home. They need to go to work outside the home; if one is a housewife she may go to the market while her husband is at work, and takes the children to school etc. She is allowed to be in offices, schools, markets and hospitals, and it makes little sense that the mosque should now be the only place she is not allowed to attend. To insist on a dry and literal application of rules, such as the religious fanatics are inclined to do, can hardly be recommended.

VI. WHAT CAN BE DONE?

Fanaticism is essentially a religious phenomenon, which is also accentuated by a variety of psychological, social and political components. Any remedies that are suggested therefore ought to take these components into consideration, and should be related to the basic causes that are identified for it. Since no individual or nation can hope to control all of the possible causes of this phenomenon, one cannot expect that fanaticism can be fought and eliminated altogether. The best one can hope for is to minimize and contain it through correct guidance, communication and understanding among the various parties concerned. All the concerned parties are therefore called upon to take part in this endeavor and consider their roles in the light of the hadith which provides that "all of you are custodians and responsible for those who are placed under your custody …"[64]

The first duty of the extremist Muslim is to rectify his thought and conduct and try to moderate his outlook through knowledge and understanding of the basic messages of Islam. If there could be a basic agreement that Islam is a religion of moderation and that it encourages rational enquiry and understanding, then the first step in the right direction would have been taken. But a step taken at the level of thought needs to be observed in one's conduct. It is not enough to respond to an idea, but then neglect to translate it into reality. The search for truth and knowledge requires self-application and sustained effort, and this search can be facilitated if the society and its intellectual leaders and governing authorities

---

[64] Yahya b. Sharaf al-Nawawi, *Riyad al-Salihin*, n.22, Hadith 658.

play their respective roles in granting access to information, encouraging openness and disseminating the right advice.

It is important that the society acknowledges the problem of fanaticism and shows a willingness to share responsibility for it. Given the inner contradictions of the materialist culture, estrangement of religious values, problems of urbanization, unemployment and education in many of the present-day Muslim societies, it is generally acknowledged that the society has become an unwilling contributor to the birth and spread of extremism, and must therefore play a positive role in the campaign to curb it. Older and more experienced people should show greater sensitivity and understanding toward today's youth and have frequent and open discussions with them. This may be encouraged both at the family level, in groups and associations, and in the society at large.

In dealing with the roots of fanaticism, government authorities and the press can contribute by opening up the atmosphere of communication and encouraging freedom of expression, so that ideas can be rationally discussed and analyzed and correct advice can be made available as a result. This might mean that problems are identified and eventually resolved, failing which hostile and false ideas are likely to thrive in secrecy and grow until they dominate the thoughts and minds of their advocates. Extremism is caused by deviant thoughts and poverty of vision, and there is little alternative but to utilize sound thinking and correct advice in its treatment. There may be a place for coercive tactics and force against those who become a menace both to society and to themselves when they resort to violence and bloodshed, but only as a last resort. It is indeed a mistake to think that extremist behavior and thought can be uprooted and remedied by recourse to brutal methods of a police state or military coup leaders—who are ready to use force against whoever disagrees with them. They may temporarily succeed, but chances are that they will ultimately fail. Violence breeds violence; if one extremist group is crushed, another even more violent is in the making.

It is important in all of this to recognize that a genuine commitment to the best values of Islam plays a central role in the advice that is formulated and given. A mere lip service and reliance on familiar clichés will fail to be convincing. Islam has a rich reservoir of ideas which may at times need to be developed and up-dated to show their relevance to the issues at hand. Steps must be taken to improve the capability of our youth to understand and interpret the Qur'an and hadith, so as to enable them to achieve a true insight into the Shari'a. Those who have this knowledge should show greater willingness to share it with others and make their teaching purposeful and relevant to the problems of modern society. The religious extremist is otherwise most likely to fall into the hands of so called 'shaykhs' with minimal knowledge, who are themselves in need of help.

Academic institutions and Islamic organizations clearly have a role to play in the training of teachers and education of young people. God Most High has assured the faithful in the Qur'an (al-Nisa', 4:31; al-Najm, 53: 31–32) that He forgives the minor faults of those who avoid major sins and may forgive even major sins of those who repent. It is therefore not recommended for the fraternity of man to be too assiduous in pursuing one another's weaknesses and failures. I agree with Aisha Lemu's observation that it is quite wrong to judge people by their appearance. One should avoid the temptation to think, for example, that when a woman wears dark colors and *hijab* from head to toe, she must be highly dedicated, and one who wears modern clothes must be a bad Muslim. For such a simplistic approach does not take into account the family background of the person. It may be that no one in her household ever wore *hijab*. It does not take into account the school where she might have spent a decade or even longer before going to university. And then it does not account for the fact that in some parts of the world, a woman in *hijab* would find it difficult to get a job or even admission to higher education.[65]

Al-Qaradawi draws attention to a story about how Hasan al-Banna dealt with a controversy in an Egyptian village where the residents were divided to the point of violence over whether *salat al-tarawih* (superogatory night prayer offered during Ramadan) was twenty or eight *rak'at* (units).

The way he treated this situation is instructive. He first asked what the juristic value of *salat al-tarawih* was. The answer was that it was a sunna. He then asked "And what is the juristic value of brotherhood among Muslims?" The people replied that it is obligatory *(fard)*, as it is one of the

---

65 Aisha Lemu, op. cit., n.4, p.21.

fundamentals of the faith. He then told them if they preserved their unity and each went home and performed *salat al-tarawih* according to his own genuine conviction, it would be far better than quarrelling.[66]

To see things in their proper perspective requires knowledge and balance and a keen awareness that conformity to rules is one thing, but to read those rules within the framework of the overall objectives of Islam is to a large extent a matter of insight and wisdom. A large percentage of the detailed rules of the Shari'a can either be read in isolation or they can be read in close association with the wider objectives of the Shari'a. A more dynamic and purposeful approach to the understanding of Shari'a should keep the following into perspective:

(1) A Qur'anic verse or a hadith should not be taken in isolation without reference to other related verses and *hadith* that may explain, elaborate and qualify it. An integrated knowledge of the Qur'an and Sunna is extremely valuable to enable one to acquire insight into the teachings of Shari'a.

(2) It is also important to distinguish between the permanent and unalterable principles of Islam and those of its parts which are directed to particular needs and circumstances.

(3) Attention must also be paid to the exigencies of social change and the developments that science and technology never cease to bring about. The Shari'a is equipped with a detailed methodology for reconstruction and *ijtihad* (the exercising of personal judgment in legal matters by one qualified to do so). Effort should be made, whenever possible, to accommodate the realities of social change within the worldview of Islam and its methodology of *ijtihad*.

CONCLUSION

I have addressed fanaticism and its adverse manifestations in the preceding pages. It is a cause for genuine concern, because fanaticism and extremism are accountable for the bad name that Islam has been given by its contemporary critics. Radical tendencies, extremism, and terrorism have become associated with a religion that rejects these outright and stands firmly for moderation and justice. God Most High has named

---

[66] Al-Qaradawi, op. cit., n.10, p.121.

this religion by the word "Islam", meaning "submission and peace" (al-Ma'idah, 5:3) which must inevitably be a reflection of the divine image of this religion. It is totally regrettable that Islam is now a target of abuse thanks to acts of misguided excessiveness carried out in its name.

I now take this opportunity to say a word about the revivification and renewal of Islam, and the efforts of many dedicated and sincere Muslims to invite attention to its true merit and the message of hope it can offer to humanity. The emphasis in Islam on God-consciousness and moral virtue is of great and lasting significance to humanity, and I believe this will override and surpass the negative currents. It is a cause for reassurance and hope that the good works of many moderate and farsighted scholars and leaders in the Muslim world are making an impact and are beginning to invite attention everywhere. There has been much misunderstanding of the true message of Islam, and this needs to be looked at and put into perspective, not just by adversaries and critics of Islam but also by those of its followers who have not restrained their anger and have found it somehow possible to seek legitimacy for their violent outrages in the name of Islam.

Lastly, I would like to note from my personal experience of university life that the vast majority of our young people exhibit a degree of openness and calm which are happily indicative of moderation. In spite of all I have said about fanaticism, it still appears to be an isolated phenomenon and has not become, as it were, a dominant characteristic of the culture and conduct of our youth. It is for me a cause of personal satisfaction to note that the International Islamic University Malaysia where I am employed and many other institutions in this country, along with academic and government leaders, are alert to the damage that fanaticism can do to all of us, and I hope that our young people will themselves again exercise initiative to make the university environment in this country and beyond even more reflective of the best values of Islam and its teachings on moderation and tolerance.

Security Strategy Foretold[1]

TOM BARRY AND JIM LOBE

I N SEPTEMBER 2000, the Project for The New American Century (PNAC) issued its strategic plan on how America should exercise its global leadership and project its military power. In its forward, PNAC's *Rebuilding America's Defenses* notes that PNAC's plan "builds upon the defense strategy outlined by the Cheney Defense Department in the waning days of the Bush administration." It credits the draft of the *Defense Policy Guidance* as providing "a blueprint for maintaining US preeminence, precluding the rise of a great power rival, and shaping the international security order in line with American principles and interests." (Wolfowitz and Libby were two of the dozen consultants involved in the report.) Among the key conclusions of PNAC's defense strategy document were the following:

"Develop and deploy global missile defenses to defend the American homeland and American allies, and to provide a secure basis for US power projection around the world."

"Control the new 'international commons' of space and 'cyberspace,' and pave the way for the creation of a new military service—US Space Forces—with the mission of space control."

"Increase defense spending, adding $15 billion to $20 billion to total defense spending annually."

"Exploit the 'revolution in military affairs' [transformation to high-

[1] This appendix originally appeared as part of "The Men Who Stole The Show" in *Foreign Policy in Focus* http://www.foreignpolicy-infocus.org.

tech, unmanned weaponry] to insure the long-term superiority of US conventional forces."

"Need to develop a new family of nuclear weapons designed to address new sets of military requirements" complaining that the US has "virtually ceased development of safer and more effective nuclear weapons."

"Facing up to the realities of multiple constabulary missions that will require a permanent allocation of US forces."

"America must defend its homeland" by "reconfiguring its nuclear force" and by missile defense systems that "counteract the effects of the proliferation of ballistic missiles and weapons of mass destruction."

"Need for a larger US security perimeter" and the US "should seek to establish a network of 'deployment bases' or 'forward operating bases' to increase the reach of current and future forces," citing the need to move beyond Western Europe and Northeast Asia to increased permanent military presence in Southeast Asia and "other regions of East Asia." Necessary "to cope with the rise of China to great-power status."

Redirecting the US Air Force to move "toward a global first-strike force."

End the Clinton administration's "devotion" to the Anti-Ballistic Missile treaty.

"North Korea, Iran, Iraq, or similar states [should not be allowed] to undermine American leadership, intimidate American allies, or threaten the American homeland itself."

"Main military missions" necessary to "preserve Pax Americana" and a "unipolar 21st century" are the following: "secure and expand zones of democratic peace, deter rise of new great-power competitor, defend key regions (Europe, East Asia, Middle East), and exploit transformation of war."

According to the PNAC report, "The American peace has proven itself peaceful, stable, and durable. Yet no moment in international politics can be frozen in time: even a global Pax Americana will not preserve itself." To preserve this "American peace" through the 21st century, the PNAC report concludes that the global order "must have a secure foundation on unquestioned US military preeminence." The report struck a prescient note when it observed that "the process of transformation is likely to be a long one, absent some catastrophic and catalyzing event—like a new Pearl Harbor."

Thomas Donnelly, the document's principal author and recently PNAC's deputy director (until he was recruited by Lockheed-Martin), expressed the hope that "the project's report will be useful as a road map for the nation's immediate and future defense plans." His hope has been realized in the new security strategy and military build-up of the current Bush administration. Many of PNAC's conclusions and recommendations are reflected in the White House's National Security Strategy document of September 2002, which reflects the "peace through strength" credo that shapes PNAC strategic thinking.